ABOUT THE AUT]

Eyal Yurconi has transformed a turbulent adolescence fraught with behavioral problems and high-school suspensions into a successful young adulthood as a college professor, trainer and entrepreneur.

For the past seven years he has dedicated his time to teaching Gen-X'ers and Y'ers from all walks of life how to unleash their inner talents and become the leaders of tomorrow. He has engaged juvenile delinquents, the academically gifted, college athletes, high-tech engineers, teachers, therapists and even the mentally challenged in diverse personal development and peak performance programs such as "The Fire Within," "Academic Excellence," and the "Teacher's Edge."

Yurconi holds a B.A. in Psychology and a M.A. in Communication and Interpersonal Relations. He is a self-taught speed reader and is considered an expert on peak performance psychology, crises counseling, psychotherapy, personal finances, strategic-thinking, negotiation and conflict resolution. He is an avid fan of Anthony Robbins, Jim Rohn, Paul Kurtz, Metallica, Hans Zimmer and Steven Spielberg and he enjoys writing music, playing tennis and traveling. This is his first literary publication.

ISBN 0-9777496-0-6

Library of Congress Control Number: 2006900630

Book site: www.being-great.com
Strength Dynamics web address: www.StrengthDynamics.com

9 8 7 6 5 4 3 2

Cover design, illustrations, pictorials, sketches, diagrams and comics by Mark Tulchinski.

Strength Dynamics Publications is dedicated to the development of generation X through training, publication of research and literary works, learning strategies and multimedia projects.

BEING GREAT

WINNING THE BATTLES WITHIN

EYAL YURCONI

and

Mark Tulchinski

Dedicated to all those who have the courage to step out of the darkness and into the light. May you roar with the lions, run with the mustangs and soar with the eagles. Your triumphs are a true source of inspiration in my life. And for that, I am forever grateful. Live Strong!

Also, to Jacob and Viorica Wexler, who have witnessed and survived the worst of mankind but never lost faith in the goodness of the human heart. Your compassion, hope and love are a monument for the best in all of us. We miss your presence dearly!

Acknowledgments

First thanks go out to my immediate support team, my mom and dad, my lady Regina, and my partner and friend, Mark Tulchinski. Thanks for being patient with this project and for taking the time to listen to my ideas. Also, I want to thank my editor, Andrew J. Craft for doing a great job. Thanks a million, Andy!

Throughout the years I've been fortunate enough to meet some incredible human beings who have influenced my life to an immeasurable affect. They believed in me and in my abilities even when I didn't believe in myself and were patient enough to coach me and teach me about the ways of the world. I want to acknowledge: Dani Bialer, for investing his time under the blazing afternoon sun of Nes-Tziona to help me become a better athlete. David Solomon, for introducing me to the wonders of the human mind and for teaching me how to think. Coach Nathaniel Warren, for giving me a second chance and showing me what true kindness and compassion really means. Dr. Jesse Pendleton and Dr. Emeka Okoly, for giving up their office hours and helping me through troubling times.

Also, I want to make a special note and recognize several individuals I've never met but whose inspiring life work has been of great influence over me: Anthony Robbins, Jim Rohn, Alan Watts, Eli Wiesel, and Yitzhak Rabin.

And lastly, a giant thanks goes out to all my friends around the world who taught me about their ways of life and through their grace and good heart I've learned the true meaning of kindness and friendship.

CONTENTS

"Greatness"

"I would rather stumble a thousand times
attempting to reach a goal,
than to sit in a crowd
in my weather-proof shroud,
a shriveled and self-satisfied soul.
I would rather be doing and daring
all of my error-filled days,
than watching, and waiting, and dying,
smug in my perfect ways.
I would rather wonder and blunder,
stumbling blindly ahead,
than for safety's sake
lest I make a mistake,
be sure, be safe, be dead"

~ Anonymous ~

Chapter I

Let's Rise to the Challenge

"The great are great to us only because we are on our knees. Let us rise"

~ Robert Collier ~

At some point in life, we must face our worst fears. It's usually a point where everything we believe, know and love, everything that used to give us a sense of comfort and security, suddenly collapses, leaving us lost and confused about who we are and what our life is about. It could be a turned down college application or the unexpected end of a relationship or the death of a loved one or a dream that has been shattered.

At first you feel as if the ground has been pulled from under you. As your confidence dwindles and hesitation takes over, you begin to second-guess every decision you have ever made. You realize that your defenses have been breached and that you are vulnerable. Very vulnerable. Desperate thoughts begin to creep into your mind. The future seems distant and hazy, too difficult to reach. You begin to question the purpose of it all and contemplate giving up. At this moment, you feel like a leaf in the wind, unable to have any influence upon your own life.

At these moments of truth, where our entire identity is being challenged, where everything we stand for and believe in is gone, we are faced with a choice: either we break down, or break through. For me, that moment came in the spring of 1999.

I was born in Israel in a small town called Rehovot. As a kid, I was always very hyper. I found school slow and boring and I always got into a lot of trouble. I had a knack for competition and I liked physical activity, so naturally I found comfort in sports. I tried everything from karate to gymnastics to swimming, until finally I settled on tennis.

As I grew older, tennis gradually became the center of my life. Winning gave my confidence a terrific boost, and I loved it. And as I began taking home trophy after trophy, the sport became a major source of power for me. The older I got, the harder I trained. I poured my heart and soul into the game and by the time I was 17, I was one of the best players in Israel.

Ever since I was a kid, I had dreamed of being able to support myself through tennis. I believed I was good enough to do so and that I deserved a chance to prove it. Then, when I turned 18, I was offered tens of thousands of dollars to play tennis and go to school in the United States. This was my dream come true. My parents were also thrilled: they wanted the education for me and I wanted the sport.

The day I boarded the airplane for the States I had goose bumps all over. I felt I was the luckiest person alive. I couldn't believe that I was about to fulfill a dream I had carried with me for more than 12 years. By the time we took off, I was glowing. When the flight attendant turned the lights off, I closed my eyes, smiled to myself with satisfaction and fell asleep to Queen's *I want it all.*

In the beginning, my life away from home proved to be everything I expected and much more. I was being paid to do what I loved, I had great friends, I was traveling all over the country and on top of it all, I even enjoyed school. My future seemed gloriously bright. So bright, that I couldn't imagine anything changing it. That's when things started to fall apart.

It started with injuries I decided to ignore and easy matches which I lost, but should have won. The pressure mounted, and I began to fail exams. As I began feeling less sure of myself I became careless. I made lousy social judgments, and said some things to key people I should have kept to myself. My dream life was gradually turning into my worst nightmare. However, I wasn't seeing it. I just figured I was going through a tough period and if I kept training hard, I'd pull out of it in no time, just as I always had.

As the weeks passed, I felt I was sinking deeper and deeper into a swamp of failure. It seemed that the harder I tried to get back on track, the deeper I sank. As the tennis season came to an end, the coach called me into his office and terminated my contract. My dream was shattered.

As I left his office I felt my entire world had collapsed. Over the next several days I lost my friends, my position, my grades, and worst of all, my self worth. I felt as if my talent had betrayed me.

As I tried to assess my situation and take inventory of what I had, I discovered I was bankrupt at just about every level. I had no education, I was overweight, all my friends had vanished, and my family was more than 5,000-miles away. And worse that that, I had lost the one thing that gave true meaning and purpose to my life. For the first time ever I felt completely and utterly lost. I couldn't see a future. My athletic journey was over- there was no question about that. But what should I do? I couldn't conceive of my life without the game. After all, it was the only thing I knew how to do.

A terrible moment of truth had arrived. I had to decide: either let go of the game and find a new meaning to my life, or end everything right then and there. This was the first time I ever considered suicide.

Both choices were untenable. On one hand, I didn't believe I could find anything that would mean to me as much as sports had. On the other, being a grandson to Holocaust survivors who found strength and resolve amidst humanity's darkest hour meant I had been brought up to believe that life had supreme value and that suicide was a violent and disgraceful act; nothing more than a weak man's attempt to escape his problems. One choice required a giant leap of faith, which I didn't feel I was capable of, and the other demanded violation of my fundamental core beliefs.

So what did I choose? I chose neither. Instead, I did something I had never done before in my life: I asked for help.

I had always believed that asking for help was synonymous with incompetence and vulnerability; two qualities no person would like to admit to. But, at that defining moment, I felt so weak and ill- prepared for this major life challenge that I had no choice. I was forced to swallow my pride and admit I didn't have all the answers. It is only with hindsight that I realize that that was the moment my life began to change.

I started searching for answers with a fierce determination that was almost manic. I searched the way a starving grizzly forages for food. Within a short period of time, I devoured more than 350 books about personal development, success, survival, psychology, physiology, relationships, communications and finances. I attended every seminar I could afford and downloaded every sound byte I could lay my hands on. I quickly developed a passion for discovering why and how some people manage to triumph against incredible odds and achieve their dreams while so many are trapped in mediocrity.

The more I searched, the stronger I became. During the next three years, I revolutionized every aspect of my life. I changed my limiting beliefs, I changed the way I made decisions, I changed my eating habits and the way I managed my finances. I changed the way I was handling my relationships, not only with other people, but also with myself. I co-founded my first company. I began teaching speed-reading and photo memory and started leading 8-hour seminar events on subjects such as self-reliance, communication skills, success, and goal-setting.

Recently, during a newspaper interview, I reflected with amazement on the pace at which I was able to transform my life. I mean, I'm far from unique. I was raised in obscurity. My parents immigrated to Israel from Romania with only $500 in their pockets. Am I athletically gifted? I wish. I'm only 5'7 and have a thick frame, which makes me prone to gaining weight. Am I extraordinarily intelligent? Unlikely. In high school, I barely finished with passing grades.

So was I simply lucky? Maybe. But since that defining day back in 1999 I have studied rigorously how people from every walk of life have managed to conquer hopeless circumstances and defy adversity. I studied musicians, POW's, presidents, inventors, artists, Olympic athletes, performers, religious leaders, teachers, philosophers and people who overcame life-threatening diseases.

Through my research, I began to notice certain patterns and distinctions. I tested these observations and implemented my findings in my own life and the results showed quickly. It wasn't long before that I had been totally lost. Now I was able to help other people with their struggles, which gave me tremendous joy. Before I knew it, I realized that I had found a new source of strength and meaning in my life. My transformation was complete.

"The fastest way to change your own circumstance is by helping other people change theirs"

~ E.Yurconi ~

I believe you and me are kindred spirits. Although I have never met you in person I know that if you have picked up this book, you are reaching out, just like I did in 1999. You are reaching out because you want more, you know you deserve more, and you know that life has more to offer than it currently does.

And you know what? You are absolutely right! It doesn't really matter where you are in your life right now or what has happened to you in the past. The important thing is that you want to rise. And rise you shall.

I know that deep inside, you feel as though you were meant to be, and do, something important. I feel the same way. And while I can't promise you that this book is going to get you there, I'm sure it's going to help you move in the right direction. I don't claim to have all the answers. However, I do know that many of the things that have worked for me can work for you as well.

I'm often asked, "Why did you decide to write this book?" My answer is that I feel that growing up and making it in the world today is tough. Very tough. We have more voices vying for our attention than ever before. From religious voices, to political voices, to advertising voices; the voices of parents, teachers, friends, relatives and of course television, the list goes on and on. How do you know which voices to listen to? Which voice has value? Which will lead you astray? This can make things extremely confusing. And confused we are. According to Rebecca and Roger Merill, authors of *Life Matters*, over the past 30 years:

- Teenage suicide has increased by almost 300 percent.

- One fourth of all adolescents contract a sexually transmitted disease before they graduate from high school.

- Out-of-wedlock births have increased more than 400 percent.

- The divorce rate has more than doubled and currently stands at 57.7 percent.

- The percentage of families headed by a single parent has more than tripled.

- One-in-three workers say they are currently dissatisfied with their jobs.

- Within 8 years of graduation 60 percent of all college graduates find occupations totally irrelevant to their major.

This is the world you and me live in today. And if this doesn't spell confusion, than I don't know what does. Who's to blame for this confusion? Take your pick. We can point a blaming finger at everything from decisions baby boomers have made, to wars and terrorism, to the lousy training we receive in school, to globalization, commercialism, racism, sexism, and so on. And to a certain extent, all would be correct.

For you and me, the world is changing in ways we can't control or entirely understand. The information economy seems chaotic and cumbersome. People become ridiculously rich (or poor) over night, companies rise and fall based on prophetic predictions, and business is made, many times, in virtual unseen markets. Today, a college graduate entering the market can expect to compete not only with his fellow graduates but with people from all over the world. According to Bernard Carl Rosen who wrote the classic *Masks and Mirrors*, "There are people who in the past had never dreamed of entering the competitive ring but now clamor to get in. Women, minorities, immigrants, once excluded from the big races for wealth, power and status, stridently demand the opportunity to compete with privileged white males for the glittering prizes that success brings." What this means to you an me is that today there is much less room for error. Whereas in the past, mistakes in the workplace were considered "expensive education," today, those same mistakes are virtually unforgivable, punished by rejection and humiliation.

There's no doubt that the marketplace has become crowded and unforgiving, a fact that will directly affect our quality of life. In *Strapped: Why America's 20- and 30-Somethings Can't Get Ahead*, Tamara Draut points out that "In 1972, a young-adult male with a bachelor's degree or higher earned on average $52,087 (2002 dollars). In 2002, young male college grads earned $48,955." That's a gloomy statistic. I think we could have taken the numbers in our stride if the cost of living would have remained the same as it was in 1972, but according to Draut:

● Between 1995 and 2002, rents in nearly all of the larg -est metropolitan areas rose astronomically: Median rents in San Francisco ballooned 76 percent; Boston, 62 percent; San Diego; 54 percent; even median rents in less costly Denver shot up 49 percent.

● Over 25 percent of college graduates in 2003 had stud- ent loan debt higher than $25,000, up from 7 percent in 1992-93.

● For middle-income families, the cost of raising a child born in 1960 to age 18 was $155,141 (in 2003 dol- lars). The cost of raising a child born in 2003 to age 18 rose to $178,590, a 15 percent increase.

● The median monthly mortgage payment for those in the 25-to-34-year-old group grew by almost one third between 1980 and 2000.

But the difficulties do not end here. While in the twentieth century, a bachelor's degree almost guaranteed a secure job and a relatively high income, today, with more than 80 million degree holders in the United States, a bachelor's degree, even from a prestigious institution, is hardly enough to secure an entry level position in the corporate world.

Am I exaggerating when I say things are tough? I don't think so. Think about the next five years of your life for a moment.

How much certainty do you have about your future? Where are you going to be? What are you going to do? How certain are you that you'll be able to finance your dreams, attract your ideal mate, or feel the passion, fulfillment and growth you know you deserve to feel?

The world is changing right before our eyes and that's not something we can or should stop. If we wish to succeed, we must not play the victim by asking "Why is this happening to *us*?" or "Why *now* and not twenty years ago?" No! The real question we must ask ourselves is "How are we going to respond and thrive in this new and changing world?" We must decide whether we are going to play by the old rules of game (carpe diem-seize the day) or whether we going to adapt ourselves to the new game (carpe cras- seize tomorrow) and take advantage of the opportunities it has to offer. We must determine whether we are going to rely on outmoded skills and irrelevant information or whether we are willing to educate ourselves and developed our own unique competitive edge. Clearly, the decision whether to become masters to of our destiny or slaves of the past is in our hands.

I wrote this book not only because I'm concerned about our generation but also because I know that in the near future, the quality of my life will be dependent on the quality of your life. You are going to be my future neighbor, lawyer, doctor, accountant, or even business partner or president. And I hope that by sharing with you the tools and distinctions that have helped me to create a meaningful change in my life, I'm actually helping to make our collective future stronger and better.

In the past, I used to carry a .45 caliber bullet in my pocket. I would point it out at a seminar participant and ask, "Are you worried at all?" The answer would usually be something like "Why should I be? That bullet isn't going anywhere." "Exactly," would be my reply. "When it's moving, this tiny bullet can kill you with ease but when it is standing still, it is powerless. People are exactly the same. When we are on the move, we are powerful. When we stand still, we are worthless."

I believe this is our time to step up. The timing is perfect. If you'll look around you, you'll notice that the world today belongs to the fast and courageous, not to those who sit in the shadows and wait for things to happen. Here's a good case in point: Have you ever used ICQ before? Do you know how on line peer-to-peer communication started? Let me tell you.

Before its $287 million acquisition by America Online, ICQ was known as Mirabilis. It was a small start up company that was founded in July 1996 when four young Israeli students, Yair Goldfinger, Arik Vardi, Sefi Vigiser and Amnon Amir wanted to introduce a new way of communication over the Internet. In their youth, they noticed the fast deployment of the World Wide Web, which was propelled by the mounting popularity of surfing and browsing, and watched the growing number of people interacting with web servers.

However, they realized that something more profound was evolving under the surface. They noticed that although millions of people were connected to the Internet, they were not connected to each other. The young team realized that if one missing component were added, all these people, in addition to interacting with web servers, would be able to interact with each other.

That missing component was the technology that would enable the Internet users to locate each other online and create peer-to-peer communication channels in a straight-forward, easy, and simple manner. Once the four guys understood the relevance of their idea, they had to make it happen. The challenge was clear: to be the first company to introduce peer-to-peer application to the market place. In order to achieve their goal, the guys quit school, moved to the United States, and for several months invested every single minute they had in developing the beta version of ICQ.

Were the guys from Israel unique in any way? Did they have some great talents you don't have? It's possible, but unlikely.

When they started out, they were just ordinary college students. They had no money, hardly any knowledge, and were totally disorganized. Nevertheless, they understood the importance of taking action. They knew that the only way their idea would materialize was if they were to be the first to introduce it to the world.

"I have been impressed with the urgency of doing. Knowing is not enough; we must apply. Being willing is not enough; we must do"

~ Leonardo da Vinci ~

You can read every book on the planet and learn every skill there is to learn, but it's not until you start implementing what you know to your life that you begin to reap the rewards. There is a huge difference between *knowing* and *doing*. Knowledge, even at its best, is not going to change your life. Only action will. With this book I can cajole you, inspire you, challenge you, but if at the end of the day you don't take action and try this stuff out then I can guarantee that you'll see no results.

I believe that this is our time to shine as a generation. And I know that if we are not going to take action now, we will fall drastically behind. If we want a better life with more passion, excitement and happiness, it's not going to be handed to us. We will need to create it, one person at a time, starting with leaders like you!

You know, we have been derogatorily labeled "Generation X," which really means a generation with no identity. The term comes from a book by Douglas Coupland, written in 1991 entitled *Generation X: Tales for an Accelerated Culture*. The book is about three strangers who decide to distance themselves from society to get a better sense of who they are. He describes the characters as "underemployed, overeducated, intensely private and unpredictable." The media found elements of Coupland's

characters' lives in today's youth and labeled them Generation
X. This stereotypical definition has led society to believe that
Generation X is made up of cynical, hopeless, frustrated and
unmotivated slackers who wear grunge clothing, listen to alternative music, and still live at home because they cannot get
real jobs. Since then, the label has stuck and our entire generation has been stigmatized and ignored. Personally, I hate this
stigma. But on the other hand, it only propels me to achieve
more.

I believe, with every fiber of my being, that my destiny is in
my own hands, as is yours. But you must realize that power
plays a major role in our society. You either control your own
life or you let other people control it for you. You either make
your own decisions, or you respond to the decisions of others.
There is no leeway or compromise in attitude here. You must
be strong and courageously claim the life you want to experience.

*"Man is made or unmade by himself. By the right choice he
ascends. As a being of power, intelligence, and love, and the
lord of his own thoughts, he holds the key to every situation"*

~ James Allen ~

Being Great is a somewhat pretentious title for this book but
as you read you'll see it really isn't. In fact, you'll realize that
greatness is something each and every one of us desperately
wants to attain. The subtitle, *Winning the Battles Within*, represents the method: greatness is attained by learning to harness
the conflicting forces within us instead of letting them run ram-
pant and dominate our lives.

This book is divided into five sections, each representing a
different aspect of our lives. These five sections are taken from
"The Major 5 Strategic Living System," which is a model we
developed in order to help people simplify their life. The five

sections are: psychological, financial, creative, physiological, and relational.

As you read this book, I want you to keep in mind that even though it is divided into those five considerably different dimensions, life is a single integrated whole. You can't do well in one area of your life, neglect the rest, and hope to be happy and fulfilled. Life doesn't work that way. The Major 5 is only a model to help you approach things in an organized manner.

So what is greatness, then? It's tempting to look at financially successful people and automatically assume they are great. However, greatness goes much deeper than that. Have you ever seen Michael Jordan in action? How about Roger Federer, or Al Pacino? If you have, I'm sure you remember the ease of motion and the effortless dexterity they display when they do their thing. It's like poetry in motion. It is as if they are tip-toeing along the edges of their potential, maximizing every ounce of ability. Can you buy that sort of personal mastery with money? You sure can't. Nevertheless, we should not make the mistake of believing that greatness is reserved only for those who have unusual talents. Greatness is something that's available in all of us regardless of our skin color, place of birth or sexual orientation. In her book, *Attaining Personal Greatness*, Dr. Melanie Brown outlines three myths regarding greatness that I'm sure will help you grasp the meaning of greatness. Let's go through them quickly:

Myth #1:
Greatness is something unusual, you either have it or you don't

Is there anything unusual about a growing tree? Hardly. We see nothing unusual about a tree growing as high as it possibly can, driving down every root it can, and stretching its branches as far as they can reach. We assume there is nothing wrong with the tree. It is simply doing what it was meant to do. As a matter of fact, whenever we see a tree that is not as high as it should be we immediately assume that it is abnormal. In nature, the maximizing of potential is considered to be the norm.

In our society, we tend to think about great human beings as "strange" or "unusual" while we consider the mediocre majority as the norm. The truth is all of us want to be normal. We don't want to appear odd or be ostracized for any reason. We tend to see people who have achieved more than us as separate from our everyday thoughts and activities. In order to make great people seem more normal, or similar to us, we like to hear about their daily lives: who they talk to, what they eat, and what problems they have. This makes them more humane, more comparable, and most of us find that comforting.

Why do we look at those who are great and think they have something that we don't? Because if we will admit that they are just like us, we will have to face our own shortcomings and complacency. So it's easier to think about them as having something that we don't.

In a sense, great people are not afraid to go against the status quo and stand out. Unlike most people, they are self-guided and self-directed, because they have a commitment to follow the calling of their heart.

"Everyone has a talent. What is rare is the courage to follow that talent to the place where it leads"

~ Erica Jong ~

It is easy to fall into the mental trap of believing that some people are more creative than us or that they have greater mental abilities or that they are simply luckier. It actually makes more sense when we realize that those we consider to be great have simply discovered how to unleash their talents with greater efficiency than most of us. Remember that somebody had to teach Michael Jordan how to dribble. Somebody had to teach Einstein how to count. When we look at great people, we don't see all the hours of training, the sacrifices, or the obstacles they had to overcome. We just see the final product. There's a lot more to greatness than what meets the eye. Just like good magic, what goes on behind the scenes is far more important than what is visible and apparent.

Myth# 2:
Greatness is being number one

In my opinion, Pete Gray is the greatest baseball player that has ever lived. And even though he only played professionally for four years and participated in only 77 games, hit no home runs and averaged only 2.18, I still think he is the greatest. Want to know why? Because Pete Gray had only one arm. When Pete was six years old, he was hit by a truck and lost his right arm. Losing his strong arm, Pete had to teach himself how to catch, throw and bat with his left arm. Commentators used to say that Pete was a study in agility and dexterity. After catching a fly ball, he would tuck his thinly padded glove under his stump; roll the ball across his chest and throw, all in one fluid motion.

Pete never made it to the hall of fame. His numbers don't even tickle baseball giants like Mark McGuire or Sami Sosa. But his achievements make him great nonetheless because he went as far as he could with the cards he had been dealt. And that's what greatness is all about.

Our society is obsessed with ranking and record keeping. We rank movies, songs, art, cars, people, and even hamburgers. But the ranking can often be misleading. When the media runs "The 10 greatest people of the year", they tend to focus on highly visible public figures while totally disregarding the Pete Grays of our society. Being great is not about being number one in other people's minds or having the best numbers, or being the quickest. Greatness is relative to each and every person's potential and ability. There is no man-made ranking scale that can determine your true worth as a human being. That's something internal, that only you can determine. Only you know whether you are truly living to the best of your ability or whether you're settling for mediocrity.

Many people are great at supporting their families. They spend every waking moment providing protection and opportunity under harsh conditions. That is admirable. Others are great surgeons, athletes, scientists and teachers. In order to be great, you don't have to change the world or feed the starving. You don't have to make gazillions of dollars or find a cure for AIDS. All you have to do is be true to yourself and always strive for the next level. Never settle or stop. Work consciously on your own personal development and don't leave it to chance. We are not born equal. Some of us have more physical power, better health or better opportunities. It's what we do with the things we have been given that makes us great. We all start from different places. That's something we do not control. But we can control where we'll go and how we'll get there. That's what being great is about.

Myth #3:
Greatness means being famous

Fame is very exciting, there's no doubt about that. I think that deep inside, we have all wished to be famous. But does being famous make us great? Not at all. There is a profound difference between being great and being *called* great. Fame is nothing more than public recognition. It simply means that a lot of people know you. It doesn't necessarily mean that you have done anything *worthy* of recognition. It just means you have it.

Today it's probably easier than ever to be famous. The media will gladly magnify any event or person that is willing to create even the slightest of controversies. Andy Warhol once said that by the end of the 20th century, every person would get at least fifteen minutes of fame. Was he right? Think. How easy it is to be on T.V.? Pretty easy. Just join a talk show crowd and you stand a very good chance of being seen nationally, if not internationally.

What else could you do to get some recognition? You could cause a ruckus in broad daylight, in a public place. Just run naked across the street. You will be all over the news. You can print a feisty flyer saying something nasty about somebody and, wham! Everybody will know you.

It is much easier to become famous than it is to become great. But it's a lousy trade off. As a matter of fact, you can have thousands and millions of people calling you great, you could even make millions of dollars, but still feel depressed and unhappy. Just think about the following people: Marilyn Monroe, Kurt Cobain, Jim Morrison, Elvis Presley, and Jim Belushi. They brought happiness to millions of people but not to themselves. While on the outside they were putting on a happy facade, on the inside they were dying a slow and agonizing death.

Many times, greatness can be entirely hidden from the public eye. For example, during World War II, Dr. Janusz Korczak operated an orphanage in Poland. In the face of the Nazi blitzkrieg and merciless killing of Jews, Korczak insisted on hosting as many surviving Jewish orphans as his orphanage could accommodate. Although he was aware of the great risk involved in caring for Jewish children, he kept operating his orphanage in secrecy long after the Nazis had stormed through Poland. Because of his courage and compassion, hundreds of Jewish and Polish children survived the terrible war years and eventually grew up to become mature adults. Sadly, Korczak never had the fortune to witness his orphans grow. On August 5 1942, Nazi soldiers came to take his 192 orphans and a dozen of his staff members to the Treblinka extermination camp. Korczak refused to let them go because he knew that the only thing waiting for them at Treblinka was certain death. When the Nazis threatened to burn the orphanage to the ground, Korczak broke down. He decided he wasn't willing to let his children go to their deaths alone and bravely, he decided to join them.

According to a popular legend, when the group arrived at the train station, a German officer recognized Korczak as the author of one of his favorite children's books and offered to help him escape, but once again, Korczak refused. He boarded the trains with the children and was never seen or heard from again.

Very few people know about Dr. Janusz Korczak. And yet, here was an ordinary person doing something great by simply following his heart. And there were no spotlights, no photographers and no newspapers to let the world know about it.

When we think about great people like Mahatma Gandhi, Martin Luther King, Yitzhak Rabin, Albert Einstein, Robert Frost, Galileo, or Mozart, we must ask ourselves "Why do we consider them to be great?" Is it because they've accumulated much wealth? Is it because they were famous? Is it because they were the best? Or is it because of the legacy they have created and the lives they've touched? To me, the answer is very clear. Greatness can only be earned by impacting other people's lives. Money, fame or being the best have nothing to do it. There are countless of men and women like Pete Gray and Dr. Janusz Korczak, people who never made a million and whose stories never made it to the front pages. And yet, by following the calling of their hearts courageously, they've exemplified the epitome of greatness- they lived it.

So as you can see, greatness is a choice that is available for all of us. We all have the ability to choose to conquer our fears and live our lives to the best of our ability. But on the same token, we all have a tendency to settle for what's comfortable and easy and give in to our environments. This is the war within us, the opposing forces that battle for our soul. And it's time for you to choose what side you want to be on. Keep in mind that greatness is something very personal. You are the only one that really knows whether you are living life the way you want to live it or whether you are just going through the motions. So be honest with yourself and choose wisely.

"To be nobody but yourself in a world which is doing its best night and day to make you like everybody else means to fight the hardest battle any human being can fight and never stop fighting"

~ E.E. Cummings ~

Before you turn the page, let me assure you that by time you'll finish reading this book you'll have the information and the tools you'll need to create the life you want. That is my part of the deal. Your part is to put this stuff to work. But let's have no illusions. The journey you're about to embark as you turn this page is not going to be short or easy. Although you won't be risking death, at times, it might get uncomfortable and even difficult. You will have to take a long hard look at yourself and the role you want to play in life and you are going to be making some of the most important decisions about the next level of your life. And while all this can be very exciting, it can also get a bit scary. But that's alright. As long as you stay the course and apply what you learn, you'll grow stronger and better and eventually be rewarded with the ultimate prize: the fulfillment of your dreams.

So let's begin by tapping into one of the most amazing forces known to mankind. A force that has created empires and destroyed kingdoms, healed nations and ruptured continents. And you know what? This is a force you already possess. All you have to do to claim it is turn the page. Let's discover how to ride the...

Section I.
The Philosophy of Being Great

Chapter II

Waves of Change:
A Flexible Philosophy for Uncertain Times

"It is not the strongest of the species that survives, nor the most intelligent that survives. It is the one that is the most adaptable to change"

~ Charles Darwin ~

For months he had been writing the software and crashing on his uncle's sofa. His idea was very simple: to develop a program that will allow computer users to swap music files with one another directly, without going through a centralized file server or middleman. However, nearly anyone he shared the idea with said it was utopian and destined to fail. "It's a selfish world, and nobody wants to share," said his friends from the IRC chat rooms. But he pressed on.

At dawn, he lay on the carpet in his uncle's office and closed his eyes. He had been awake 60 straight hours, turning the Windows API protocols and UNIX server commands into a polished and simple application. Once he was done, he e-mailed the beta-program to several friends in the hacker community saying, "Do NOT share this with anyone. This is still in test phase." Within months, hundreds of thousands of people were forwarded that e-mail. Within one year, more than 25 million people downloaded the program making it one of the greatest Internet applications ever, along with e-mail and instant messaging.

Love it or hate it, Napster has changed the world. It unleashed the mischievous power of the Internet, leaping over legal barriers and transforming our common assumptions of music and information sharing. Moreover, it forced record companies and recording artists to rethink radically their business models and find new ways to defend their intellectual property.

Most of us live and think as if life was static, or as if it should be. We believe that tomorrow will be much like today; that we'll slide by all right if we just get a little better or a little smarter at doing what we are already doing. But life is far from static. Over the next several years, most of the elements that make up what you think of as your "self," will change radically; what you do for a living, how you carry out that career, what you call yourself professionally, the shape of the organization you work for, whom you claim as spouse or mate, the flavor of that relationship, your financial situation, where you live, your relationships with your parents, children, and friends, your health and even your beliefs and assumptions about yourself and the world around you. Some will change drastically, some subtly. Some will change incrementally, some cataclysmically. Some will be changed by outside forces, some from within. However it happens, change is absolutely certain.

It's enough to take a quick glance at the last hundred years to realize the significance of change in our lives. During this time we have witnessed two world wars, been to the moon and experienced dramatic transitions in our economy; from agriculture to mass production and industrialization, and lately into the information revolution.

Over the past twenty years alone we have seen the rise of mobile communication, laptop computers, palm pilots, mp3, iPods, DVD players, Blogs, P2P sharefarms, surround sound, laser surgery, and the decoding of the human DNA.

Today, change on a massive scale is not something attributable to a particular scientist or the leaders of industries. It is something that people, normal people, like you and I create. When Shawn Fanning created "Napster," he didn't have any visions of grandeur. According to journalist Karl Greenfeld, "Fanning never intended to hijack the music industry. The idea for Napster just came to him as he was sitting in his dorm room at Northeastern University in Boston, hanging out with his bros, drinking a brew and listening to his roommate whine about dead MP3 links." Little did he know that his simple idea would eventually force the entire music industry onto its back legs.

That's the kind of world you and I are living in today; one in which a 19-year-old college drop-out writing computer codes in his uncle's office can change the world and force a billion dollar industry to reconsider its business agenda.

When we look at the trends underlying the rate of change, nothing suggests that things are going to slow down or get easier. In fact, as we look forward to the new century and examine demographic forces and technological shifts, the signs are that the ride will get much wilder.

"We live in a world where what you earn depends on what you can learn, where the average 18-year-old will change jobs eight times in a lifetime, and where none of us can promise any of you that what you do for a living is absolutely safe from now on"

~ Bill Clinton ~

The bad news is that there is no easy way to master change. There is no one web site, or book or even an exceptional trainer who can teach you how to cope with change. It's a path you'll have to discover on your own. As the ancient saying goes,

"Many paths, one mountain." Change is slippery, pliable and complex. It moves about in an unpredictable fashion and is nearly impossible to predict. Let me give you an example. Remember the days when you used to follow ants and examine anthills? Now visualize an anthill. No single ant knows how to make an anthill. The anthill emerges from the much simpler interactions of the ants. No one decides which way the stock market will go. Its activity emerges from millions of decisions made by stockholders. Another example I can think of is global terrorism. Here is a consistent pattern; random attacks on civilians around the world. But this "movement" has no public leadership or organized infrastructure. Nobody knows exactly who's in charge, where or when it will strike or who's involved in it. Among futuristic researchers this phenomenon is known as "Spontaneous Emergence."

Spontaneous Emergence represents the unpredictable nature of change. But for most of us, change is something that simply happens. And when it does, it usually catches us off guard and unprepared. So what do we do? The most natural thing to do when faced with uncertainty about the future is to try to predict what will happen. Is this the right career for me? Should I get an MBA? What will happen if I move to the city? Is this a good time to invest in stocks? Will I be promoted? Will I find the perfect mate?

Predicting change is tricky and difficult. For starters, you must have a point of reference that provides you with trustworthy information. And what is that point of reference for most of us? Our past experience. It's hard to deny that most of us have a bias towards our own personal experience. That is, we tend to believe that our own past experience is the best and most reliable source of knowledge because it actually happened to us. Therefore, when change strikes, we go to our most trusted knowledge bank: our past. In the business world this is known as classic trend analysis; looking at yesterday's performance in order to prophesize tomorrow. This approach works fine short-term, when things are relatively stable and when only one major variable changes at a time.

Imagine yourself in a race car blazing through the track at heart-stopping speeds. At 220-miles-per-hour, you are betting your life on an analysis of the short-term future. You are focused on one thing and one thing alone: what the other drivers are doing. So when a collision occurs in front of you, your sharp and well trained instincts steer the car towards the imaginary spot where the accident began since that is the least likely for the wreckage to be when he gets there. Great move, trouble avoided. But what if there's an oil puddle immediately after the collision? And what if, at the same time, a plastic bag flies from the stands and lands on top of your windshield? And what if, completely out of the blue, your pit manager tells you over the radio that the radiator is about to give out and that they forgot to bring a spare one? And what if suddenly it starts to rain? You're in big trouble. Nothing prepared you for this scenario.

The reality is that life jumps at us from all directions simultaneously. Problems don't wait politely in line. And as we continue to progress and increase the amount of variables that are changing in our lives, the more turbulent our future will become and the less we'll be able to predict it using conventional linear thinking or trend analysis.

Throughout our lives we develop different coping strategies for dealing with unexpected change. For example, when some of us face an impending change, be it a newly hired CEO, a friend who has become addicted to drugs, or a change in our personal relationships, we try to dodge the situation. We say "I'm not going to let this affect me," or we completely ignore the situation in hope that it will fade away on its own. This attitude works in minor matters. To use a nautical metaphor, it will allow a breaker to pass you by. But when a gale is coming your way, you'll find yourself heading back to the shore. You can't ignore change. When a train is coming, it's best to get off the track. When opportunity knocks, it's best to open the door. You must be able to respond to change, regardless of how powerful or complex it might be. Picture yourself dancing with a giant gorilla. You don't ignore the gorilla's strength, you respect it and adapt to it. And if you are wise enough, you will let the gorilla lead and do all the work for you.

Some people try to dominate or overpower change. This approach seems reliable and effective but unfortunately, it is short lived. Winning is always about outdoing an opponent when the rules of engagement are clear and the road to victory is visible. The reason that dominance or winning does not work is simple: it is aimed at the wrong target. Whatever the change that is headed our way, whoever the "attacker" may be, what we truly have to struggle with is ourselves.

In a garden, the plants compete for water, sunlight, and nutrients. Yet we do not measure the success of one plant by the failure of the plants around it. We measure it in its own terms: its size, the flavor of its fruit, the lushness of its foliage and the beauty of its shape and color. In their study of eighteen "visionary" companies that were experts in survival, James Collins and Jerry Porras of Stanford University found that "Organizations that survive and thrive over a long period of time do not ask themselves, "How can I beat the competition?" They ask themselves, "How can I outdo myself?"

Those who are driven by competition against others are always in reaction. They are never ahead of the pack. Success in dealing with change is about profiting from it, about using the energy that it brings into your life to challenge yourself, to become larger, stronger, more fruitful and more useful to those around you. It's a lot like sailing. To be an effective sailor, you must learn how to harness the power of the wind. But while most people only know how to sail when the wind is at their back, the wise skipper knows how to take advantage of the storm, the rain, the waves, the head wind, the side wind or even instances when there's no wind at all.

The good news is that you already posses all the necessary resources for mastering change. However, those resources lie deep within you, hidden beneath your fears and confusion at the unfamiliar and unknown. Consider your attitude towards success, as an example. Success is something will we all strive for. But we all fail on occasion. In fact, if we are honest with ourselves, we fail quite often; we make a bad decision, or end up hurting a friend, instead of just listening. These failures are all about us, and they are exquisite teaching devices equipped with powerful wisdom. And yet, most of us avoid failure like the plague. When I fail, I have a powerful impulse to distance myself from the failure, to tell myself all the ways in which it was not my fault, mention it to no one and "put it behind me," or try to just "forget about it." But I know that it does no good when it's behind me. My mistakes are full of information, exactly tailored to me, because they are my mistakes, and no one else's. And if I am determined not to commit the same mistake over and over, I must put failure in front of me, look it in the eye, and pump it for every bit of information it can bring me about how I failed and how I can do better.

There's no doubt in mind that we need a new and dynamic way of dealing with change that will allow us to react to life "on-the-move" rather than stay chained to old and limiting patterns. We need a way of thinking that's adaptable rather than predictable. In San Francisco, because of the interaction of ocean currents and winds, the inland heat, and the city's famous hills, the summer weather can vary wildly from one neighborhood to the next, from wind-blown fog to balmy sunshine to drizzle. So the experienced San Franciscan doesn't try to predict the summer weather, but instead, he dresses in layers: shirt, sweater, jacket, with a windbreaker folded into his bag. He becomes adaptable, moment to moment.

"Change has considerable psychological impact on the human mind. To the fearful, change is threatening because it

means that things may get worse. To the hopeful, change is encouraging because things may get better. To confident, change is inspiring because the challenge exists to make thing better"

~ King Whitney, Jr .~

I'm sure you've noticed that some people deal well with change. In fact, they seem to thrive on it. They take its challenges as sources of enormous energy to drive them forward like a surfer riding the face of a thundering comber. Other people fall apart in the face of change. They seem well organized, confident and may have a desirable spouse, a nice home and a positive outlook until one day they get laid off or discover their child is doing drugs. That's when their life crumbles, revealing their inability to deal with change in their environment.

So let me ask you, what's the real difference between those who thrive on change and those who fall apart, clawing and scrabbling their way down a slippery slope? Is it just luck? Could be, if it happened just once. But if we look closer, we will notice that people develop certain patterns of behavior throughout their lives. We all know people who seem to shoot themselves in the foot every chance they get. On the other hand, we all know people like Nelson Mandela or Lance Armstrong who experienced monumental adversity in their lives on more than one occasion and still managed to triumph every single time. That takes far more than luck.

People who thrive on change share common fundamental abilities. And since change is fractal, its basic nature looks the same at different scales. So the abilities or skills that make a relationship deal effectively with change are the same as those which make a community livable, an organization successful and an individual creative, adaptive, and confident in the midst of turbulence. There are four such abilities, let's go through them quickly.

First is the ability to preserve resources and energy. According to Joe Flower, founder of the Change-Project, "Like an army that does not get too far ahead of its supply train, like a family that stays out of short-term debt and builds up savings, like a man who reaches his seventies with a body he has never abused, an organism that does not waste its capital has more options when it is threatened."

It's important we do not confuse preservation with stinginess. Preservation is not about being thrifty, it's about being penny-wise and "need- conscious" rather than impulsive. It's also critical to develop an awareness of our current limitation. Individuals, families, companies and even countries who constantly over extend their means are vulnerable and are ill prepared for change.

Preserving strength, money or any other resource is an intelligent practice. It's the awareness that change, in any way, shape or form, may strike at any moment and any time. It can be a horrible accident that leaves a close relative paralyzed and in need of expensive care, or a son or a daughter who has just been accepted to a costly university, or a new business idea that requires immediate funds.

Preserving resources means that at whatever financial level you currently exist you must keep debt down and savings up, so that you have resources on which to draw when you need them. In individuals, this means staying in good mental and physical health. In couples and families this means working constantly to keep the relationships strong long before any crisis comes.

Second is the ability and willingness to share knowledge and power. Most of us keep secrets from colleagues, friends and even family members. But to what benefit? Certain types of information such as Coke's secret formula and the design of Intel's next chip are truly trade secrets and must be guarded. But typically we tend to restrict information and power far beyond those narrow boundaries.

We tend to horde information and power out of our fear of

losing control and being vulnerable. This can be costly. On august 12, 2000, the Russian submarine Kursk sunk to the bottom of the sea after an internal explosion had ripped a hole in its hull. Most of the submarine crew survived the explosion and remained trapped at the bottom of the sea awaiting rescue. The Russian military refused immediate American assistance, which could have saved the lives of the 118 crewman, and preferred to wait for a Dutch salvage company. Unfortunately, by the time the Dutch team arrived, the crew had tragically died of asphyxiation. The decision to refuse American assistance was clearly driven by the Russian military's fear of letting American officers inspect the submarine.

When we are afraid to share knowledge and power, we are making a big risk. One-brain, one-track decision making ignores other brains and their creative inventive and entrepreneurial experience. In order to harness all the brain power in your family, business or even circle of friends, you must give them decision-making power where they can feel secure enough to voice their opinion and try different solutions. In a family, this means considerable autonomy for each individual, within the broad sense of the family's spirit and purpose. In an organization, this means considering what everybody thinks, including line employees and maintenance crew.

In times of change, the need to share information grows dramatically. When computer programmers and analysts get stuck in their work, they turn to blogs and forums for answers. The latest fad of 3-D animation movies is largely the result of flowering on-line communities such as *www.renderocity.com*, where amateur and professional animators troubleshoot and exchange tips and strategies about their work.

Are there dangers to sharing? Sure. I know that revealing facts about yourself may leave you vulnerable, especially in cases were your strategy is based on manipulating other people to do what you want. But when you reveal facts or even personal mistakes in order to set the record straight or to apologize, or find a way to overcome a challenge, you show incredible inner strength and you communicate trust to your listener. People will respect and admire you for this.

Third is the ability to develop strong and dependable relationships. We tend to develop relationships with people in our immediate environment, those around whom we feel comfortable. We tend to avoid those who are different. In college, freshmen tend to hang out with freshmen, sophomores with sophomores and juniors with juniors. In the workplace, we form bonds with our immediate superiors and subordinates, those we work closely with. We don't form strong bonds with people in the next work unit over, or several levels above or below us in the hierarchy. Yet organizations in which people have multiple bonds and a lot of history together do better in times of difficulty.

In the early 1980s, John Kotter, author of the classics *Leading Change* and *Force for Change*, examined the management styles of CEOs and division directors who were generally acknowledged as excellent organizational leaders. One of the attributes these leaders had in common was that they seemed to know not only their peers, subordinates, and superiors, but people in other divisions, clergy in the town, the union leaders, their counterparts at other organizations, the janitor who vacuumed their offices. And when the time came, each of these relationships was useful, often in unpredictable ways. Think about the most powerful families in the country: the Kennedy's, the Bush's, the Rockefellers and the Vanderbilts. What do they have in common? Strong bonds both inside and outside the clan.

Fourth is the ability to create, commit and maintain a vision for the future. Victory does not always go to the largest armies, or those with the best deployment and the most firepower. It goes as often to the smaller force with the greatest imagination, flexibility, and boldness, with the vision to make something happen. Every vision of the future sets off its own feedback loop. One prepares for what one believes will happen. At the same time, that preparation makes it more likely that this particular future will happen.

Vision, the ability to visualize the future we want to experience, is an important factor in surviving change and triumphing over difficult times. During the time he was imprisoned in Auschwitz, the infamous Nazi death camp where more than 20,000 Jews were exterminated every single day, Viktor Frankl could not help but notice that among those who were not sent to the gas chambers and were given a chance for survival, it was those who held on to a vision of the future - whether it be a significant task before them or a return to their loved ones - that were most likely to survive their suffering.

After surviving the horrors of Auschwitz, Frankl wrote *Man's Search for Meaning* where he explained how we derive strength from envisioning intensely what we want to happen in the future. Once a picture or vision is clear in our mind, we intuitively take whatever steps are necessary to make the vision a reality. The man determined to survive and reunite with his family will take care of himself to guarantee that the dream comes true. The company determined to keep its people employed in the years ahead will stake out new markets, make changes in processes, and lay out strategies and tactics to make it so.

"He who rejects change is the architect of decay. The only human institution which rejects progress is the cemetery"

~ Harold Wilson ~

The four attributes we covered are essential for dealing with change effectively. But how do you develop and apply them to your life? It's a two step process.

Step 1:
Run Towards the Roar

The first step you'll need to take is to muster the courage to leave your comfort zone and learn to swim in unfamiliar waters. In one of his outstanding lectures, philosopher Alan Watts observed that " Today, we are finally beginning to realize that our "rock" is worn out in an age where it becomes more and more obvious that our world is a floating world. It's a world floating in space where all positions are relative and any point may be regarded as the center, a world which doesn't float on anything, and therefore the attitude of our time should not be one of 'clinging to rocks,' but one of 'learning to swim.'" That's a powerful insight.

In order to learn to swim, we must let go of everything that's stable and secure; the shore, the docks, the rocks, and trust ourselves to the water. In our case, the water is life itself. And the question I want you to consider is: How much do you trust it? Most people don't trust life. And so, they don't take any chances. They spend their lives seeking safety and security, not realizing that by doing so, they are excluding themselves from the game. They cling to their strengths like an inexperienced mountain climber might cling to a piece of rock in fear that he might fall.

What I'll be asking you to do more and more throughout this book is to let go. Let go of what you know and what you're familiar with for the sake of introducing something greater and bigger into your life. I know it's not easy to let go of our strengths. We all have our favorite moves, the ones that really work for us and that we fall back on time after time. The temptation is to play it safe by repeating those moves over and over, and seeking out the situations where they work best. But to really grow, we have to do the opposite. We have to seek out the situations that are the most difficult for us, work them through, hang out with them long enough to begin to be at home in with uncertainty, with not knowing. This represents a paradoxical, ambiguous, and strange circumstance

Consider the following lesson. When lions hunt antelopes, the dominant male stays where he is while the female lions, the real hunter, swifter than the male, sneaks around to the far side of the herd and lies down in the grass. Too big and slow to catch the antelope by himself, he takes on the job of suddenly leaping up and roaring at the antelope. Terrified, the antelope runs in the opposite direction, straight into the trap laid by the waiting female.

For the antelope, salvation would lie in running towards the roar, in deliberately picking out the thing that is most terrifying, and moving towards the source of the fear. While this behavior is counter-intuitive, it is the only way for the antelope to survive. This is true for us as well. What you fear, what your family or your organization instinctively avoid, becomes a useful marker of the direction of the most powerful change that you could make. This paradox, your fear as a guide to change, is especially evident in our relationships with other people. Ask yourself "What do I fear most? Deeply committing myself to my mate? Expressing my emotions, even the graceless ones? Learning to hear without judgment?" That's the direction in which you will find the most powerful engine of change. Always remember: the places of weakness are the places of the greatest growth potential.

Step 2:
Look in the Mirror

The second step you must take is to discover who you are, or rather, who you *think* you are. Why is it important to discover who you are? Because it's those internal forces; our values, beliefs and our sense of our selves that can act either as an anchor holding us back, or as a rocket that propels us forward. Ideally, having a deep sense of who we are should allow us to go into uncharted territories with supreme confidence. But more often, mistaken ideas about who we *think* we are prevent us from exploring new possibilities, like the circus elephant held by his short ankle chain linked to a huge stake driven deep into the ground. One of the first and most important parts of any personal transformation program is to bring to the table all your hopes, fears, beliefs, assumptions, values and goals. This is the essential process of identifying who you are and where you are at this particular point in your life. Later on, this will become your "Anamnesis," a place you can reach out and touch in the midst of turmoil. Anamnesis or "True soul-memory" is the skill of keeping touch with what is deep and constant in the midst of change.

Imagine you and I are having a one-on-one conversation. After talking for about 15-minutes, what kind of a person would I see? How would you describe yourself? What do you stand for? What do you believe in? What are your strength and weaknesses? How would you define yourself? Are you a lover? A procrastinator? A giver? A taker? A winner? A loser? Are you sexy? Funny? Are you a shy person? Are you loud and flamboyant? Are you a Christian? A Jew? Are you spiritual? A millionaire? A student? Are you single? Involved? Married? How do you identify yourself?

Usually when I ask people who they are I get one of three answers. I get either a blank stare, which means they just ran into a mental brick wall, or I get a superficial retort like, "I am me and that's it," which means they simply don't want to think about the whole issue, or, in the best case scenarios, I get something like "I don't know," or "I'm not sure."

What's important to know is that who you think you are, the qualities, talents, character and personality traits you believe you possess, the things you stand for, (and against) the beliefs you have about the world and other people, the views and values you carry, the way other people behave towards you, the feedback you receive from your environment, and the emotions you feel, all those form the fabric of your being. This fabric is also called your "identity."

The quickest way to discover your identity is to look at your patterns of behavior. Aristotle said: "We are what we repeatedly do." Think about it, don't you define other people according to their actions? If you have a friend who sleeps a lot and likes to take things easy, how do you describe him? Maybe you'd call him a "sleepy head," or "laid back," or even "lazy," depending on how much you value that sort of behavior. Don't you do the same thing with yourself? If you find yourself being late all the time, how would you describe yourself? If you went out a lot and enjoyed being around other people, you wouldn't call yourself shy, right? You'd probably identify yourself as outgoing and easy to get along with or something of that sort.

The music you listen to is another good indicator of the things you identify with. What kind of music to you like? Slow and mellow? Energetic? Aggressive? What do you like about it? How does it make you feel? Alive? In love? Lonely? Powerful? Remember, the music you like tends to express how you feel about certain things. When you identify yourself with certain lyrics, you immediately internalize their meaning and consequently you feel the emotional state they were meant to induce.

Another way to find out what makes you feel unique is by looking at your friends. There is an old saying, which goes "You are the average of your five best friends." There's plenty of truth to that. That's because in many cases, your friends are a reflection of who you *think* you are. Think about it for a minute, what attracts you to your friends? What are the qualities you share in common? What are the things you do together? If you examine this seriously, I'm sure you'll find patterns that will give you an indication as to what you value.

One more way to discover your identity is by examining how other people behave towards you. The way in which different people behave towards you is a result of the person *they* think you are. If they think you are smart, they'll act towards you in a certain way. If they think you are irresponsible, they'll treat you differently. If they think you are a loving and compassionate person they'll treat you differently once again.

Lastly, you can always look at your past for references. As I said earlier, tennis was an important part of my past and a huge part of my identity. Today, however, even though I maintain an athletic life style, I don't see myself as a tennis player because it's not a part of my present experience. But it's a resource I still have within me that I can tap into whenever I'm in competitive situations.

Alright, I think you are ready for a little bit of real-time training. Understanding new concepts requires intelligence but it's not until we put those concepts to practice and apply them to our lives that we actually begin to reap the rewards. This will be a great opportunity to exercise your ability to take the initiative and push the procrastinating voice inside of you into a corner.

Go grab a pen please. Put some music on and sit up straight. Now, on the other side of this page you'll find a blank page. That's where you'll be writing. Your goal is to fill the page within two minutes with all the words that describe and identify who you are. Try to think about the things you like, the talents you have and the values and principles you stand for. Write as fast as you can for two minutes without lifting your pen from the paper. It's important you don't postpone this activity and don't say "I'll come back to this later," because you won't. Take charge and do it now. You'll feel great once you're done. Ready? Go!

Who are you?

I am:

Your identity plays a monumental function in your psychological make up. It defines your uniqueness and individuality. It sets the boundaries for your everyday experience. It informs your ideas about what you can and cannot do. It determines what emotions you will feel or avoid feeling. It guides your behavior in social situations, dictates how you will react to other people, and how you will respond to unexpected events. Let me give you a few examples.

Were you ever invited to do something you considered to be totally nuts? If you answered the invitation with something like, "I could never do that," or "that's just not me," you ran into the boundaries of your identity, which means that you do not identify with that sort of behavior and you don't see yourself as "that kind of a person." Therefore, you probably won't do it. But on the other hand, if you view yourself as a crazy risk taker, chances are that you'll go for it.

It's crucial to understand that we tend to behave in accordance with what we *think* we are capable of achieving rather than what we are really capable of. An experiment Rosenthal and Jacobson conducted a while ago illustrates this best. They took elementary school children from 18 classrooms and randomly chose 20 percent of the children from each room and told the teachers they were "intellectual bloomers." They explained that these children could be expected to show remarkable gains during the year. What do you think happened? Well, even though there was no difference in the amount of time the teachers spent with the different student groups, the "intellectual bloomers" really did bloom! This phenomenon is known as "the Pygmalion effect."

According to Rosenthal "We may say that by what she said, by how and when she said it, by her actual facial expressions, postures and perhaps by her touch, the teacher may have communicated to the children of the experimental group that she expected improved intellectual performance. Such communication together with possible changes in teaching techniques may have helped the child learn by changing his self concept, (identity) his expectations of his own behavior, and his motivation, as well as his cognitive style and skills."

The Pygmalion effect is not only prevalent among children, but in every aspect of life. When we enter a new job, we have a "job description" which is nothing more than an expectations list that sets the boundaries of our job. How many times did you face a clerk who refused to help you beyond his "job description"? The identities we assume determine the quality of our performance; be it in bed with our spouses, out with our friends, at our jobs or when we compete.

It's important to remember that the Pygmalion effect also operates in reverse. It's called "the set-up-to-fail" syndrome. When we expect to fail at something, we usually do. How many times have you succeed in something when you said to yourself, "I can never be good at this"? Not very often, right? That's because when you think you are not good at something, you program "failure" into your nervous system.

Many people cling to identities that limit and rob them of the future they deserve to experience. Ever wondered why?

For starters, many people think about their identity in the same way they think about their skin color; that it's a part of their genetic makeup. Therefore, they can't even imagine tampering with it. That's absurd. We don't inherit traits like "anger" or "shyness," we develop them. We model them. And we spend years perfecting them as defense mechanisms. The reality is that all it takes to change our identity is to behave in a way that contradicts who we think we are. For example, if you tend to be shy, you must practice acting sociable and outgoing. (Remember "Running towards the roar"?) If you are afraid of dogs, go visit the local animal shelter. This is how I overcame my fear of public speaking. When I was younger, you couldn't pay me enough to stand in front a group of people and speak. I was mortified at the thought of it. But after I did it again and again and again I began to feel more and more comfortable and the fear and anxiety gradually retreated.

The second reason people don't change is because in our culture, we have been strongly conditioned to associate inconsistency and change with massive pain. We've been taught that change suggests instability, chaos, lack of certainty, insecurity and vulnerability.

Just think about it, how do we describe people who say one thing today, and tomorrow something totally different? We call them fakes, two-faced, and hypocrites. Not labels you want to have attached to your name, right? On the other hand how do we describe people who are consistent? We call them reliable, trustworthy, loyal, dependable and balanced. Sometimes we might even go as far as calling them fair or honest. Now who wouldn't want to have their name associated with those qualities?

Most people do not change because they find it easier to blame others for their circumstances than take responsibility. For example, a person who has frequent anger bursts can blame them on "the way he is" instead of facing the fact that getting angry is a conscious choice. Ignoring the fact that we can change allows us to live in denial and accept our weaknesses as character flaws rather than *opportunities for improvement.*

In order to change effectively, we must be brutally honesty with ourselves and admit our shortcomings (and we all have plenty of them) so we can eradicate them before they become malignant and contaminate other parts of our personality. Sure, getting real with ourselves can be uncomfortable, but trust me when I say that it will pay off tremendously in the long run. The sooner you get real, the faster your life will embark on a new road.

"Identity would seem to be the garment with which one covers the nakedness of the self, in which case, it is best that the garment be loose, a little like the robes of the desert, through which one's nakedness can always be felt, and, sometimes, dis-

cerned. This trust in one's nakedness is all that gives one the power to change one's robes"

~ James Arthur Baldwin ~

The real secret in mastering personal change lies in choosing our identities *consciously* instead of simply allowing different traits stick to us without our awareness. Just think about it, what if right now, you decided to do something you've never done before? What if you decided to step up and became a leader? How would that influence your life? As a leader, what would you do? Would you organize social awareness rallies? Would you organize safe sex seminars? Would you commit to helping disadvantaged kids? How about fundraising for your childhood elementary school? Would you start a business venture?

One of the most powerful resources we have at our disposal is the ability to design our own identity and to expand it. When we expand our identity, when we see ourselves for more than what we currently are, we are creating a vision and are automatically pulled in its direction.

The best way to expand our identity is to claim who we are when we are at our best. When we claim our highest standards and see ourselves not only as whom we are at the moment, but also as whom we want to be in the future, we give ourselves unconscious permission to grow. Remember, you must be willing to claim not only who you are, but also who you want to be. If you don't claim it, how can you ever become it?

Let me show you how it's done. I'll use myself as an example. Check out the box on the next page.

Who am I when I'm at my best?

When I'm at my best, I am a force of nature. I'm an example of possibility and freedom for everything that is strong and good in life. I'm an outstandingly courageous, fear-crushing leader with the power to influence and the wisdom to learn. I'm a steaming locomotive. I'm funny, outrageous, happy, playful, inspiring, smart, sophisticated, admirable, beautiful, sexy, attractive, intriguing, and forever passionate. I'm a treasured son, brother, uncle, and lover.

But that's not enough. I'm also an extraordinary teacher, facilitator and communicator. I'm an accelerator of human growth, a designer of futures and creator of destinies. I'm an author, a learning machine, a supreme scholar, a feisty philosopher, a devastating DJ, an innovator, businessman, visionary, agent of change, and most importantly, towering above everything else... I'm a human being!

Seeing yourself as more than you currently are is not about being arrogant, aloof or narcissistic. It's about identifying with the best in you and striving to make it even better. Claiming who you want to be, forcefully and with absolute certainty is nothing but a method of self empowerment. It is a primary tool in your mental arsenal, one that if used persistently will ultimately take you to where you want to go.

For myself, I choose the characteristics that bring out the best in me. Do I live all of them, all the time, every second of every minute of everyday? No. But I try hard to. My "best" identity acts as a standard of behavior, a compass, which reminds me to step up whenever I feel negative or pessimistic.

Please read carefully what Nelson Mandela said in his 1994 inaugural speech and let his immortal words wash away any traces of self-doubt or unworthiness from your consciousness: "Our deepest fear is not that we are inadequate. . . . Our deepest fear is that we are powerful beyond measure. It is our light, not our darkness, that most frightens us. We ask ourselves, who am I to be brilliant, to be gorgeous, talented, and fabulous. Actually, who are you not to be? You are a child of God. Your playing small doesn't serve the world. There is nothing enlightened about shrinking so that others won't feel insecure around you. We are born to make manifest the glory of God within us. And as we let our light shine, we consciously give others permission to do the same. As we are liberated from our fear, our presence automatically liberates others." Internalize the message. Cement it in your brain.

Now it's your turn. It's time to step up and claim the person you want to be. Give yourself a clean slate. Forget about the past, forget about your environment. Focus for a minute on who you want to be right now. Let me remind you that living your life through your past is like using a rear view mirror to guide you into the future. You're bound to crash. You might as well drive blindfolded.

Same drill as before. Put some music on, relax and have fun. Don't censure or evaluate your thoughts. Just write them down as soon as they pop into your head. Again, your goal is to fill the page within two minutes. Remember that you won't be graded on this so don't hold back.

Before you start, let me ask you a few stimulating questions that will get your mind going in the right direction. Please tell me, when you are at your very best:

How would you breathe?

How would you talk?

How would you stand?

What would other people say about you?

What will they see when they look at you?

What will they feel when they talk to you?

What resources will be available to you?

What will you share?

Take two minutes, do the best you can. Hit it!

Who am I when I'm at my best?

When I'm at my best, I am:

Now, let me ask you, are you limited to having only one identity? Of course not. You can develop as many identities as you want, as long as you don't get them mixed up. Researchers into cases of "multiple personalities" tell us that these cases are only extreme versions of ourselves. In "multiples" the relationships between the parts of the personality have broken down. Often one identity, a controlling one or a victimized one, comes to dominate the personality while other parts are ignored. This kind of personality is brittle and inflexible. Strong and flexible personalities bring all parts to the table, from the "inner child," full of wonder, delight, and sadness, to the controller, arbiter of order and purpose.

Personally, I have many different identities. For example, I have an identity of a "Sexual sensei" that I use when I'm intimate with my significant other. Whenever I slip into this identity my entire physiology changes; the tone of my voice the way in which I breathe, the way I touch.

When I'm about to go on stage or lead a training session I go into my "Omega Supreme" identity, which is a combination of an actor/leader/teacher/coach/facilitator. As a result, I have access to specific resources within myself that empower me and allow me to perform at my best. My speech becomes clearer and louder, I move with certainty and force and my entire body becomes a communication device.

When I'm training my body, I'm in a "Warrior" mode. I move as though I was chasing prey in the jungle. I conjure intense focus. I breathe rhythmically and move fluidly. And as a result, I not only enjoy the workout but I also get the feeling as though I'm preparing for a challenge, much like a warrior before battle.

Which one of those identities is the *real* me? The answer is: all of them. In order to play our different roles to the best of our ability, we have to change our identities, just like actors do. Because after all, aren't we all actors? Don't all of us have different roles to fulfill? And isn't the entire world just a big stage?

There is virtually no limit to the blends and flavors of identities you can create for yourself. And as long as *you* determine what they are, they are going to make you better, stronger, and more adaptable to the trials and tribulations ahead.

One of the most important identities I have for myself is that of a chameleon. It's an identity that allows me to shift patterns of behavior swiftly and assimilate with my environment quickly. It's an important identity for me because during the last six years, I had the privilege of living in Jewish, Asian, African-American, Latino, and Chicano communities, and without an ability to assimilate and adapt to new customs and cultures quickly, I would have never been able to fit in and make myself or the people around me feel at ease with my behavior.

Remember, your identity is what you believe it is. If you believe it is cemented and unchangeable, then that's how you'll experience the world. But if you believe it is something fluid and dynamic, something agile and flexible, capable of adapting and adjusting quickly to any situation, than your experience of the world will change accordingly.

"Now you put water into a cup, it becomes the cup. You put water into a bottle, it becomes the bottle. You put water into a teapot, and it becomes the teapot. Now water can flow or it can crash! Be water, my friend"

~ Bruce Lee ~

My goal in this chapter was to encourage you to take a closer look at the reflection you see in the mirror and examine your own sense of existence. Why? Because it's your sense of being, the sense of knowing who you are that will ultimately determine whether you will stand strong or crumble in the face of impending change.

I believe you and I are much more than the sum total of our identities. We are much more than the collection of our behaviors, our fears, our emotions and our bodies. If you ask an ordinary person to point at themselves, you know where they'll point? To their heart. Not their head, their heart. Don't you find that interesting?

If you look back at your life, I'm sure you'll realize that even though throughout the years everything about you has changed, nevertheless at the core, something still remains stable and unflinching. Some people call it "mind," others call it "soul" or "spirit." In *The 8th Habit*, Stephen Covey called it "the gap between stimulus and response." He referred to it as "our freedom to choose." He also describes it as "Our first birth-gift."

Personally, I believe that within each and every one of us resides a powerful, eternal and unchanging force, a force that nobody can take away from us. This force is our ability to decide who we want to be. It is a force that transcends our genetic makeup and our social conditioning. And it's this force, the ability to decide and direct our lives that will eventually determine our destiny.

I don't know if you saw the movie *21 grams* but if you did, I'm sure you remember the final scene where Sean Penn's character is lying on his death bed tied to a respirator, thinking his last thoughts about who and what we really are as human beings. It's a heart breaking scene because the entire movie is about an unfortunate series of ironic accidents that portray how fragile, temporary and vulnerable everything in life really is. As Penn's breath is about to give way, we can hear his broken voiceover reflecting philosophically about the life:

" *They say we all lose 21 grams at the exact moment of our death. Now how much fits into 21 grams? How much is lost? Why do we lose 21 grams? How much goes with them? How much is gained? How…..much…. is …. Gained?*

21 grams. The weight of a stack of five nickels. The weight of a humming bird. A chocolate bar."

What are those 21 grams? I believe that's our power of choice. And we can use this power to change and grow or hang tightly to our limiting identities. Clearly, the decision is clearly ours. In *Pathfinders*, author Gail Sheehy wrote "If we don't change, we don't grow. If we don't grow, we aren't really living." She is absolutely right. You have been given the power to choose who you want to be and how you want to respond to life. Use it wisely.

"We are given one life, and the decision is ours whether to wait for circumstances to make up our mind, or whether to act, and in acting, to live"

~ Omar Nelson Bradley ~

Alright, we've laid the philosophical foundation for dealing with change and we learned about the power of identity. It's time to continue our quest and dive into the deep realms of human behavior. Let's discover...

Chapter III

The Forces That Shape Our Lives:

What Drives Human Behavior?

"If you deliberately plan on being less than you are capable of being, then I warn you that you'll be unhappy for the rest of your life"

~Abraham Maslow~

At about 3 A.M. his boat capsized. He quickly sealed himself in his waterproof cabin and began pumping water into the outside containers that were supposed to turn his boat back up. But the waves were just too high. He reached for his telex transmitter, his only means of communication with the world, and pressed the SOS button. Nothing. This meant serious trouble.

He had already been under water for nearly two hours, relentlessly working the pump. But now the oxygen was running low and he began to feel disoriented. For a minute, he let go of the pump and surrendered to the storming Pacific. He was exhausted and about to give up.

In a last desperate effort, he decided to give the water pump another try. He felt his way through the darkness, cutting and bruising his skin and occasionally loosing his footing. As he clinched the handle, he remembered all the things that mattered to him most; his wife, his two children, his family, his home in France and even the people at Sector who agreed to finance his ambitious journey.

Suddenly, the storm began to subside. He felt a rush of energy and began pumping like crazy. This was his last chance at survival. Within a few minutes, the "Sector" flipped over and Gerard could finally open his cabin and breathe the fresh night air. For now, it seemed that everything was going to be OK. As he collapsed unto the deck, drenched and tired, he whispered a prayer of gratitude and fell into a deep sleep.

Several weeks later, as he approached Washington State shoreline, he saw his family in the distance, surrounded by several hundred cheering spectators. At that point, he could no longer hold back the tears. His journey was over.

On July 11, 1991 Gerard Daboville set sail from Japan towards the western shores of the United States alone, in a boat with no engines or sails. The grueling 1,350- mile journey lasted 134 days in which Gerard had to row an average of 14 hours a day and face 40-foot waves that caused his boat to capsize more than 30 times. By the time he reached the shores of the United States, Gerard had lost more than 25 pounds. He had cuts and bruises all over his face, a dislocated shoulder, and was suffering from dehydration. But, as he writes in *Alone*, at that moment, he was "One happy man."

Gerard's story is pretty amazing, isn't it? But it's also strange. Why would a man risk his life by rowing across the vast Pacific alone? It sure wasn't to save on a plane ticket. Was he after fame? Attention? Money? Was he outright crazy? We'll get back to Gerard later on in this chapter.

What do you think drives us to do the things we do? Why do we cross the Pacific in a row boat? Why do we buy cars? Why do we sing? Why do we climb mountains? Why do we build airplanes? Why do we fall in love? Why do we paint and play music? Why do we get married and have children? Have you ever wondered why we do all those things?

One thing is absolutely clear to me: it doesn't matter how mundane or bizarre human behavior may seem at times, be it crossing the Pacific or smashing a plane full of innocent people into a skyscraper; there is always an underlying reason for our actions. Human behavior is not random or coincidental. Sure, we may not always be aware of the reasons for our behavior but nevertheless, they are still there. And if we can understand what drives our behavior, we can take charge of our lives and shape our destiny according to our will.

"What we believe to be the motives of our conduct are usually but the pretexts for it"

~ Miguel de Unamuno ~

To begin our quest into the mysterious realms of human behavior and motivation, let's take a quick look at what we already know about the subject. In the beginning of the twentieth century, Sigmund Freud, who studied the mentally ill and the neurotic, suggested that human behavior was motivated by unconscious instinctual impulses which he called "life instincts." For example, we can't control the feeling of hunger. It simply "pops-up" or emerges whenever your body needs food. By the same token, we can't control our instinct to squint whenever we look at sun; our body does that automatically to protect your eyes. Today we know that those life instincts are bioelectrical messages our nervous system sends to our brain in order to ensure our survival i.e. move us closer to pleasure and away from pain. This is also known as the "Pain-Pleasure principle." When we touch a hot stove, we immediately feel a burst of pain and we pull back. On the other hand, when we think something will make us feel pleasure, our nervous system automatically attempts to move us closer to it. What's your favorite dessert? How about warm chocolate raspberry trifle with French soft cream? Or apple cake with delicious caramel sauce and vanilla ice cream? Or strawberry cheese cake with dripping Belgian chocolate sauce? Is your mouth getting watery? That's your "pleasure" buds trying to move you closer to that desert. When we examine Freud's view carefully, we discover there's plenty of truth to it.

In the 1930's, Burrhus Frederic Skinner, a Harvard psychology graduate, who experimented primarily with pigeons and rats, suggested that human behavior was predominantly driven by external factors in the form of rewards and punishments. By offering food to pigeons and rats in different experimental settings, he was able to control, shape, and modify their behavior. In Skinner's view, people do not commit crimes because they fear the consequences of getting caught. In this case, the judicial system serves as an external deterring agency. On the positive side, many people would gladly change their jobs if offered higher compensation. Higher compensation in this case, acts as an external motivator. Obviously, there's plenty of truth to Skinners' theory as well.

In the 1950's, Abraham Maslow broke new ground. He felt that Freud and Skinner's theories were sufficient in explaining simple, primordial behaviors such as copulation or aggression but inadequate in explaining complex behaviors such as playing the violin or writing a poem. He felt that human beings had a unique yearning, unlike animals, to express their abilities and realize their own unique individuality. Unlike Freud and Skinner, Maslow did not study the mentally ill and based his views strictly on animal research. "The study of crippled, stunted, immature, and unhealthy specimens can yield only a crippled psychology and a crippled philosophy," he wrote in *Motivation and Personality*. So he chose to study exemplary people such as Albert Einstein, Jane Addams, Eleanor Roosevelt, and Frederick Douglass in an attempt to find out what really drives human behavior. His studies led him to discover that even though we are capable of a wide and diverse array of behaviors, we are all driven by a deep desire to feel certain emotions. Think about money, for example. Why do people want money? Is it because they like the way a dollar bill looks like? Of course not. People want money because they believe it will give them a sense of security and freedom. Why do people want relationships? Is it because they want another person to split the bills with? Not really. People want relationships because of the love, the passion the excitement and the intimacy they think relationships will give them. Why do people contribute to charities or do volunteer work? Is it because they enjoy doing things for free? No. It's because they want to feel that they are making a difference through unselfish contribution.

If you could have all the money in the world right now but without the feeling of financial freedom and security, would you still want it? What if at this moment, you could have the relationship you really wanted but without the passion or intimacy? Would you still want it? What if you could help the unfortunate, feed the hungry and cure the sick without the sense of contribution and influence? Would you still want it?

There's ample truth to Maslow's insight. It's obvious that we don't buy a house just to have a place to sleep; we buy a house because we want to feel secure and comfortable. We don't buy a car in order to get from point A to point B. If this were true, we would save our money and take the bus or the train. We buy a car because we want to feel dynamic and stylish and free. It's the same with marriage. We don't get married so we can have a big party and spend lots of money; we get married because we want to feel a sense of commitment and deep connection with another person.

"Let's not forget that the little emotions are the great captains of our lives and we obey them without realizing it"

~ Vincent Van Gogh ~

Human behavior, Maslow believed, is primarily driven by emotional needs. When he worked with monkeys early in his career, Maslow noticed that they constantly tried to satisfy specific emotional needs. He also observed that some needs took precedence over others. For example, a monkey would try to meet his need for food before he would attempt to meet his need for sexual pleasure. Later on in his career, Maslow recognized that just like the monkeys he studied, human beings seemed to be driven by specific emotional needs as well; the need to feel security, variety, significance, love, growth and contribution. However, Maslow noted, while we all have the same six emotional needs, we were trying to fulfill them in different ways.

In order to grasp the profound meaning of this insight, we need to take a closer look at the needs that drive us and the different ways we have for meeting them.

The first need is the need for comfort and security. This is a need to feel certain that in any situation we can avoid pain and gain pleasure. This is a survival need. It's non negotiable. It is not something we can ignore or undermine. It is the first need we try to meet in any new situations we encounter, in every area of our lives. For example, in our relationships, the first thing we are trying to achieve is a certain level of certainty that our spouse loves us and that love is safe and secure. In our job, the first thing we strive for is a certain level of competence that can make us feel comfortable and secure.

What happens when we can't meet this need sufficiently? If you've ever been in an earthquake or in a car accident or any other situation where your life was threatened, then I'm sure you know exactly what I'm talking about. When we don't have the certainty that we can be comfortable, when we don't feel as though we can control what's going on around us and protect ourselves from pain, then our brain goes into survival mode and our lives are in danger of falling apart. Have you seen Spielberg's *War of the Worlds*? That is a great example of what happens to people when one day, comfort and security completely vanish.

So what do we do to feel comfortable and secure? Well, some of us build houses with high fences and expensive alarm systems. Some of us relocate. Others may get a dog or buy a weapon. In social settings, some people grasp for control. They may try to control their environment, or their spouse or their colleagues because by controlling events and people they feel that we can predict outcomes. And if they can predict outcomes, then we can be secure. Some people try to feel comfort by doing the same thing everyday. They feel that if they can create consistent patterns in their lives, then nothing would surprise them or knock them off balance.

Another way for some people to feel comfortable and secure is by eating. Why eating? Because by eating, especially when they are stressed, they get to feel momentary comfort. It's a way to grasp for control and move away from pain and towards pleasure. What else do we do to feel secure and comfortable? Have you ever rented a movie you've already seen? Why did you? After all, you already know what's going to happen, right? You did it because you were confident that it would make you feel good. It's the same reason people use drugs or listen to the song over and over again; because they know those things will make them feel good.

I think that one of the best and most positive ways to have certainty in our day and age is to develop hope. What do I mean by hope? Hope is about knowing that you have ability to respond with courage and creativity to whatever life throws your way. It is the unshakable confidence that you can control how you feel at any moment in time, under any conditions, regardless of what the future may impose. Dr. David Mayers who teaches at Michigan Hope's college described it as "A deep and abiding sense that, despite the day's woes, all is, or will be, well. Even when the surface waters churn, the deep currents run sure." Life has an unpredictable dimension to it. There will always be things we can't control. We can't control other people, we can't control the weather, we can't control terrorists, and we can't control the economy. Nobody really knows what tomorrow will bring. This sort of shaky reality forces us to constantly negotiate a certain level of insecurity in our lives. Hope is the antidote.

It's really up to you to decide how we want to respond to the future. You can either allow fear and worry to dominate your life or you can choose to take charge by getting stronger, smarter and better. In the following chapters, I'm going to give you the distinctions and strategies that will help to take charge and be in control of your life. But, if you're not going to put them into action, you'll stay exactly where you are. John Schaar observed that "the future is not some place we are going, but one we are creating. The paths to it are not found but made, and the activity of making them changes both the maker and the destination." Schaar is absolutely right. It's your responsibility to create the future you want to experience. Yours and no one else's.

Tell me, what would happen if you could predict the next several days of your life with precise accuracy? I'll tell what will happen, you'll get bored. We get bored when we have too much comfort and security. And this can be destructive as the next story illustrates.

Once there was a king who, while standing at the window of his palace, happened to notice a man in the town square below. He was an average man, walking home at night, who had taken the same route five nights a week for many years. "I wonder what would happen if a man were kept in cage like the animals in the zoo?" the king thought to himself.

The next day the king had a cage brought from the zoo. The cage was fairly large since it that had been occupied by a lion when it was new. The cage was put in an inner private court in the palace grounds, and the average man, whom the king had seen from the window, was brought and placed therein.

At first the man was simply bewildered. He kept saying to the king, "I have to catch the tram, I have to get to work, look what time is, and I'll be late for work!" But later on in the afternoon the man began to realize his circumstance, and then he protested vehemently, "The king can't do this to me! It is unjust! It's against the law." His voice was strong, and his eyes full of anger.

The king's personal psychologist was interested by the man's anger. He had encountered anger often in his work. "Yes," he realized, "this anger is the attitude of people who, like the healthy adolescents of any era, want to fight what's wrong, who protest directly against it. When people come to me in this mood, it is good. They can be helped."

During the rest of the week the man continued his vehement protests. When the king walked by the cage, as he did everyday, the man made his protests directly to the monarch. But the king answered, "Look here, you are getting plenty of food, you have a good bed, and you don't have to work. We take good care of you; so why are you objecting?"

Every day the king, as he walked through the courtyard, kept reminding the man in the cage that he was given food and shelter and taken good care of. The psychologist noticed that, whereas at first the man had been entirely impervious to the king's statements, it now seemed more and more that he was pausing for a moment after the king's speech- as though he was actually thinking about what the king said.

After a few more weeks, the man began to discuss with the psychologist how it was a useful thing that a man is given food and shelter and that his health is taken care of; and how a man had lived by his fate in any case, and the wisdom of life was to accept fate. He soon developed an extensive theory about security and the acceptance of fate and circumstances. He was very talkative during this period, although the talk was mostly a monologue.

The psychologist noticed that now, the corner of the man's

mouth always turned down, as though it was some gigantic pout. One day, a research team of several graduate students came to visit the palace. Instead of lecturing to the group about psychology and behavior, the psychologist thought that a conversation with the victim himself would be much more interesting. The man was friendly toward the students and explained that he had chosen this way of life, that there were great values in security and in being taken care of, that they would of course see how sensible his life was and so on.

As time progressed, the man became more solemn and morose. His grand philosophical theories vanished and instead, he only uttered simply sentences saying, "it is fate," and "this is life." Shortly thereafter, the man completely stopped using the word "I." He had accepted the cage. He had no anger, no hate, and no rationalization.

When our lives become redundant, when we feel we know exactly what's going to happen in our work or in our relationship, we satiate our need for comfort and security and we become complacent and indolent. Gerard felt this way an 1990, a year before his great expedition:

> "*A feeling that I was not getting any younger, a general sense of wear and tear on mind and body, business ventures that had turned sour, plus I had to admit, an overall feeling of boredom.*"

Luckily, we have a second need that is designed to balance our need for comfort and security and inject zest and spice into our lives.

The second need is the need for change and variety. Let's face it, we all need a little excitement and surprise in our lives, right? Do you like birthdays? How about visiting new places and meeting new people?

The need for change and variety usually kicks in when we

feel our lives have become repetitive. It is an urge we have to experience new things, to be surprised, to be challenged, to feel alive and to face risks and dangers. Let me show you what people do to meet this need. Let's take relationships, for example.

What do people do when they get bored in their relationships? Some people may begin to lie or cheat. Other people may pick a fight, or even leave. Other people may decide to go on a second honey moon or do something they've never done before like go horseback riding.

How about professionally? What do people do in order to feel change and variety in their work? Well, some people ask to be moved to a different position. Others may ask for new responsibilities. Other people may choose to leave and start something on their own.

The need for change and variety is the reason we go to movies and concerts. It's why we visit new places and meet new people. It's the reason we read books, join clubs or learn a new set of skills. In essence, any new experience can help us meet our need for change and variety. But perhaps the best way to do so is by choosing to face a new challenge. Here, we can learn from Gerard:

> "I vaguely knew that I needed to cleanse my mind, refocus my priorities, and engage in some real combat. A combat in which I would invest all the daring, tenacity, and courage I could muster; all my considerable experience; all my profound knowledge of the sea, a combat into which I would throw my self body and soul, its success dependent solely upon me."

The third need is the need for significance. This is the need to have validation for our existence, to feel that we are unique and special and that people recognize and respect who we are and what we do.

What are some of the things we do to meet this need? We achieve. We chase degrees and diplomas since our society regards formal titles such as "doctor," or "lawyer," with high respect.

Another way to meet this need is by wearing unique clothes. By dressing in a particular fashion, by having tattoos or piercing ourselves, we can feel unique and different. Also consider the way we walk, talk and gesture: some people, like actors, comedians or people who like to tell jokes, meet their need for significance by communicating in unique ways. Other people feel significant because of the interests they have. They may do crazy things like bungee jumping or collect baseball cards or toy trains.

There are also negative ways to meet this need. Take violence, for example. When we are violent, we get immediate attention and we get to feel important instantly. How about joining a gang? Could that make you feel significant? Of course. Not only that, it also gives you a strong, though dysfunctional, sense of emotional comfort and belonging.

One of most bizarre behaviors we have witnessed in the last few decades is that of suicide bombing. We first saw it during the Second World War with the Kamikazes, then we saw it on 9/11, and today, it happens all around the world. Don't you find it perplexing and bizarre that an individual, usually in his twenties (the average age of most suicide bombers is 24,) will strap himself with explosives and blow himself up on an airplane or a bus or a train? Some experts believe that environmental factors such as extreme poverty or hopelessness towards the future are the driving forces behind suicide bombings. But these factors are questionable. First of all, there are millions of young people around the world who live in extreme poverty and deprivation and yet they do not blow themselves up in the middle of civilian populations. And second, people who feel hopeless and destitute and want to commit suicide do not try to kill others in the process.

The latest research suggests that the most influential factor in motivating suicide bombers is the sense of significance that's associated with martyrdom. Through their actions, suicide bombers become heroes and gain the respect and admiration of their community. They are idolized in posters and pictures and they have songs written about them. By committing to a suicide mission, they feel a strong sense of purpose and divine justice and they bring respect and dignity to their family. It is known that the Kamikaze pilots were among the most honored of the Japanese air force.

Self sacrifice is an extremely powerful way to meet the need for significance and importance. It makes you feel as though your existence has a higher meaning, that you are contributing beyond yourself and that you are displaying courage and love for those you love.

This sort of extreme behavior teaches us an important lesson: Our brain will find a way to meet our needs either consciously or unconsciously, even at the expense of our own mortality.

"The significance of a man is not in what he attains, but rather what he longs to attain"

~ Kahlil Gibran ~

By the way, can we feel too significant? Can we become too different? Of course. In fact, when we feel too significant, we begin to feel alienated and disconnected from other people. Kurt Cobain and his band Nirvana had a meteoric rise during the early nineties. Within one year, they went from being a garage band from Seattle that nobody knew about, to performing all over the world in front of millions of people. Suddenly, they had to do interviews and photo shoots and to respond to public demands. This was too much for Kurt. It created in him a strong sense of alienation, of being too different and of not being able to connect with other people and it led to depression and eventually suicide.

What do you do to feel significant? What makes you feel special and unique? I'll tell you what it is for me. My life style. I feel significant because of the way I choose to treat other people, because of the way I work out, and because of the challenges I undertake. This brings me an enormous sense of purpose and importance. It makes me feel alive and unique.

The key thing to remember here is that in order to meet the need for significance, we have to *do* or *be* different from other people. And usually, by doing different things, we separate and distance ourselves, from the crowd. We stand out. But we have to be careful, because if we stand out too much, we may hamper our ability to meet our fourth need which is the need for love and belonging.

The fourth need is the need for love and belongingness. In the movie *Cast Away,* Tom Hanks plays Chuck Noland, a Federal Express employee who survives a plane crash and finds himself alone on a desert island. In order to meet the need for love and belonging he creates Mr. Wilson. Mr. Wilson is actually a volley ball onto which Hanks paints a face with his own blood. It becomes his constant companion, giving him silent advice and quiet friendship. We realize how powerful the need for love is when the connection between Hanks and Wilson ruptures as they are trying to leave the island on a small raft. As a wave hits the raft and knocks Mr. Wilson into the ocean, Tom is torn apart between trying to bring him back and staying on the raft. Eventually, Mr. Wilson drifts away and Tom begins to cry in despair.

The need for love and belonging is a fundamental human need. We all want to feel love and be accepted by other people. In chapter 13 we are going to talk about relationships and I'm going to share with you some interesting researches about love. What you'll learn is that love is crucial to our survival. For example, babies who do not get sufficient love develop failure to thrive syndrome. But more on that later.

What do we do to meet this need? We get into relationships, we get married, we have children, we have pets, we grow flowers and we join clubs and organizations such as fraternities or the Rotary club where we can share common interests with other people.

We can also meet this need by connecting with ourselves. By taking the time to listen to our own needs and doing something that's just for us, we can meet and even satiate the need for love. How do people connect with their inner selves? They may take a trip on their own or they may set aside some private time for prayer or contemplation, or even take a long bath. Gerard for example, connected with himself deeply when he decided to cross the pacific because he chose to do it for himself, not for others.

We all have a need to belong. We all need to feel that we are not alone and that we are accepted unconditionally for who we are. In healthy families, children tend to be emotionally happy and loyal to the family core since that is where they feel they belong. But when the family is dysfunctional and does not meet the child's need for love and belonging, what do children do? They "Look for love in all the wrong places," as Marc Almond's song goes. They may join a gang or form a social circle that gives them the unconditional acceptance and connection they need. One way or another, we must fulfill this need. The only question is what vehicle are we going to use and what will be the consequences.

By the way, can this need be satiated? It sure can. This can happen especially in romantic relationships where one side begins to feel suffocated by the other. That's when we begin to pull away in order to cool off the relationship. The key to meeting this need properly is by measured affection. It's just like hugging a pet. If we hug too hard and too long, the pet may suffocate. If we hug to little and not often enough, it will feel unloved. We'll talk more about this on chapter 13.

The fifth need is the need for growth. This need is the need to fulfill the first four needs to best of our ability. The need to grow exists in people in different degrees. Although people have the same needs, they are driven to meet those needs at different intensities. For example, people meet their needs for comfort, change, significance and love to different degrees. For example, some people need security guards, alarms and watch dogs in order to feel secure and comfortable while others are content with leaving the front door open. Some people don't handle change and variety very well and are tend to go into shock if too much is going on at one time, while other people enjoy doing ten new and exciting things in a single day. Some people feel significant by wearing unique clothes while others have a need to be on stage in front of millions of people. Some people need to be hugged and kissed every five minutes while others are perfectly comfortable having long distance relationships with an occasional get together.

Whatever your level of needs are, know that in order to be happy and fulfilled, you must meet your needs at full capacity. If there is one characteristic that is common to all the people we consider great, it's the relentless ambition to fulfill their first four needs to their full capacity. Abraham Maslow called them "self-actualizers," and he believed that "A musician must make music; an artist must paint, a poet must write, if he is to be at peace with himself. What a man can be, he must be. This is the need we may call self-actualization. It refers to man's desire for fulfillment, namely to the tendency for him to become actually what he is potentially: to become everything that one is capable of becoming."

"Happiness is neither virtue nor pleasure nor this thing nor that but simply growth, we are happy when we are growing"

~ William Butler Yeats ~

Maslow believed there are two processes necessary for self-actualization: self exploration and action. And that the deeper the self exploration, the closer we come to self-actualization. In order to be happy and fulfilled, we must grow. And the only way to fulfill this need is by overcoming new challenges, learning new things and pushing our limits.

In 1980, Gerard crossed the Atlantic Ocean. In 1984, he crossed the Niger River and in 1986 he rode his motorcycle in the Paris-Dakar. Now do you begin to understand what drove him to cross the Pacific? When we take a look at Gerard's life, we understand that for him, crossing the pacific wasn't crazy or unreasonable. On the contrary, it was perfectly logical. Just another step upward towards a new challenge. And since he was an expert seaman, the Pacific proved to be perfect ground to test his capacities.

The sad reality is that most people do not strive to grow and meet their needs to their full capacity. They let fear and complacency dominate their life and they make every excuse possible in order to feel OK. And usually, you can see immediately that their life is not working out for them because they are either bored or angry or depressed or cynical or they put other people down, or over-drink or over-eat or they spend to much time watching T.V or do anything else to try and distract themselves from the fact that they are not happy.

This sort of complacency and compromise can lead to a situation Stanley Milgram, a former psychology professor at Harvard University, called "learned helplessness." In one experiment, he put a monkey in a small cube made of glass. The cube's floor was made of wire that was carrying low voltage electricity. At the top of the cube, Milgram planted a button that once pressed, would disable the electric current that was moving through the wire floor for several minutes. The intelligent monkey quickly learned that whenever he pressed the button repeatedly, the current would stop. Once the monkey mastered this skill, Milgram moved him to a new box that was a replica of the old box, only here the wire connecting the button and the floor was disconnected.

In the new box, the monkey began pressing the button hoping it would disconnect the current but nothing happened. The monkey tried again and again until finally he realized that pressing the button had no effect on the current. Defeated and tired, the monkey slumped in the corner of the cube, accepting his electric reality.

Once Milgram was convinced that the monkey has given up, he moved him back to the first glass cube. Back in the first cube, what do you think happened? Did the monkey reach for the button when the current was administered? No. The monkey had a new defeated reality where he learned that the button could no longer save him from the current. It wasn't until Milgram physically took the monkey's hand and pressed it against the button that the monkey began to regain faith in his ability to control his environment.

All of us try to fulfill our needs. But we don't always succeed. The question is what we do when we can't seem to meet our needs at the level we think we ought to meet them. We'll learn all about dealing with failure and frustration in chapter 4. But for now, I want you to realize that if you want to be truly happy and fulfilled, you must challenge yourself. You can't allow yourself to become cynical and negative about trying new things. Now, I don't suggest you try to cross the Pacific like Gerard did, but I know that there are challenges for you out there, experiences that will stretch your abilities and make you grow and feel like a winner. But those experiences won't happen out of the blue. You're going to have to walk towards challenges instead of waiting for them to come to you. Because one way or another, you'll get challenged.

If you truly want to be happy, you must understand that the responsibility to make your life fulfilling is strictly yours. Life owes you nothing. If you are not having fun, if you are bored, it only means you have been taking it easy for far too long and that it's time for a change. And I think that time has come.

Go and do things you've never done before. Get out of your comfort zone. Read philosophy, poetry and self help books. Become self educated. Talk to an elderly person. Go to seminars, learn surfing or snowboarding, get a pilot's license, learn to play the piano, run a marathon, write a book, record a song, join a political group, lift weights, start a business, offer a service, learn web design, learn how to draw or learn to cook, just do something you've never done before. Soon, you'll fall in love with taking on new challenges because they not only increase your sense of self-esteem; they also build up your personal and social confidence and make you a light of inspiration to others.

The sixth need we have is the need to contribute to something greater than ourselves. We all have a need to know that what we do in life helps in some way to the greater good. It doesn't matter if you are a mailman, a heart surgeon or the president of the country. We all need to feel that we contribute to life in some significant way. That's because on an unconscious level, all of us are connected and depend on one another. When people don't feel they contribute enough through their work, they may get involved in charity work or practice altruism. They may tutor a child or coach little league or volunteer for the local neighborhood security watch. But perhaps the best way to meet this need is by meeting the fifth need, the need to grow, to the best of our ability. The best contribution you can possibly make is to overcome your fears and be the best you can be at what you love to do. You don't have to give away a million dollars or do community service every weekend in order to contribute. Let me remind you that the best contribution you can possibly make to the world is to inspire others to shatter their fears and fulfill their dreams. And to do that it's enough to take your passion and push it to the limit. I guarantee that will be enough to inspire others to do the same. Let's turn to Gerard one last time to firmly grasp just how powerful and influential inspiration can be:

> "*After the hundredth letter, I began to wonder. Thanks for what? When I set out from Choshi, my goal had not been altruistic. But slowly, I began to realize that despite myself I had given hope to all kinds of people: prisoners, the unemployed, the downtrodden, and the homeless. And I also saw, I had brought a ray of hope and sunshine into the lives of the aged, those who so often were, as I had been, distressingly alone.*
>
> *The discovery that people were identifying with me did raise a question of conscience in my mind. But when I think back, when each stroke of the oars found its place in my mind, when all that happened has been pondered and sifted through, if then I will have proven that you can fulfill your personal goals by digging deep into your own inner resources, that is already something.*"

As I said earlier, we all have the same needs and desires, but we use different vehicles to meet them. The most rewarding experiences in our lives are the experiences that meet all our needs simultaneously. When that happens, we truly feel fulfilled and happy. In this chapter, I offered you some practical ways to meet your needs in a positive and empowering way that can enhance your quality of life and bring your happiness to whole new level. However, there is one short cut, one that surpasses our emotional needs that I haven't shared with you yet. Can you guess what it is?

I'm talking about gratitude. Every religion promotes the practice of giving thanks in one form or another. Have you ever wondered why? Other than its religious value of recognizing a higher authority, psychologically, being grateful reminds us that we are standing on the shoulders of giants. Today, we enjoy luxuries that the kings and queens of ancient times could not even dream of having. We have gourmet restaurants, theme parks, cable television, fancy cars, ice cream, bookstores, perfumes, movies, rollerblades, advanced medicine, electric guitars, iPods, eBay, and thousands of other things we did absolutely nothing to obtain. It's all a part of our inheritance from past generations.

Just think about it. If you want a new shirt, you simply go to the store and buy one, right? You don't have to fetch a sheep, shave its fur, turn it into wool, and than tailor it into a shirt. That process has been shortened for you by innovation and technology. Do you drive a car? Would you rather ride a horse and buggy on your way to work? How about traveling? In the past, traveling across the ocean was a sixty day ordeal on a crowded boat infested with disease and with no guarantee of a safe arrival. However, today, we can fly across the ocean in less then six hours and enjoy food and movies all along the way.

How about music? Do you listen to mp3's? Today, you can get any song by any artist at anytime on the Internet. It wasn't long ago that you had to spin a handle on a squeaking gramophone if you wanted to enjoy some tunes and even than the quality was horrible.

My final point is this: either you can take everything around you for granted and behave as if the world owes you something or you can respect the efforts of those who came before you. You can either focus on what you don't have and feel empty or you can focus on all the abundance of knowledge and wisdom that you've inherited and feel instantly fulfilled.

So, make a daily habit of reminding yourself that you are truly lucky for being alive today. The world may not be perfect. Sure enough, there's plenty of filth and dirt that needs to be cleaned up. But nevertheless, things are getting better. Much better than they were ten years ago and much better than they were a hundred years ago, mostly due to people like you.

"Let us rise up and be thankful, for if we didn't learn a lot

today, at least we learned a little, and if we didn't learn a little, at least we didn't get sick, and if we got sick, at least we didn't die; so, let us all be thankful"

~ Buddha ~

I truly believe you and I were born with all the resources we will ever need in order to be happy and meet each and every one of our needs abundantly. But unless we commit to growth, unless we commit to following our own hearts courageously, we'll discover that happiness eludes us. Happiness is not something we can buy or get or achieve. It is something we have to experience by climbing the mountain of life. As Bertrand Russell once said, "The happiness that is genuinely satisfying is accompanied by the fullest exercise of our faculties and the fullest realization of the world in which we live."

We talked about a lot of things in this chapter. We talked about Freud, Skinner and Maslow. We talked about our physiological need to move away from pain and towards pleasure. We talked about the six human needs and learned that we all have different ways for meeting them. And we talked about gratitude. In the next chapter, we are going to learn how ordinary people overcome extraordinary challenges and end up triumphant. Don't you find it strange how…

Chapter IV

Every Winner has Scars

"Every great achievement is the victory of a flaming heart"

~ Ralph Waldo Emerson ~

On December 23, 1987 nineteen-year-old Jami Goldman and her friend Lisa Barzano got up at 6 A.M., grabbed a six-pack of Diet Pepsis and a cinnamon roll and left Gallup, New Mexico towards Scottsdale, Arizona in a red Chevy Blazer. The drive was supposed to take a little over four hours.

Two hours into the drive, the girls lost their way. They stopped at a gas station only to learn that they were four hours away from where they were supposed to be. They couldn't find a map and on a stranger's advice they decided to get back on the road before an impending snow storm. But they were out of luck. Within thirty minutes, heavy snow began to fall. The temperature dropped considerably. The girls put the car in four-wheel drive and slowed down to five miles an hour. Visibility was nearly zero. Suddenly, the car slid on a patch of ice, hit a snow bank and stopped. Jami put the car in reverse and gently pressed the gas. The car slid for several inches more and than came to a dead stop. She tried to rock the car by shifting from drive to reverse but it wouldn't move. Panic set in. The girls stepped out of the car and tried to break the ice under the tires with ski poles but their effort proved fruitless.

It was slightly after noontime. The girls assessed their situation and decided it was too dangerous to walk and that they would be better off waiting for rescue. "A plow will be here any minute," Jami reassured Lisa as the girls climbed into the backseat of the Blazer. But by nightfall, the weather has only gotten worse. No rescue had come. The car battery had died and the girls realized they would probably have to spend the night in the frozen car. But this was only the beginning of a challenge that would test the girls' courage and faith amidst impossible conditions.

For the next ten days, Jami and Lisa were forced to stay in the frozen car desperately struggling to survive as temperatures plummeted to 21 degrees below zero. They had no food or water other than the frozen six-pack of Diet Pepsis and cinnamon roll they grabbed when they left Gallup. When nature called they used plastic bags. Once, when the storm seemed to let up, they even made an attempt to leave the car and call for help but the snow was thigh deep and they returned quickly.

On the morning of the eleventh day the girls were found by a father and son traveling on their snowmobiles. By that time, they were on the brink of death, extremely dehydrated, and suffering from severe frostbites.

Once at medical care, the girls received steaming whirlpool treatments for their legs. A day and a half later, they were flown to Scottsdale Memorial Hospital where they underwent painful hyperbaric chamber treatments were highly pressurized oxygen was forced into their damaged skin tissue.

Lisa showed quick signs of recovery and gradually her frostbites were reversing. But Jami's weren't. In fact, the gangrene in her feet started to spread towards her knees. After three weeks of unsuccessful treatments, the doctors concluded that the only way to prevent the infection from spreading further was to amputate Jami's legs below the knee.

Recovery proved to be a grueling process. But slowly, Jami began to find her inner strength. She invested every available minute in physical therapy and quickly learned to use prosthetics. And as soon as she felt strong enough, she went back to school. Life seemed to slowly get back on track.

One day, while Jami was visiting her prosthetic adjuster for a routine adjustment, he told her about the Paralympics and how disabled athletes competed, set world records and won medals. Jami decided to give it a try and fell in love with a new set of prosthetics called "Cheetah Legs" that allowed her run. She decided to begin training and discovered she had a natural talent for sprinting. It wasn't long before she found herself traveling around the world, competing relentlessly, until one day she set a world record in the hundred-meter dash (14.1 sec).

Her achievements attracted Adidas, the sporting goods company, who decided to make a commercial with her in the lead role. That was her first television exposure. As a result, she caught the attention of Hollywood and was invited to audition for Steven Spielberg's A.I. She ended up playing a female robot in the flesh fair scene. A while later, she also began touring as a speaker in efforts to raise awareness for people with disabilities. She volunteered her time, gave talks and promoted special causes and became a symbol of hope and courage for thousands worldwide.

Jami is remarkable, isn't she? I believe that all of us have an inborn talent for success and survival. But, within most of us, this talent lies dormant and waiting to be awakened, much like the sleeping beauty who awaits the prince.

Whether you like it or not, you'll have to face many unexpected challenges throughout your life. That's just the way life is. It can be the sudden death of a loved one, a spouse walking away on us unexpectedly, a car accident or the loss of a job. Such events affect the core of our being, not only because they happen unexpectedly and send our lives into a tailspin, but also because they remind us that we are vulnerable and not in complete control. Can we avoid such challenges? Sometimes. But we must remember that life is a full contact sport. At some point, we all have to cross paths with pain, death, loneliness, disappointment, broken hearts, and broken dreams. Therefore, the question we must consider in this chapter is not "Will we get hit?" but "How are we going to respond when we do?"

Think about it for a minute, how do you respond to the unexpected blows of life? How do you handle tragedy? Some people feel victimized and blame other people for their plight. Others dive into depression. Others may get angry or try to hurt the people around them. Others, however, have the incredible ability to reach inside and find a way not only to cope with adversity but also to gain from it.

In this chapter we are going to take a look at those unique individuals who have managed to find a way to overcome incredible obstacles. We'll consider people like John Larkin, who suffered from a severe stutter which led to an emotionally traumatic childhood. Ashamed to converse with other people, John took to music at the age of 12 and by 1970's and 80's he was a professional jazz pianist. But his career failed to take off. Playing small gigs in murky jazz clubs around Los Angeles, John was depressed and alcoholism and drug addiction began to take a hold of his life. But things would soon change for the better.

In 1990, Larkin moved to Berlin, Germany in order to give himself a fresh start. Appreciative of the jazz culture of the city, he continued playing gigs as a jazz pianist on cruise ships and in bars and clubs around Germany. But things still weren't clicking. Desperately, he decided to add singing to his act for the first time and to his amazement, his audience loved it. Nevertheless, John was scared that listeners would realize he stuttered, so his wife Judy suggested that he talk about his stutter directly in his music. John decided to go for it. Working with prominent dance producers, he recorded "Scatman," a song intended to inspire children who stuttered to overcome adversity. The single took off to massive proportions, reaching #1 in nearly every country it was released in and selling over 6 million copies worldwide. John's stutter, once a weakness, has become his most reliable strength.

How was John Larkin capable of turning a debilitating physical condition and a traumatic childhood a successful music career? What were the insights and understandings that helped him maintain a bright outlook on life even at his toughest hour? And, are there any similarities between him and Jami?

It is my hope that by learning about people like Jaim and Scatman John, you'll begin to discover and practice your own ability to overcome challenges and deal with the unexpected blows of life, because I believe that transforming tragedy into success is not a random or accidental process, as you'll discover in the following pages. There are specific insights and distinctions, as well as patterns of language and behavior that survivors like Jami Goldman and John Larkin use in order to transform dire circumstances into incredible triumphs. Let's find what those insights are.

"To overcome difficulties is to experience the full delight of existence"

~ Arthur Schopenhauer ~

Insight #1
Life is unfair, but you can still beat the odds

We would like to believe that there's a certain element of fairness in life, that we will, (or at least should be) rewarded for good deeds and punished for bad ones. But when we hear about children being born with severe disabilities or young people who discover they have a terminal disease, this sense of fairness becomes questionable.

Great winners and survivors realize that life is not fair. And because life is unfair, they accept the fact that sometimes bad things happen to good people for no apparent reason. That's just a part of life's set up. Dr. Burlage ,the author of *Lessons in Living* observed that "There are simply too many tragedies that befall innocent people to conclude that there is an essential justice at work in the affairs of humanity- innocent children racked with pain from all sorts of killer maladies, good parents being literally tortured to death by wayward and evil offspring, millions of people being killed and starved to death in the wartime environments, innocent children being gassed in Hitler's Germany, children being born with crack addiction or irreparable damaged by a mother's alcoholism during pregnancy. With these, and in thousands of other instances, it becomes quite clear that there is no basic justice system that applies to the affairs of humankind."

Most people take life's tragedies very personally. When tragedies strike, they feel victimized by life, as if God is punishing them intentionally. But that's absurd. God has no favorites and he doesn't prey on people for his amusement. Think about the winter. In the winter, we know that the bad weather is not trying to "get us." We are intelligent enough to know that stormy skies and strong winds are not the result of a mistake we made or an unpaid parking ticket. Bad weather occurs with total disregard to our existence. This is why we never take it personally. We simply acknowledge the fact that it is not in our control and we make the best out of it.

This reminds me of a story about a gazelle who spots a lion in the distance and asks God "Oh God, why is this lion after *me* when there are hundreds of gazelles in the field?" to which God answers "Well, he's hungry and you just happened to be in sight. Now, if you don't want to become dinner I suggest you use those quick legs I gave you instead of asking silly questions."

Here's another anecdote on a similar note: A man who can't

swim has fallen into the river. As he cries for God's help, a young swimmer spots him from the river bank and offers to jump to the rescue. "That's fine, God will take care of me," says the drowning man. A short while thereafter, a man in a fishing boat goes by and offers his help. Again, the drowning man says, "Don't bother, I'm a good person and at the Lord's mercy. He'll take care of me." Not ten minutes go by and a helicopter flies by and spots the drowning man. With his last breath, the man shouts," Go away, my faith is strong, I'll be rescued by the Almighty." A short while later, he drowns. As he enters the pearly gates he asks God, "Oh God, I've been a good man all my life. Why did you let me drown?" to which God answers swiftly, "What do you mean? I sent a helicopter, a boat and swimmer for you."

What's the point of those stories? Yes, life is unfair. Sometimes, you're the first gazelle in sight and sometimes you fall into a gushing river. But it's up to you to use what you have and make the best of it.

Let me share with you a remarkable true story that demonstrates how you can use life's unfairness to your advantage. On May 7 2000, Mary Ann Stephens was shot dead in Florida during an armed robbery while walking along with her husband on a sidewalk. Two and a half hours later, the police apprehended Brenton Butler, a 15-year-old black kid, who was on his way to drop off a job application at the local Blockbuster. The police took Brenton back to the crime scene where Mr. Stephens, who was still overwhelmed by the morning's events, identified him as the murderer. Brenton was then taken to the police station where he was interrogated for more then nine hours. During those nine hours he was threatened, beaten, humiliated, and denied access to food and water as well as his rights to an attorney. After nine relentless hours of psychological and physical torment, Brenton broke down and signed his name on a confession sheet that had been written by the police, using their words to describe what had happened.

Brenton was then thrown in jail for the duration of the trial. Finally, after six and a half months of deliberations, he was acquitted of all charges due to the relentless work of public defender Patrick McGuiness who exposed how the interrogating detectives lied, intimidated and abused Brenton for more then nine hours. Ironically, only 45 days after his acquittal, the police caught the assailant and convicted him.

Was life fair to Brenton? Did he deserve to spend six and a half months in jail for something he didn't do? Of course not. But he didn't make a big deal out of it. He didn't take it personally. In a situation where most people would feel victimized by the system and angry at the world, he kept his cool. As soon as the trial ended, he went back to school and wrote a book entitled *They Said It Was Murder.* He also established "The Brenton Butler Foundation for the Wrongfully Accused and Convicted." Will he carry an emotional scar from that incident for the rest of his life? Probably. But, like Jami and Scatman John, he has grown stronger and better since the incident because he never took it personally.

Insight #2
Events have no meaning except the meaning we give them

Let me ask you something. Is rain good or bad? Tricky question, isn't it? If you're a farmer, rain is great. But, if it's your wedding day in the great outdoors, rain is horrible. But what if you lived on the moon? What would rain mean to you then?

In order to make sense of the world, our brain has to assign meaning to the events that happen to us. What is meaning? Meaning is simply the way we interpret events. Whenever something happens in our life, the first thing our brain tries to figure out is what and how that event will influence us. And in order to figure that out, our brain must interpret; that is, decide whether an event is potentially dangerous, (pain producing) or safe (pleasure producing).

Since it is our brain doing the interpretation, we have the tendency to feel that our interpretation is right and truthful and that it represents life the way it really is. But is that true?

Let's think about rain one more time. Rain is nothing more than water falling from the sky, right? Now, water falling from the sky has no meaning in and of itself. It's merely water. It is neither good nor bad. However, once we insert our personal point of view into the equation and consider the impact that water falling from the sky has on our lives, we begin to interpret and judge it.

On September 11, 2001, more than 3,000 people lost their lives when the Twin Towers collapsed in a vicious terror attack. But interestingly, people around the world interpreted that event in many different ways: Some rejoiced, others cried, and some didn't care. How could people interpret an event so obviously tragic to most Americans in so many different ways? The answer is simple. It's because people interpret life from their own unique point of view. For example, a New Yorker would most likely feel angry or cry and would want to retaliate. An Iranian, on the other hand, might rejoice and feel a sense of divine justice. Meanwhile, an Israeli father who lost his family in a terror attack may feel a sense of compassion and understanding while a tribesman from Borneo may feel indifferent because he has never been to New York, never met a New Yorker, and most likely, doesn't even know where New York is. Who's right? They all are. Why? Because all of them interpreted and judged the event from their *own* unique point of view. In reality, our notion of truth is nothing more than our subjective interpretation of reality. There are as many truths and realities to life as there are people. But we will talk about this more in the next chapter.

*"There is no meaning to life except the meaning man gives
to his life by the unfolding of his powers"*

~ Erich Fromm ~

So let me ask you, if meaning is something that we assign
to events is it possible to change what things mean to us? In
other words, is it possible to change the way in which we interpret and judge different events in our lives?

In 1920, Watson and Rayner did an interesting study with
baby boy named Albert and a gentle white rat. At the beginning of the study, Albert was happy and enjoyed playing with
the rat. After a while, the experimenters took the rat away.
When they brought the rat back, they carefully timed a loud
noise that frightened Albert whenever he tried to touch the rat.
Soon, Albert became startled and began to cry. After repeating
the experiment several times Albert began to cry at mere sight
of the white rat.

If you noticed, the scientists were able to change Albert's
reaction to the rat by changing what he associated to it. At
first, the rat meant joy and fun. But after the loud noise treatment, the rat meant fear, anguish and suffering. This proved
that we, even as babies, have the ability to change what things
mean to us.

Unfortunately, most of us interpret and judge events unconsciously without ever really considering the long term impact those judgments would have on our lives. In many cases,
we unconsciously assign generalized meanings to events just
to protect ourselves from pain. While I was working as a counselor at the Pines Treatment Center, I had a conversation with
one of girls that had recently arrived. Sadly, this girl was raped
in her early teens, and now, almost 9 years later, she was convicted of sexually molesting a 7-year-old boy. When I asked her
how she interpreted her rape she said, "There's nothing to interpret. All men are beasts. They are evil, brutal, and should be

thrown in jail as soon as they're born." Now that's more than an interpretation. That's a harsh, generalized judgment. I decided to challenge her. "Do you really think *all* men are evil?" I asked, "Even me?" "Well," she paused shortly, "You are nice. But that's only because you get paid to be nice. I'm sure that deep inside; you are just like the rest of them." I couldn't believe it. Here I was being labeled a beast just because I was a male.

Let's examine this closely. Obviously, the girl had experienced serious trauma in her teens. And in order to protect her from pain, her brain created a generalized judgment about males. However, she wasn't aware of the fact that this judgment was costing her dearly. For more than nine years she had been in and out of juvenile institutions, mostly for assault charges against boys, teenage boys, and even adult males whom she said were "trying to get too close her."

Now, as a trained counselor, I carry no judgment towards this girl since I've never been in her shoes. But, it doesn't take a genius to realize that the meaning she assigned to her rape almost 9 years ago was causing her life to spiral out of control. It shaped the way she treated males of all ages. It affected the way she dressed and carried herself. It influenced her body language and erased her femininity. And as a result, it greatly diminished her chances to succeed in life.

What would have happened if this girl had chosen a different meaning to her rape? What if she decided that because she was raped, she could help other girls who had also been raped to recover faster? What if she decided that because she was raped, she now had the opportunity to educate young males about sexuality and increase their awareness of the psychological and physical damages caused by rape? Do you think her life would have turned out differently? I'm sure it would have.

Consider Candy Lightner. When Cari Lightner died at the age of 12 by drunk driver, her mother Candy could have responded by diving into deep depression and self pity. Nobody would have held that against her. But Candy decided to respond in a unique way. Instead of thinking that her daughter's death was "the end of her life," Candy decided to use it in order to empower and protect other people.

Within four days of her daughter's death, she decided to create MADD (mothers against drunk driving) with a crystal clear goal in mind: to stop drunk driving, support the victims, and prevent underage drinking. Since it was founded in 1980, MADD was the catalyst behind more than two thousand new pieces of legislation that have been passed against drunk driving.

Another powerful example is that of Scott O'Grady. After his F-16 was shot down in Bosnia in 1995, Scott O'Grady had to survive for six days in hostile Serbian terrain. He slept by day, covering himself with camouflage netting, and moved only between midnight and 4 a.m. Armed Serbs were never far away and he often heard gunfire. He used a sponge to soak up rainwater to fill a container and he ate grass and bugs. However, as scary and tragic as most of us would find this experience, O'Grady found that "The entire experience, as funny as this sounds, those six days were, well, the most positive experience of my life. It was just quite amazing."

We have the ability to choose what things mean to us. The key to overcoming difficult situations is to choose the meanings that empower us the most. People like Candy Lightner and Scott O'Grady approach every challenge in life as if it were a growing experience. By asking themselves questions like: "How can I grow from this? How can I use this to my advantage? What can I learn from this?" and "How can other people benefit from this?" both Scott and Candy were able to turn difficult situations into meaningful experiences. Survivors have the incredible ability to turn tragedies into learning experiences. They believe that there is a lesson to be learned in every situation in life. And it is because they treat tragedies as lessons that they are able to bounce back so quickly.

It's important to remember that the major premise of this book is that you and I are not helpless in our existence. We are not leaves in the wind. And although there are many events we can't control in life, we can always choose our reactions to them. Viktor Frankl recalls that "We who lived in concentration camps can remember the men who walked through the huts comforting others, giving away their last piece of bread. They may have been few in number, but they offer sufficient proof that everything can be taken away from a man but one thing, the last of the human freedoms; to choose one's attitude in any given set of circumstances, to choose one's own way."

"Although a man may have no jurisdiction over the fact of his existence, he can hold supreme command over the meaning of existence for him"

~ Norman Cousins ~

When Jami lost her legs, she could have told herself that it was the 'end of her femininity' or that she 'could never have children' because 'nobody wants a wife with no legs.' This type of helpless affirmation would have destroyed her chances for a quick physical and emotional recovery. Luckily, she was smart. She focused on the things she could do, on helping others, on getting back to normal functioning, and on pursuing new dreams. And it's by focusing on empowering meanings that she gradually began to realize that losing her legs might not have been such a terrible loss after all.

An important tool that helps survivors overcome hard times is reframing. Reframing is the ability to change negative statements into positive by altering the words we use. For example, while most people use the word "tragedy" or "disaster," when describing certain painful events, survivors use the word "challenge" or "test" or "lesson." The word "tragedy" presupposes something bad or sad has happened. It already assigns a negative meaning to an event even before it has been thoroughly examined. A "challenge," on the other hand, presupposes that indeed there is a difficulty but it can be surmounted. It also implies that there's an opportunity for growth within the situation. We all get excited by challenges, especially those we know confidently we can overcome.

Another good example is the word "failure." The word implies that we are not good enough. We tend to associate it with lack of intelligence, lack of resources, lack of ingenuity, and an overall feeling of inadequacy. Survivors don't use the word "failure." To them, it doesn't even exist. They know that whenever they are confronted with a challenge or try something new, there is a pretty good chance they are not going to get the results they are looking for on the first try. So they register it as a learning experience. They use the feedback of an experience in order to refine their approach and make further distinctions about what they need to do to achieve the results they are after.

In 1984, an English teacher at the prestigious Harrow school wrote on a report card, "A conspicuous lack of success," but that didn't stop Winston Churchill from leading England to triumph in World War II. In 1902, the *Atlantic Monthly* returned the poems of a twenty-eight year old poet saying, "Our magazine has no room for your vigorous verse." But that didn't stop Robert Frost from becoming one of the most influential poets of our time. In 1905, the University of Bern rejected a dissertation saying it was irrelevant and fanciful. But that didn't stop Albert Einstein from publishing his theory of relativity. It took Colonel Sanders almost a hundred rejections before he finally managed to sell his chicken recipe and it took Thomas Edison almost 10,000 tries to invent the incandescent light bulb. If any one of those individuals had believed in 'failure,' you and I would not enjoy many of the luxuries we have around us today.

"Success is the result of good judgment, good judgment is the result of experience, experience is often the result of bad judgment"

~ Anthony Robbins ~

The only way to become better at dealing with life's difficulties is to face more of them. Most of us live pretty comfortable lives. Rarely do we go outside our comfort zone. And when we do, it's only because we have to. But we must remember that the quest for greatness lies not only in finding out who we are but also in what we can become. And the only way to do so is by a process of trial and error, by putting ourselves and our ideas on the line even when we are not certain we can deliver.

Nobody will force you to climb mountains, start a business, run a marathon or be the best father or mother you can be. Somebody may encourage you to try (if you're lucky) but chances are that if you want greatness, you'll have to motivate yourself. And I don't know what you are passionate about, but I do know, beyond a shadow of a doubt, that it's out there waiting for you. Maybe your passion is to become the best teacher you could possibly be or the best fireman or the best mom or dad. Maybe your passion is to establish your own software business or complete a marathon. Maybe it's to make a movie or record an album. If you are alive, then I know there's a challenge out there that will light such a fire in your belly that you will never feel bored or jaded again in your life. But it's up to you to find it.

By the way, do you have to win the Tour de France or the U.S. Open in order to be great? Do you have to go out and do something spectacular? You sure don't. We tend to think that unless we can dunk like Jordan, putt like Tiger, paint like Picasso or compete like Gates, our talents aren't meaningful and our contribution doesn't really count. That's nonsense.

Ever hear of Ray Gatchalian? I doubt it. Not many people

have. Ray was a fire fighter in the Oakland fire department. Once, while on a vacation at El Salvador, he was introduced to a four-year-old child named Francisca. Francisca suffered from cancer and her right hand was painfully swollen. In that time, El Salvador had no medical facilities that could help Francisca, and unless she received appropriate medical treatment, it was obvious she would soon lose her life.

Ray decided to take on the challenge. He knew the only way Francisca would survive was if she received treatment in the United States. He couldn't afford to pay for the specialized operation, nor did he have the necessary connections among the medical community to find anyone who would agree to perform the surgery.

But Ray was a true survivor. He was driven by passion and was determined not to let anything stop him. First, he turned to government officials and other public servants in order to cut through the clutter of red tape and bureaucracy that stopped him bringing Francisca into the United States. His passion and enthusiasm prompted everyone he came in contact with to go the extra mile and soon, he found a person willing to provide transportation, and another who was willing to provide a home for Francisca before and after the operation. At the last moment, Ray managed to recruit a doctor and a staff of six at Stanford Medical center in Palo Alto to perform the surgery without charge. The operation was considered a smashing success and within weeks, Francisca was back at home with her family.

Sadly, Ray passed away at the age of 57 in a car accident in Chile. But helping out Francisca was just one act in the incredible legacy he left behind him. He was a Vietnam veteran and a peace activist. He directed a month long anti-violence vigil in Oakland, worked with incarcerated youth in Alameda and ran across the country to raise money for a memorial to Francis Scott Key. He filmed several documentaries, including the international award winning *Survival Run* and the emotionally moving *Unheard Voices* which has been featured in congress.

In 2001, Ray told the San Francisco chronicle that, "Optimism enables us to claim the future for ourselves and not abandon it to chance. When I meet people who believe the problems they face are too huge and complex, that they can't make a difference - that's the worst notion you can have." Regarding people like Ray, Professor Paul Kurtz of the State University of New York wrote that, "Humanists are not overwhelmed by the "tragic" character of the human condition; they must face death, sorrow, and suffering with courage. They have confidence in the ability of human beings to overcome alienation, solve the problems of life, and develop the capacity to share the goods of life and empathize with others."

"Good timber doesn't grow with ease, the stronger the wind, the stronger the trees"

~ J. Williard Marriott ~

Ray didn't win any Olympic Gold medals and he never wrote a best-selling book. His movies never reached the big screen and he never became a house hold name. But nevertheless, he was great. He lived his life fully, doing things that made him proud, constantly taking on new challenges and searching for new ways to grow and contribute. He wasn't searching for the lime light and he wasn't out there to make a million dollars. But the way he lived made a difference to a lot of people.

Life is not about being first or being better than others. It is about being the best human being you can be. Much too often, we compare ourselves to other people. We either look up at those who are doing better or down at those who are doing worse. What I'm asking you to do is forget about other people and look inside, into your own heart and soul. Pete Strudwick was born with only partial hands and no feet. Yet, at the age of forty-one, wearing special boots, he ran the Pikes Peak Marathon. Although he knew he would arrive at the finish line hours after the last contestant, he considered himself a serious competitor. And when he finally reached the finish line, he was proud of his achievement. Why? Because he conquered his disability. Even before he began the race, it was clear that he would "lose" in conventional terms. But Pete did not see it that way. Disabled though he was, he did not let it interfere with his plans. He was motivated because he did not see coming in last as a contradiction to success, as long as he gave it his best effort. There are many disabled and elderly people who compete in all types of tournaments. They don't let their handicaps stop them, and they are proud of it. Another example is the twenty year old dyslexic who, after years of instruction, finally learns to read. Indeed, other people learn to read at a much younger age, but he is not deterred. Although he cannot take pride in coming in first, he can take pride in conquering his limitations. That's what being great is all about.

We all have disabilities and weaknesses. Not necessarily physical, but psychological. We all fear failure to a certain extant. We all procrastinate at times. We all have the tendency to be complacent. And we can either allow these weaknesses to dominate our lives and define who we are and what we can do, or we can conquer them. The decision is up to us.

For great people, overcoming weaknesses and disabilities is a way of life. They constantly fight an internal war to be the best they can be at what they do. In his book, *Alone*, Gerard Daboville, the Pacific sailor, captured the mind set of those truly unique individuals who strive for ultimate complete self mastery when he explained:

> *"My motor is not so much my muscles, but my stubbornness, my tenacity, my loathing of discouragement, which I have to fight day after day, hour after hour, stroke after stroke, as each arc of the ors grows more difficult than the last. I am a resistance fighter in a war I invented for myself. The enemy is*

me, with all my physical shortcomings, my temptation to give up. That temptation, by the way, does not consist of sending up my distress signal and throwing in the towel as one might think. It is a thousand and one little daily temptations that lie in wait for us all: to get out of bed five minutes later than usual; to stop a minute before the bell rings singling the end of the working day; to pull a trifle less vigorous on the oar next time; even to stop shaving. These are the kinds of minor abandonment's, the easing off just a little here and there, which in and of themselves are insignificant but which, taken together, ineluctably lead to ultimate surrender. And it is these same minor, ridiculous battles, these repetitive, fastidious inglorious battles that, if I persist, will eventually lead me to victory."

The challenge of being great is to hold yourself to a higher standard in your behavior, your personal ethics, in the way you treat other people and in the way you communicate with yourself. And as you struggle daily to be better, you unconsciously strengthen the core of your spirit. Think about the most rewarding experiences of your life for a minute. What were they? College graduation? A long project you completed at work? Maybe it was an important race you won? Maybe it was an organization you started? Or maybe it was a girl or a guy who you were desperately trying to date who finally said "Yes"?

What made those events valuable? Was it the compliments you received afterwards? Or was it the self knowledge that you worked hard, kept pushing against the forces of resistance, and didn't give up even when a part of you wanted to? I think you know the answer.

What if you made a decision, right *here* and *now* to step up and take on a new challenge? What if you decided to learn how to dance or master singing or maybe take an investments course or learn to fly a plane? What if decided to turn your body into an inspiration and join a cycling team or a swimming team? What if you decided to learn French or read books to blind kids in the local children's hospital? What challenge would make you grow and expand? What would make you feel like a hero?

Remember that life throws challenges at us all the time. But it's the challenges we take on *by choice,* the extra battles we are willing to engage in and the extra effort we are willing to exhort that ultimately gives us the deepest sense of fulfillment.

Alright, let's recap. We learned that challenges are something we all must go through regardless of our socioeconomic status, skin color, age, gender, or religious conviction. We also learned that life is frequently unfair and that bad things can happen to good people. Next, we learned that survivors have the incredible ability to transform desperate situations into opportunities by choosing the meaning those events will have for them. We learned that any event or object has an infinite number of meanings and that if we are committed enough, we can always find a meaning that will empower us.

We also learned that survivors pay attention to how they

> *"It is not the critic who counts, not the man who points out how the strong man stumbled, or where the doer of deeds could have done better. The credit belongs to the man who is actually in the arena, whose face is marred by dust and sweat and blood, who again, who knows the great enthusiasms, the great devotions, and spends himself in a worthy cause, who at best knows achievement and who at the worst if he fails at least fails while daring greatly so that his place shall never be with those cold and timid souls who know neither victory not deafet."*

When you were young, did you believe in Santa Claus? How about the tooth fairy? Do you remember the day you discovered they don't really exist? How did you feel? Cheated? Disappointed?

For many adults, believing in Santa or the tooth fairy is considered naive and childish, even downright stupid. But that's not the case for children. As children, we don't care if what we believe in is real or not as long as it makes us happy. Where am I going with this? Well, the next chapter in our journey is about beliefs. Why beliefs? Because in the long run, our beliefs, what we think is true or untrue, will determine the way in which we will experience the future. As novelist Anatole France observed, "To accomplish great things, we must not only act, but also dream; not only plan, but also believe." Is there any truth to his words? Let's find out.

CHAPTER V

Beliefs:
Pathways to Power

"Man is made by his belief. As he believes, so he is"

~ Bhagavad-Gita ~

"How many of you believe I can cross the Niagara Falls on a tightrope?" He asked an ecstatic crowd of five thousand. The answer was quick to come. The crowd cheered and applauded with belief and support. Can you imagine yourself crossing the Niagara Falls on a tightrope? Sounds crazy, right? But not for Charles Blondin.

The French born entertainer had been walking a tightrope since the age of five and performing for the public since the age of nine. Crossing the falls had been a childhood dream of his and now it was about to come true. The day before the crossing, Blondin stretched a three-inch hemp cord from one bank of the falls to the other. The cord was 1,100 feet long and about 160 feet above the falls. To make a comparison, that's like crossing four football fields sixteen stories above ground, on nothing more than a waist belt. Falling down meant instant death.

It was time. Blondin hushed the crowed and began crossing the falls. The crowd held their breath until Blondin reached the end of the tightrope. Then, to their amazement, he immediately turned around and returned. The crowd responded with more applause and adoration. Blondin thanked them for their support and then asked, "How many of you believe I can cross the falls pushing a wheelbarrow?" The cheers and applause knew no limit. To their astonishment, Blondin not only crossed the falls pushing a wheelbarrow, but he also did it two more times, once on stilts and once blindfolded.

By this point, the crowd was frantic. It seemed that with each crossing, Blondin was growing more and more confident. He became steadier, faster, and there was a certain aura of invincibility about him. But then, he asked what appeared to be a subtle question. "How many of you believe I can cross Niagara Falls with somebody on my back?" Well, that didn't seem like much of a feat after what they have already seen. They cheered and applauded once again but by this point, they believed Blondin could do almost anything on a tightrope. Blondin decided to test their belief. "Then who would like to volunteer?"

The crowd became dead silent. Not one hand rose. Not a single soul who just moments earlier expressed total belief in Blondin's ability to carry a person across the falls truly believed. After about ten minutes of silence and no volunteers, he ended up carrying his assistant on his back while performing antics on the way.

When most of us hear the word "beliefs," we immediately think about religious dogmas or doctrines, something that's usually imposed on us from a pulpit or by a teacher or a parent. And that's what many beliefs are. In the most basic sense, a belief is any guiding principle that we feel is truthful. It can be something we believe in without any real evidence, like believing that aliens exist, or it can be something as subtle as liking yogurt. Do aliens really exist? Does yogurt really taste good? Obviously, not everybody believes in aliens and not everybody likes yogurt. So who's right? Those who believe or those who don't? Beliefs about aliens and yogurt are somewhat insignificant to our everyday life, therefore it doesn't matter whether one believes in them or not. But what about beliefs about God, creation, life, humanity, the inferiority or superiority of other cultures, or even beliefs about our own personal abilities? Are those insignificant as well? As you will discover in this chapter, some beliefs have the amazing power to control, direct, and determine the entire course of our lives while others are inconsequential.

It's important to understand that beliefs are something we all have. We have beliefs about what is true and untrue, we have beliefs about ourselves and other people, we have beliefs about what makes life worth living and what doesn't and we have beliefs about our past and our future.

Another important thing to consider is what we mean when we say we believe in something. Do we mean that we consider it to be factual and true? Do we mean that we are willing to apply it to our lives? For Blondin, real belief meant complete trust in his abilities in the face of incredible danger. What do you mean when you say "I believe"?

The Potency of Beliefs

Throughout history, Hitler, Stalin, and other dictators realized that if they could control what people believe, they would have a method of coercion better than a thousand tanks. They understood that without the freedom to think critically, human beings would quickly become obedient automatons, blindly trusting authority figures.

The more we learn about the human mind, the more we discover the power that beliefs have in shaping our experience of reality. For centuries we believed that there is only one, strict particular reality, the reality we perceive through the senses. If we can see it, feel it, smell it, taste it or hear it then it is real, and if we can't, than it's not. But then Albert Einstein came along and changed the way we view reality forever. With his theory of relativity, he proved mathematically that reality was not "out there" but rather, that it is the result of our own relative perception of what's "out there."

"Reality is merely an illusion, albeit a very persistent one"

~ Albert Einstein ~

Today, the medical community, the scientific community, the athletic community and even the academic community are finally beginning to accept that beliefs are the force that creates reality. Our beliefs are so potent in their ability to affect our brain and nervous system that they literally control our physiological experience. Take the Placebo effect, for example. The placebo effect is where a dummy preparation, which a person believes to be the active treatment, achieves the same or similar effects as a real treatment would. In 2000, Margaret Talbot wrote in the *New York Times* that "a young Seattle cardiologist named Leonard Cobb conducted a unique trial of a procedure commonly used for angina, in which doctors made small incisions in the chest and tied knots in two arteries to try to increase blood flow to the heart. It was a popular technique — 90 percent of patients reported that it helped — but when Cobb compared it with placebo surgery in which he made incisions but did not tie off the arteries, the sham operations proved just as successful."

Here is another example. In 1998, Irving Kirsch, a psychologist at the University of Connecticut analyzed 19 clinical trials of antidepressants and concluded that the expectation of improvement, not adjustments in brain chemistry, accounted for 75 percent of the drugs' effectiveness. "The critical factor," says Kirsch, "is our beliefs about what's going to happen to us. You don't have to rely on drugs to see profound transformation."

While the Placebo effect is a well known phenomenon among medical and psychology professional, the "Nocebo effect," its evil twin, is far less known. In 1992, researchers stumbled upon a striking finding. Apparently, women who believed that they were prone to heart disease were nearly four times as likely to die as women with similar risk factors who didn't hold such fatalistic views. The higher risk of death, in other words, had nothing to do with the usual causes (age, blood pressure, high cholesterol, obesity) of heart disease.

In another important study conducted fifteen years ago, researchers at three medical centers undertook a study of aspirin and another blood thinner in heart patients and came up with unexpected results that said little about the heart and much about the brain. At two locations, patients were warned of possible gastrointestinal problems, one of the most common side effects of repeated use of aspirin. At the other location, patients received no such caution. When the researchers reviewed the data, they found striking results. Those warned about the gastrointestinal problems were almost three times as likely to have side effects. Though the evidence of actual stomach damage such as ulcers was the same for all three groups, those with the most information about the prospect of minor problems were the most likely to experience the pain.

In *Unlimited Power*, Anthony Robbins states that "When we congruently believe that something is true, it is like delivering a command to our brain as to how to represent what is occurring." That is precisely why the Placebo and Nocebo effects work. When we believe that something is true, either about ourselves or about others, we unconsciously formulate the fabric of the reality we will experience.

"Nothing is easier than self-deceit. For what each man wishes, that he also believes to be true"

~ Demonsthenes ~

Our beliefs not only affect our immune system and physiology, they also determine the quality of our behavior and performance. When we believe that there is something we *can't* do, it literally becomes true for us regardless of our true ability. When we think something is impossible, our brain, out of need for consistency, will cause us to behave in accordance with our limiting belief. For example, most people don't believe they can complete a marathon. They think it's a physical impossibility for them because they are either overweight or too old or because they never run more than 2 miles in their entire lives. However, doctors have proven beyond of shadow of a doubt that the human body, even at the age of 80, is perfectly capable of running 26.2 miles. If we look at someone like Jordan or Einstein and say to ourselves, "I could never do what they do," than we immediately handicap our ability and cage ourselves in mediocrity. Most of us have never trained like Mike or solved as many math problems as Albert, and we haven't devoted the time or diligence in perfecting a particular skill. It's far more intelligent to affirm that there are some things we can't do *at the moment*, than it is to shut the door of possibility forever.

Ever heard the story of the four-minute mile? For decades people believed it was impossible for a human being to run a mile in less than four minutes. Physiologist thought the body and mind would rebel against the strains they were being forced to endure and thwart the attempt. However, one man, Roger Banister, refused to adhere to the common belief of the time. In 1954, he finally managed to run a mile in under 4 minutes. But here is what is interesting. In 1955, 37 runners broke the 4 minute mile barrier. In 1956, more than 300 other runners did the same thing. Again, was this a question of ability? Didn't all those runners who broke the 4 minute mile barrier in 1955-56 had the ability to do so in 1954? Of course they had. But, because they all had a powerful limiting belief, their brain did not let them access the necessary resources to break the 4-minute mile. Since they believed it was impossible, it became their reality.

Whether we believe we can do something or not, we are right. But, that doesn't mean that if we believe we can do anything, we can really do it right here and now. I don't care how much you believe in your boxing skills. If I would throw you in the ring with Mike Tyson without proper training, you'll see stars in bright daylight. Great people believe and acknowledge their unlimited potential. But, at the same time, they realize that the fulfillment of that potential depends upon planning, learning, training and patience. Great people believe that it is only when those disciplines are diligently cultivated that they can do anything they want. And they are absolutely right.

Just think about the people that have shaped the way we experience life today, people like Galileo Galilee, the Wright brothers, Jesus Christ, Mahatma Gandhi and Leonardo De Vinci. Those individuals changed the world by changing our beliefs about what is possible for human beings to achieve. It is only because they believed in unlimited possibility while everyone else focused on the limitations that we get to experience the abundance and freedom of the 21st century, and we must be greatly thankful for thier courage.

In most instances, we posses enough intelligence, skill, and ability to get the job done, ace the test, win the race and achieve anything our hearts desire. But it's our limiting beliefs about our capabilities that prevent us from taping into our full potential. We believe that we are "shy" so we miss out on social events where we could have tons of fun if we were outgoing. We believe we are "not good with money," so we never try to balance a budget. We believe we are "too old," "too young," "too ugly," "too dumb," too short," "too tall," "too poor," or "too depressed," we believe we are being treated unfairly and that we don't get enough breaks and we believe people discriminate against us and put us down. The horrid reality is that at the moment we believe any of those things, our brain goes to work to make sure we experience them.

"In the province of the mind, what one believes to be true either is true or becomes true"

~ John Lilly ~

John Boe, a top sales trainer and motivational speaker tells a story about an eager, new insurance agent who had just received his license and was looking for prospects. He met with a successful businessman who had agreed to provide him with referrals. As he handed the salesman ten prospect cards, the businessman instructed him to call the prospects immediately and report back after he had finished. One week later, the enthusiastic salesman decided to drop by the businessman's office to give him feedback and to ask for more referrals.

The insurance agent was pleased to inform him that he had been very successful! He said he had already contacted and sold insurance policies to eight of the referrals and was still trying to contact the other two. He enthusiastically thanked the businessman for providing him with the ten prospects and then asked him if he had thought of any other people to refer. The businessman smiled and said that he was very busy at the moment and shocked the insurance agent by handing him a phone book. The businessman explained that he had selected the previous ten prospect names at random out of the phone book and that the insurance agent could go ahead and gets the next ten for himself.

This story teaches us an important lesson. First, our beliefs and expectations are true for us even if they are not real. The young insurance agent believed in the businessman and his referrals even though they were taken out of a phonebook. Had he known that in advance, would he still be eager to make the calls? Not likely. Second, we learn that success is greatly determined by our expectations and beliefs about how we are going to perform rather then external factors such as equipment, referrals, leads, conditions etc.

We already discussed one critical form of beliefs when we learned about the power of identity (Chapter 2, remember?) We learned that identity is nothing more than the beliefs you have about who you are and what you are capable of doing. Physicist Jeremy W. Hayward assures us that, "To a very large extent men and women are a product of how they define them-selves. As a result of a combination of innate ideas and the inti-mate influences of the culture and environment we grow up in, we come to have beliefs about the nature of being human. These beliefs penetrate to a very deep level of our psychoso-matic systems, our minds and brains, our nervous systems, our endocrine systems, and even our blood and sinews. We act, speak, and think according to these deeply held beliefs and be-lief systems."

Your identity represents only a small portion of the wide vista of beliefs that compose the fabric of your life. Just think for a minute, you have certain beliefs about love, about health, about wealth, about your ability to solve problems and face challenges, about success and failure; you have beliefs about learning, about your relationships, and even beliefs about life and the world.

The beliefs you currently have are the compass that guides your life. They tell you what will lead to pain and what will lead to pleasure, they govern your behavior and expectations and they determine how you respond to the world around you. Dr. John Chaffee, a professor of philosophy at the City Univer-sity of New York claims in his book, *The Thinker's Way*, that "in the same way that you use road maps to guide you towards your destination, your belief system constitutes the "map" you use to inform your decisions. If your mental map of the world is reasonably accurate, then it will provide reliable guidance in helping you figure things out and make intelligent decisions. On the other hand, if your mental map is not accurate, then the results are likely to be unfortunate and even disastrous."

It is important to understand that regardless of the quality of our beliefs (limiting or empowering,) our brain will always attempts to guide us in the direction they point by producing a consistent behavior. For example, if you believe that all dogs are potentially evil and unpredictable creatures that can attack you at any time, chances are you are not going to have a dog.

In fact, you probably won't even pet them. On the other hand, if you believe that apples are great, healthy and tasty you will probably reach for one as soon as you can.

Only lately have scientists been able to identify the part of the human brain that is involved in producing behavior in accordance with beliefs. It's called the Reticular Activating System. The RAS is a net-like group of cells that compares all the information we receive through the senses with the existing beliefs we have in order to determine their validity. Interestingly, they also discovered that our beliefs screen our perception in that we tend not to notice or register information running contrary to what we currently hold as truth. They concluded that we tend to assimilate information in such a way as to reinforce our beliefs.

Ultimately, your beliefs will determine how much of your inner resources and abilities are going to be available for you. Strong, empowering beliefs allow you to take advantage of your mental, physical and spiritual resources and draw unlimited strength and creativity from them while limiting beliefs will drive your mind into a narrow reality vision which ultimately will confine your perception and limit your existence. Let me share with you a remarkable finding that exemplifies the destructive force beliefs can have in shaping the reality of teenagers.

Leon Bing, the author of *Do or Die*, spent several months among two of America's most notorious teenage gangs, the "Crips" and the "Bloods." She interviewed veteran gang members, she met with teens that were locked up for violence and assault charges and she spoke to former gang members and in her conclusion, she uncovered a fascinating pattern: "in every interview, with every youngster I talked to, the same theme ran through the conversation. They all said that if they didn't have an enemy to go after, they'd fight themselves, that, "you got to have somebody to fight with."

Can you imagine the rage and turmoil that a belief like "You must always have somebody to fight with," creates in someone's life? Where do you think that sort of belief will eventually lead to? That's right, constant fighting. The brain will constantly be looking for existing "threats" and "enemies" and in case it doesn't find any, it will make some.

There is no doubt that for many kids who are involved in gangs, the way out to safety is blocked not only by limiting beliefs about life but also by physical/existential threats. In most cases, gang members provide the feeling of trust and connection many teens should experience at home but don't. By choosing to join a gang and accept the love, most teens also accept an extreme set of beliefs about how life should be lived and what living is ultimately about.

The most frustrating way limiting beliefs can affect us is when they lead to self sabotaging behavior. We self-sabotage when there is no logical or rational explanation for why we can't do the things we want to do or why we can't have the things we want to have. Here's a practical example. If you really want to exercise after work, but the moment you get home to change clothes, you start thinking of all the other things you "should" do instead, you are definitely self-sabotaging. In fact, anytime you hear yourself say, "I want to do this, but I can't because…." or whenever you try to rationalize why something can't or shouldn't be done, *you* are the one shutting the door on success.

"When we argue for our limitations, we get to keep them"

~ Peter Mcwilliams ~

Self-sabotaging behavior will leave you frustrated, discouraged, and trapped in negative situations. It feels like being caged in a cell with invisible walls.

What is the source of self sabotage? Why do we sometimes ruin our chances for success and happiness? The answer lies in an internal conflict between our will power and our unconscious limiting beliefs.

Let me give you an example of this conflict. 155 years ago, the Women's Rights Movement began to form in upstate New York. Elizabeth Cady Stanton, a young housewife and mother, was invited to have tea with four women friends. Out of this meeting, a document called the Declaration of Sentiments was forged. The Declaration of Sentiments soon became the framework for a campaign designed to better the lives of women in America. In the beginning, there was much excitement about the document. Many women happily volunteered their names and were glad to support a worthy cause. But as the movement began to gather strength, several women mysteriously decided to withdraw their signatures. Within several days, more and more women withdrew their names from the Declaration of Sentiments. Within weeks, the movement came to halt and then completely fell apart. What happened here?

As we study the history of these women, we learn that their goals were indeed to make life better for themselves and other women. And that's exactly what they achieved. However, when they began to gather strength, the issue of voting rights began to surface. That was never a part of their original agenda. From colonial times until well into the 19th century, women were considered the property of their husbands. They were required by law to turn over to their spouse any earnings they made and they were denied the guardianship of their children in case of divorce. In those times, most women were conditioned to believe that voting had nothing to do with them personally and that it would not affect their lives. So when Stanton decided to raise the issue of voting rights, many women backed off because they didn't believe it was worth fighting for. Sadly, it wasn't until 80 years later, in 1920 that women finally gained the right to vote and influence political affairs.

Can a single, limiting belief ruin an entire social movement? Of course. We must never underestimate the power of limiting beliefs and the impact they can have on our lives. Here's another example. Many guys experience "cold feet" syndrome just before they get married. Have you ever wondered why it happens? In most cases, guys who get cold feet at the altar love their girlfriends and want to marry them with all their heart. However, they have certain limiting beliefs about marriage and commitment that prevent them from making the eternal vow. They believe things like "marriage is the end of freedom," and "marriage is a ball and chain." Such (ridiculous) limiting beliefs will hinder anybody from taking a step towards marriage, be it men or women.

"The mind is its own place, and in it self can make a Heav'n of Hell, a Hell of Heav'n"

~ John Molton ~

Now that we understand the incredible power beliefs have in determining the reality we experience, let's take a minute to understand how we form beliefs.

Initially, all beliefs are nothing but an **idea**. Ideas are pretty basic; they are merely a mental representation of a certain concept, be it from a book, television, our own observation, or things we've been told by others. After we ponder a particular idea and compare it with the information we have in our head, we form an **opinion** about it. Opinions are conclusive thoughts. However, they are usually still open for dispute. As we receive references that strengthen our opinions, our feelings of certainty and confidence about its truthfulness and validity increase and we go on to form a world view, or, a **perspective**. A perspective is a unique, subjective way of looking at the world. Once a perspective is being reinforced, either by other people or by our own observations, we intellectually accept it as truth and it becomes a **belief**. At this point, we no longer question its truthfulness or validity and we accept it as a solid fact in our life.

In some cases, our beliefs can also become **convictions**. Convictions are beliefs intensified by emotions, which usually cause us to act with blind obedience on what we think is true. The Japanese Kamikazes are an excellent example of people who displayed strong convictions. Another example of the immaculate power of convictions was horrifyingly displayed in 1997, where 39 members of Heavens Gate committed suicide because they believed a spaceship, allegedly hiding behind the comet Hale Bopp, was coming to take them to the next life.

World renowned psychiatrist Erik Erickson discovered that we form the majority of our beliefs about ourselves by the age of fourteen. Most of those beliefs we model from our parents, teachers, friends, media, books, and other information sources we have been exposed to. The problem is that at fourteen, most of us never actually question whether those beliefs are good for us or whether they support who we want to become. We never consider the long term implications they will have on our lives or the things we might miss out on because of them.

Many of the beliefs we form as children can greatly hinder us in adulthood. For example, I was raised to believe that boys should not cry or show emotions such as pain and love since that sort of exposure indicated weakness and vulnerability.

This belief made me grow up to be emotionally tough and cold which served me greatly in sports and professional competitions. However, it came back to bite me later on in life in my personal relationships, especially romantic ones.

Romantic relationships depend on your ability to share emotions. If you're unable to share emotions, rest assured your relationships will die quickly. I found that out the hard way. For years, I just didn't seem to have the ability to share how I felt with the people I loved. And I had no idea why. It wasn't until I experienced a painful breakup with a very special girl who called me "emotionally handicapped" that I began to realize that my emotional blockage was nothing more than a limiting belief I developed as a little kid. Mad with rage, I challenged that limiting belief (with the 9 questions I'll share with you soon) and decided to transform it once and for all from "showing emotions is a weakness," to "showing emotions means courageous trust." Sure enough, since then, things have never been the same.

Our beliefs are often hidden. We are not aware of them because we do not analyze the contents of our minds on a regular basis. Therefore, we may carry unconscious beliefs for years, even decades, without ever realizing how they influence our behavior. I'm talking specifically about things we learned as young children. We tend to regard our parents and the education we have been given with such high respect that we don't even consider questioning the beliefs we were raised with. Nevertheless, we must remember that our parents, grandparents, or anyone else for this matter, see the world from their particular perspective and that perspective may not fit the path we want to take in life. We, as people who seek growth and greatness, must always keep in mind that times are changing. And because times are changing we must also change. Beliefs that have worked for our parents or grandparents may not work for us. In fact, beliefs that have worked for us as kids or teenagers, probably won't work for us today either. Therefore, we must leave no stone unturned and question all our beliefs regularly. We must not become mentally lazy and accept everything that's being thrown our way. What are some of the questions you should ask yourself when trying to evaluate a certain belief? Here are nine questions I use on a regular basis.

1) What is the source and evidence for this belief?

2) Can the evidence be interpreted differently, and if so how?

3) What are the circumstances under which this belief was initially formed?

4) Were mistakes in perception possible?

5) What's a contradicting belief I could create?

6) What will this belief cost me?

7) Does this belief work for me?

8) Is there an exception to this belief, and if so why?

9) Are there any external sources pressuring me to adopt this belief?

In order to deeply comprehend the inner workings of our beliefs, you and I must do three things.

First, we must develop the awareness that our beliefs are a choice. Most of us tend to think that beliefs are cemented, unchanging conceptual truths about life. But nothing could be further from the truth. When applied properly, beliefs are dynamic, interchanging guidelines that are constantly refined due to our growth and greater understanding of life

Second, we must realize that most of our beliefs are nothing more than generalized misinterpretations of reality and not reality itself. Our brain doesn't have the ability to distinguish between an experience that truly happened and one that is vividly imagined. Think about the last time you had a bad dream. How did it affect you? Did you wake up in a cold sweat? Did you feel frightened? How is that possible? After all, you were lying in bed the whole time.

It's important to realize that our senses act only as transducers. A transducer is a device that converts one form of energy to another. Our brain cannot process direct energy waves like sunlight or the smell of roses. It can only process electrical signals. So functioning as transducers, our senses merely record the stimulus around us, convert it, and send it to our brain.

Second, I challenged my limiting beliefs by using the 9 questions I shared with you earlier on in this chapter.

Third, I created new beliefs that I thought were empowering for me and with which I could replace my old limiting ones. For example, I changed the limiting belief "I don't have enough education," into "I have a PhD in self education." "After all," I rationalized, "during the past 3 years, I had read more than 350 books, taught myself speed reading and photographic Se

However, our senses are far from perfect. Our eyes, for example, are relatively small in size and therefore have limited light gathering capacity. They can only see electromagnetic radiation in the visible wavelengths. We can't follow a flying bullet. We can't see x rays or electricity or even germ cells, but nevertheless, we know they exist.

In the past, many of our false beliefs about the world have been based on misinterpretations. Up until 1492 we believed the world was flat, and therefore, we did not sail oceans from fear of falling off the edge. Luckily, Columbus had the courage to show us we were wrong. Up until 1553, we still believed the earth was the center of the universe until Copernicus came along and knocked us off our cosmos-centric pedestal.

The range of detection of our senses is narrow compared to the almost infinite spectrum of stimuli. Therefore when we rely on the usual sensory method of defining reality, we limit ourselves to only a fraction of what comprises the universe.

"There are no facts, only interpretations"

~ Friedrich Nietzsche ~

Take a look at the picture on the next page and try to determine whether you are seeing a floor or a ceiling.

Tricky, isn't it? Let me expose the trick for you. If you will notice, both edges of the floor/ceiling are incomplete. Had they been complete, the little fence had to connect on both ends and the illusion would be ruined.

When our brain receives information from the environment, it begins to create a representation, or a map of how the world is. In *Science and Sanity*, author Alfred Korzybski observed that "Important characteristics of maps should be noted. A map is not the territory it represents, but if correct, it has a similar structure to the territory, which account for its usefulness." Therefore, what we ultimately see is not reality but rather, a *re*-presentation of reality (which is never precisely accurate) as it is perceived by our senses.

It's important to understand that we never experience reality in its totality. We only experience what our beliefs allow us to feel and think. Our beliefs allow only selective strings of information to trickle to our brain in much the same way we use a strainer to drain pasta. As a result of this filtering process, we end up experiencing a very slim version of reality.

Third, we must realize that our beliefs are neither morally right nor wrong. They are simply our own interpretations of reality. Several weeks ago, I lost my wallet on the subway in New York. Amazingly enough it was returned to me anonymously after several days. Needless to say, I was surprised. If there was one place on earth I would not expect to have my wallet returned with all its contents, that was it, the subway in New York. What would you do if you found a wallet with $500, three credit cards, a driver's license and an I.D.? Would you leave the wallet where you found it? Would you take the money? Would you try to contact the owner? Would you take the money and then contact the owner telling him there was no money in the wallet when you found it? What if there was no driver's license and no ID in the wallet? What would you do then? And what if your rent was due the morning after and you had no money to pay for it? Would that change your course of action? The way you choose to behave in this sort of situation depends on your morality; your belief about what is right and wrong. Morality is a tricky thing. For years, philosophers have been arguing back and fourth about whether there is a true universal scale of right and wrong or whether right and wrong are merely personal preferences, strictly dependent on one's inner values. But in my view, the argument is futile because both views are right. Please read the following questions:

- **Is it right to believe in God?**

- **Is it wrong to be a Muslim?**

- **Is it right to be a democrat?**

- **Is it wrong to be a homosexual?**

- **Is it right to go to war?**

- **Is it wrong to kill?**

- **Is it right to allow a baby to be born severely disabled?**

These are tough questions to which no one has indefinite answers to. Is it right to believe in God? Depends who you're asking. A catholic minister would say "Yes" while an atheist would say "No." Is it wrong to be a Muslim? Opinions defer. But let's assume it is wrong. In that case, would it also be wrong to be Jewish or Christian or Hindu? Are the democrats right? The answer is "Yes," if you're a democrat. But if you are a republican, the answer is "No." Is homosexuality wrong? No one can truly determine. Other than ridiculous religious arguments driven by fear and ignorance, it has not been scientifically documented that heterosexuals live a day longer or are happier than homosexuals. Is it right to go to war? Again, no there's no definite answer. It probably wasn't the best move to go to war against the North Vietnamese but on the other hand, no one questions the necessity of going to war against Germany in WW II. Is it right to allow a baby to be born disabled? I have some personal insight about this one. I used to volunteer at St. Mary's, a hospital for severely disabled children. Some of the children there were cortically blind, deaf, and in a vegetative state while others had the ability to communicate with their environment to different degrees. Now, I'm a humanist at heart. I strongly believe in the sanctity of life. But the time I spent at St. Mary's made me think whether we were doing the right thing by bringing to this world a child who will never get to stand on his own feet, wash his own body, get a job, hear music, see the sunset, feel love and intimacy or experience or any of the things you and I experience on a daily basis. Is there a purpose to such a life? I'll let you decide. Take a look at the next illustration and tell me if you see a duck or a rabbit.

Well? Which one is it? The obvious answer is both. You are right if you think it's a rabbit and you are right if you think it's a duck. One of the keys to greatness is not to cling to a particular set of beliefs for the sake of being "right" but rather, to find the beliefs that work for you best and use them. In simple words, don't be "right" at the expense of being smart. Imagine yourself standing on a sidewalk, waiting for the light to turn green so you could cross the street. As the light turns green, you notice a speeding car heading straight towards you. What do you do? Do you start crossing or stay on the sidewalk? If you are one of those people who insist on being "right," than you should cross. After all, the law states that when a pedestrian has a green light, an incoming car should yield. However, common sense tells you that being "right" in this case is not worth the risk of getting run over. So intelligently, you give up being "right" for the sake of being smart (staying alive.)

"The belief that becomes truth for me... is that which allows me the best use of my strength, the best means of putting my virtues into action"

~ Andre Gide ~

The best way to find the "right" beliefs (those that will em-power you) is to find people who are achieving the results you want to achieve and model their belief system. For example, if you see someone who has extraordinary relationships, simply go and ask him, "what do you believe makes your relationship different?" "What are the beliefs that make your relationship work so well?" "What do you think are some good beliefs about relationships?"

Another effective way to model other people's beliefs sys-tems is by reading biographies and autobiographies. By read-ing biographies and autobiographies, we get a chance to see the mental makeup of a person, even as far back as the Greek scholars of antiquity. You can do this on an afternoon stroll to the library. You can read the biographies of artists and musi-cians you enjoy, of athletes you admire, of statesmen you re-vere or any other human being that has achieved the results you are interested in.

The Courage to Believe in Yourself

Christy Brown was born in Dublin in 1932 to a family of 10 children with parents of particularly modest means. Several weeks after his birth, the doctors diagnosed him with a severe case of cerebral palsy. His cerebral palsy was so debilitating that other than his left foot, Christy couldn't control any other part of his body. He couldn't speak, he couldn't walk, and he couldn't use his arms. His future looked abysmally hopeless.

Since he could not communicate with his environment and had a distorted expression on his face at all times, (he was al-ways drooling and foaming at the mouth) everybody soon be-gan to treat him as if he was retarded. However, within that crippled body, Christy's soul was burning with self determina-tion and belief. Even though he couldn't communicate with his environment, he knew he wasn't retarded. He knew his mind was perfectly fine and he believed that if he could only have a chance, he could prove he was just like everybody else.

One day, his younger sister left a piece of chalk in the living room. Christy spotted the chalk and dragged himself across the room. He grabbed the chalk with his left foot and with much effort drew the letter "A." The family stood aghast. They believed Christy was beyond hope. But Christy knew what he was capable of. By the age of ten he learned how to read and write. He gradually learned to use different tools and instruments around the house and make himself useful wherever he could. In his early teens he began to paint and read poetry, using nothing but his left foot to hold the brush and turn the pages.

When his father died and the family came under severe financial hardship, Christy urged his brothers to take his poetry and pictures and try to sell them. That move proved to be extremely successful. Several publishers wanted to publish Christy's work and a short while later, Christy was given the opportunity to show his pictures in a private exhibitions. But the story doesn't end here. Throughout the years, Christy Brown continued to portray his own unique perspective of the world as a severally disabled individual. Today, he is considered Ireland's foremost poet/writer and has received many awards and distinctions for his work. In fact, his autobiography, *My Left Foot*, was a world wide best seller which was eventually adapted into an award winning movie in which Daniel Day Lewis won an Oscar for playing Christy Brown.

Many times, our beliefs may come under fire. Christy Brown had to face not only a barrage of limiting social expectations, but also a debilitating physical disability that severely limited his ability to function independently. But Christy held on to his belief in his own ability and talent, and did not allow the world to move him from his conviction.

Arthur Shopenhauer, the famous german philosopher observed that every belief goes through three steps before it becomes commonly accepted. First, it is ridiculed, second, it is violently opposed, and third, it is accepted as self-evident and taken for granted. When we think about the courage to stand up for an empowering belief we can't help but remember a small Indian man who had an unshakable conviction that the British could be driven out of India without the use of violence. At a time when World War II was raging in Europe, causing millions of casualties, Gandhi's method of civil disobedience seemed ridiculous and unrealistic. Nevertheless he refused to compromise and almost single-handedly drove the British occupiers out of India.

Fifteen years after Gandhi's death, Dr. Martin Luther King embraced his principles of nonviolent civil disobedience and decided that they would become the fundamental corner stones of the civil rights movement. Since then, hunger strikes, walkouts, marches and parades have become common strategies of resistance for students, academicians, and even prisoners throughout the world who wish to oppose higher authorities without using violence.

"A man who won't die for something he believes in is not fit to live"

~ Dr. Martin Luther King, Jr. ~

Here are several more examples of great ideas that initially encountered strong resistance:

"The wireless music box has no imaginable commercial value. Who would pay for a message sent to nobody in particular?"
—David Sarnoff's associates in response to his urgings for investment in the radio in the 1920s.

"We don't like their sound, and guitar music is on the wayout."
—Decca Recording Co. rejecting the Beatles, 1962.

"The concept is interesting and well-formed, but in order to earn better than a 'C,' the idea must be feasible."
—A Yale University management professor in response to Fred Smith's paper proposing reliable overnight delivery service. (Smith went on to found Federal Express Corp.)

"A cookie store is a bad idea. Besides, the market research reports say America likes crispy cookies, not soft and chewy cookies like you make."
—Response to Debbi Fields' idea of starting Mrs. Fields' Cookies.

If there is one thing I want you take away from this chapter it's this: *you can have and do anything you want as long as you are willing to shatter the limiting belief about why you can't have it.* I truly believe in the truthfulness of this and think it is one of the most important life lessons I have learned.

I often think about that terrible dark period in my life when I felt destitute and hopeless about my future in order to remind myself of how mischievous and destructive limiting beliefs can be. I clearly remember dreaming about what I would do with my life and knowing it would never happen because I believed I didn't have the necessary resources; I was alone in a foreign country with no family or friends, I was young and inexperienced and had no money or education.

It wasn't until I was exposed to some incredible transformation stories of people who managed to rise from the gutter to the top that I began to understand that the only resource I really needed to make my life better was the four pounds of gray tissue between my two ears. The excuses and the stories I made up about why I couldn't have things my way were nothing more than self imposed limitations I created to support my own limiting beliefs. It was at that point I realized that unless I dealt with the root of the problem immediately (changing my limiting beliefs,) my dreams would never come to pass and my existence would be meaningless.

And here's how I did it. First, I identified four limiting beliefs that were keeping me from having what I want and I wrote them down.

Limiting belief #1:

I don't not having enough education

Limiting belief #2:

I don't have enough money

Limiting belief #3:

Nobody would want to listen to

somebody as young as me

Limiting belief #4:

I am not a native speaker of English,
my accent will drive people away

Second, I challenged my limiting beliefs by using the 9 questions I shared with you earlier on in this chapter.

Third, I created new beliefs that I thought were empowering for me and which I could substitute with my old limiting ones. For example, I changed the limiting belief "I don't not having enough education," into "I have a PhD in self education." "After all," I rationalized, "during the past 3 years, I read more than 350 books, thought myself speed reading and photographic memory."

I changed the limiting belief "I don't have enough money," to "I have as much money as I must have." "If I don't have enough," I concluded, "it's only because I did not make money a necessity." And so, I bought a small coupon sales kit and started selling coupons. I went to work in the school cafeteria and struck a cord with the general manager who quickly made me his personal assistant.

The third limiting belief, "nobody would want to listen to somebody as young as me," was a bit harder to change because most adults tend to discard young people's opinion due to lack of life experience. I ended up transforming that one into "youth is power." "I might be young," I thought, "but I have traveled more, seen more, and experienced more in the last five years than most people have throughout their entire lives. I've worked with juvenile delinquents, the academically gifted, college athletes and high-tech engineers as well as the mentally and physically challenged. I've traveled extensively around the world and had the unique opportunity of living within the Amerindian, Jewish, African-America, Asian-American and Latino communities."

And lastly, I transformed "I am not a native speaker of English my accent will drive people away," into "My accent is my trademark. I distinguish myself from other people by the way I speak."

As you can see, every limitation can be transformed into an advantage because limitations are only real in our mind. And just like Christy Brown, Jami Goldman and John Larkin, who turned an apparent physical limitation into a powerful advantage, so can you and I transform our limitations into our strengths.

"By believing passionately in something that still does not exist, we create it. The nonexistent is whatever we have not sufficiently desired"

~ Nikos Kazantzakis ~

Alright, let's quickly recap. We learned that beliefs control our reality. What we believe literally becomes true for us. We learned that our brain will back up all our beliefs with consistent behavior, even if the behavior is not in our best interest.

We learned how beliefs are formed and how most of our beliefs are hidden from us. We discovered that our senses are not perfect and that we must be able to evaluate all beliefs with questions to determine the value they have for us. We discovered that most of our beliefs have been embedded in us as children when our ability to evaluate information was very limited.

We found that most people form their beliefs haphazardly and without real intention which often leads to a confusion that infuses doubt and uncertainty. We also learned that limiting beliefs often lead to self sabotaging behavior, robbing us of our chances for success. And lastly, we studied how great people have the courage to stand up for something they believe in despite insuperable odds and extreme opposition.

As we finish chapter five, I hope that by now you understand that you either control your own beliefs and perceptions of reality or you respond to the beliefs and perceptions of other people. There is no middle ground. So make it your personal mission in life to shape your own reality and shatter all limiting beliefs. In the next chapter, I'm going to share with you seven powerful beliefs that I think will greatly enhance your ability to deal with life's challenges and thrive. I call them...

CHAPTER VI

The Seven Beacons
of Greatness

"The real challenge in life is to choose, hold, and operate through intelligent, uplifting, and fully empowering beliefs"

~ Michael Sky ~

The first and most important step one has to take in order to unfold his human potential is to become aware of the beliefs that control one's life. You've already done that. The next step is to expose yourself to empowering and consider implementing them in your life.

While there are many empowering beliefs that can affect the quality of your life, there are several fundamental beliefs that all great people have in common regardless of occupation, sex, race, or religious convictions. I call those beliefs "the beacons of greatness" and I'd like to share them with you.

In this chapter, I put together seven primary beliefs that many great people choose to live by. Those beliefs should give you a firm understating of the inner workings of great people and provide you with internal strength.

As you begin to read this chapter, it is important you keep in mind that great achievers, leaders and change makers come from every walk of life, every religious persuasion, every race, every gender and every level of education. The beliefs you will read about in this chapter are beliefs about life and people in general. They are not about worshipping or conforming to a higher power. They are merely general, empowering, positive observations that have worked in the lives of thousands of people and most likely will work for you too.

It is also important to remember that the following seven are just appetizers. Even though they have allowed many people to achieve and become more, they are by no means a "formula" for success. You can choose to adopt all, some, or none of those beliefs. That's strictly up to you. My hopes are that you will take the time to think and ponder them and then, try to implement them in your life. If they work for you, great! And if they don't, get rid of them quickly and find new ones. Here are the seven beacons of greatness:

Belief #1: Life is a metaphor.

Belief #2: I control my destiny.

Belief #3: In life, everything counts.

Belief #4: There are no desperate situations, only desperate people.

Belief #5: The past does not dictate the future.

Belief #6: Change happens instantly.

Belief #7: Life is a team sport.

As you read, try not to think about the seven beacons in terms of "right" or "wrong" but rather, in a practical and pragmatic sense; "Are they going to work for me or not?" and "How are they going to affect me?"

This chapter should also be a good chance for you to re-evaluate your current beliefs and compare them with the ones you will be reading. Try to imagine how your life would be if you had different beliefs five years ago. And then, try to think how your life will look like five years from now if you choose to implement them in your life.

Try to invest at least five minutes thinking about each belief before you move on to the next one. Don't rush. This chapter should provide you with a change of pace because I designed each and every belief to stand-alone, meaning, that there is no particular sequence you need to follow in order for the chapter to make sense. You can either read the entire chapter beginning to end or you can jump around from one belief to the other. Again, it's up to you.

Alright, let's get moving. Remember to take your time and evaluate each and every belief in the context of your life. Apply what makes sense and discard what doesn't.

"If you develop the absolute sense of certainty that powerful beliefs provide, then you can get yourself to accomplish virtually anything, including those things that other people are certain are impossible"

~ Anthony Robbins ~

Belief #1: Life is a metaphor. What is life for you? Is it a game? Is it a battle? Is it an opportunity? A quest? We use many metaphors to describe how life is. For some, life is a game, for others it is a war, while for others it is a journey or a passageway, or maybe even a test. Life can also be a stage, a ball and chain, it can be a sentence, or it can even be a dance.

We usually don't pay much attention to the metaphors we use to describe how life is. When life is good and things are going our way, then we "catch a wave," and life turns into a game. When the going gets rough and tough, we call life a challenge or a war, and it becomes "a fight to the finish." When we are forced to face circumstances we don't quite understand, like accidents or natural disasters, we look at life as a "mystery."

We use life metaphors because metaphors help us make sense out of life, much like a pair of three-dimensional goggles allows us to make sense of a stereoscopic picture.

However, life metaphors have a powerful effect on the quality of our beliefs because each life metaphor represents a complete set of beliefs about our selves, other people, the environment and the unknown.

Every time we adopt a life metaphor we automatically adopt both the limiting and the empowering beliefs that that particular metaphor is made of. For example, what if you believed that life is like a war? What kind of beliefs will you adopt as a result? In war, people must die. Survival is the only thing that counts. Everything is fair game. There are no morals, no values, and no guiding principles. When life is a war, you must always watch your back because you believe people are out there to "get you." You use phrases like "dog-eat-dog," and "it's every man for himself," and "today's friend is tomorrow's foe." How would this life metaphor affect your life? How would it affect the way you treat other people? Or the way you do business? How about the way you handle your relationships? Or the way you raise your kids?

What if life is a test? Can you imagine the amount of pressure you would experience if you believe everything you do is a test? In a test, it's either black or white. You either pass or fail. Everything must always be judged, compared, and evaluated. Expectations are the order of the day and the only thing that counts is performance. There are always deadlines to meet, objectives to achieve and people to please.

Our metaphors for life change as we grow. And just like our beliefs, we adopt them unconsciously, borrowing from what we hear, see and experience without really considering the cumulative long term impact they will have on us.

The key to being great is to choose the life metaphors that empower you the most- deliberately, in a conscious manner. It's just like Andre Gide, the French author who received the Nobel Prize in literature said "the belief that becomes truth for me... is that which allows me the best use of my strength, the best means of putting my virtues into action."

> *"Life is an opportunity, benefit from it.*
> *Life is beauty, admire it.*
> *Life is bliss, taste it.*
> *Life is a dream, realize it.*
> *Life is a challenge, meet it.*
> *Life is a duty, complete it.*
> *Life is a game, play it.*
> *Life is a promise, fulfill it.*
> *Life is sorrow, overcome it.*
> *Life is a song, sing it.*
> *Life is a struggle, accept it.*
> *Life is a tragedy, confront it.*
> *Life is an adventure, dare it.*
> *Life is luck, make it.*
> *Life is too precious, do not destroy it.*
> *Life is life, fight for it."*
>
> *~ Mother Teresa ~*

One of the most powerful life metaphors I know is the metaphor of life as an adventure. Just think about it, how did you feel when Alice went down the rabbit hole and when Frodo Baggins left the Shire? How about when Indiana Jones went to find the Lost Ark and Harry Potter left for the Hogwarts School of Magic? Remember the anticipation and excitement you felt?

Adventures are exciting. They are the fabric of the human drama. We create it in movies, we cherish it in folklore tales, we sing about it, and we admire the courage of the hero to go through the unknown in search for his destiny. Isn't that how our lives really are?

Humanistic philosopher Paul Kurtz observed that," The drama of human life is unpredictable, as human dreams and expectations are realized and shattered. At any one moment, the future is either promising or foreboding. The vista beyond in unclear; we may be inspired or frightened by what lies around the next corner or far down the road. We constantly wonder about what awaits for us: victory or defeat, prosperity or adversity, achievement or failure."

Like any great adventure, much of our lives are unknown. Many times we must make decisions without having all the information we need, and without knowing what the long term implications will be. We are not really sure what our purpose is or what role we play in the larger scheme of things but nevertheless, like any great hero, we choose to make a courageous, committed effort to do whatever it takes to find out. In part, going through the unknown is scary. Life is in part dangerous, unpredictable, chaotic, and unfair and in part glorious, magnificent, full of opportunity and excitement.

When we begin to think about life as an adventure, we are giving ourselves permission to peer into the unknown with curiosity rather than fear. We allow ourselves to become the protagonist in our lives. Immediately, we adopt a set of empowering beliefs that acknowledges the fact that risks, challenges, obstacles, and setbacks are a natural part of the journey towards finding our destiny, and so are triumph, glory and happiness. We understand that just like any adventure, sometimes the wind might be in your face, the rain will be pouring hard, and the sun will be hiding behind dark clouds, and at times, the wind will be at your back, the rain and darkness will retreat and the sun will illuminate our way.

"Adventure isn't hanging on a rope on the side of a mountain. Adventure is an attitude that we must apply to the day-to-day obstacles of life - facing new challenges, seizing new opportunities, testing our resources against the unknown and, in the process, discovering our own unique potential"

~ John Amatt ~

Adventure is not something savored only by astronauts and scientists, those who live on the edges of human knowledge; it is something each and every one of us must experience everyday since we all have a part to play in the larger quest for human destiny. The late Helen Keller wrote "Life is either a daring adventure or nothing. To keep our faces toward change and behave like free spirits in the presence of fate is strength undefeatable." I believe she is absolutely right.

You can make your life an adventure or you can make it a predictable bore. It is really up to you. In all the greatest human stories, the hero learns to trust his heart courageously through the darkness in order to discover who he really is. And as a result, he is rewarded with his destiny.

Greatness does not come to the bored and the lazy. You must be willing to live it daily, ask new questions, confront new obstacles, and stretch the limits. Meaning and destiny do not come to those sitting on the sidelines. They must be searched for, hunted down, and captured in order to be enjoyed.

George Leigh Mallory was a father of three and a school teacher by profession with an insatiable love for challenges and adventures. He died leading a British expedition up Mount Everest and was arguably the first person to reach to peak. But for him, the mountain was only a metaphor, "If you cannot understand that there is something in us which responds to the challenge of this mountain and goes out to meet it, that the struggle is the struggle of life itself - upward and forever upward - then you won't see why we go. What we get from this adventure is just sheer joy. And joy is, after all, the end of life. We do not live to eat and make money. We eat and make money to be able to enjoy life. That is what life means and what life is for."

Belief #2: I control my destiny. Who's in charge? Who's in control of your life? Is it you? Is it your parents? Is it other people? Who determines how your life is going to turn out?

Great people focus strictly on their strengths, on the things they *can* do in order to advance their lives. They don't worry about what's outside their spectrum of control. They acknowledge the fact that external forces do influence their lives; however, they don't let those forces *determine* the final outcome.

John Wodden, the legendry UCLA basketball coach was quoted saying, "If you get caught up in things over which you have no control, it will adversely affect those things over which you have control."

John Wooden didn't only coach basketball, he coached life. He coached the UCLA basketball team to 10 national titles and is currently one of only two men to be honored by the Hall of Fame as a player and as a coach. However, tenacious competitor you might think he is, he didn't do many of the things other coaches do. He didn't scout, he didn't focus on the media, he didn't focus on the officials, and he didn't focus on winning. His only focus was to get his players to play to the maximum of their potential. He knew there was no point in worrying about external factors since neither he nor they could control them. He realized that when his players focused on the things they could control, which was themselves, instead of the things they could not, his team would never lose, even if the final score was not in their favor. Peace of mind means lack of worry. And the moment you acknowledge that you are the one in the driver's seat, charting your own course, you acknowledge that your life is really up to you- within your control.

This leads us to another important aspect of control: responsibility. Responsibility is our ability to respond to life situations. In many cases, we find it easy and comforting to blame external factors for how we feel. We say,"It's your fault I'm failing," or "you make me angry." But blaming others doesn't make things better for us. The only person that can change your life for the better is you. And to do that, you must be willing to respond to situations even when you do not initiate them. When your company is forced to downsize due to fierce competition and you end up losing your job, that's not your fault. But it's your responsibility to do something about it. Whenever something bad happens to you, you have a choice: either stay a part of the problem, or become a part of the solution. You never have to stay in pain. But you do have to become responsible and exercise control.

Control is not something that's given or can be handed out. It's something you claim and take. And it's only those people who take the initiative and are proactive that ultimately get to control their own lives. In order to take control, you must focus your energy on the things that you can directly influence. Things like your free time, the books you read, the people you choose to talk to, the habits you choose to adopt, and the places you choose to visit. When we focus on the things we can control instead of those we can't, we free ourselves from the shackles of worry and fear. We don't care for what other people think about us, or how the market is doing because we are prepared and ready to respond to whatever happens.

The professional term for the amount of control you believe you have over your life is called *locus of control*. Psychologists have distinguished between two different types of control: internal and external. Internal locus of control means you believe internal factors, such as, beliefs, decisions, and attitudes determine the outcome of your life, while external locus of control indicates you believe that outside factors, such as other people or the weather determine your life's outcomes.

In his research, Dr. Michael K. Meyerhoff discovered "People with a strong "internal" locus of control tend to be highly successful and quite happy in life. People with a strong "external" locus of control tend not to do well and, more importantly, tend to be chronically miserable.

Here's a short exercise that will give you some reflection about who's in control in your life. It will only take a minute and I'm sure you will enjoy it. Although I tend towards a healthy cynicism conventional psychology, it does have its bright moments and this is definitely one of them. Here's how to do it: read the statements below and circle either true or false, what-

1. I usually get what I want in life.	True/False
2. I need to be kept informed about news and events.	True/False
3. I seldom know where I stand with other people.	True/False
4. People's misfortunes result from the mistakes they make.	True/False
5. I think that I could easily win a lottery.	True/False
6. When somebody doesn't like me, there is little I can do about it.	True/False
7. I usually convince others to do things my way.	True/False
8. People make a difference in controlling crime.	True/False
9. The success I have is largely a matter of chance.	True/False
10. Marriage is largely a gamble for most people.	True/False
11. People must be the master of their own fate.	True/False
12. It is not important for me to vote.	True/False
13. Life is a series of random events.	True/False
14. I never try anything that I am not sure of.	True/False

15. I earn the respect and honors I receive.	True/False
16. A person can get rich by taking risks.	True/False
17. Leaders are successful when they work hard.	True/False
18. Persistence and hard work usually lead to success.	True/False
19. It is difficult to know who my real friends are.	True/False
20. There will always be wars, no matter how hard people try to prevent them.	True/False

Want to see how you did? Turn to page 167 for the answer analysis.

Belief #3: In life, everything counts. Every decision counts. Every action, word, thought and event has an impact on the way your life unfolds and the direction it takes. There is no "small stuff." Every breath we take counts. Every letter we write counts. Every apology we make counts, every trip we take counts, every conversation we have counts, and surely, every person we come in contact with counts. You will never live a day that doesn't count. It is only in our neglect and laziness, in not returning a phone call, in promising and not fulfilling, in saying "it doesn't matter," and in letting things slide that we devalue ourselves and make life less than it really deserves to be.

Whenever you hesitate calling somebody, sending a thank-you note, or apologizing for something you did, don't. Just go ahead and do it. In the final analysis, we must always keep in mind that things add up, both big and small. Many people tend to focus only on the big things, the big promotions, the big hits, the big investments, and they neglect the smaller stuff, like greeting others or holding the door for a stranger. Thinking that only the big stuff matters is a tragic mistake. Greatness is achieved with acute attention and care for both the large and small details.

"Human felicity is produced not as much by great pieces of good fortune that seldom happen as by little advantages that occur every day"

~ Benjamin Franklin ~

Many people don't turn the lights off and television when they are staying at a hotel. They figure that since they've already paid a hefty price for the room, they might as well leave everything on. After all, it's the hotel's expense, not theirs.

But what if everybody were to turn the television and lights off? Maybe the price of the room would come down. What would happen if tomorrow, every person in the country were to throw one piece of thrash into a garbage can? Would that make a difference? What if every person donated one dollar for AIDS or cancer research? Small things can make a big difference.

Positive deeds, regardless of how small, have a tendency to multiply. Remember the movie *Pay It Forward* with Haley Joel Osment and Kevin Spacey? It's about a social studies teacher who challenges his 11-year-old students to come up with an idea that will change the world. One of the kids decides to step up to the plate and offers the concept of "paying it forward." Essentially, paying it forward means that every time somebody does a favor for you, instead of paying him back, you pay it forward to three other people. At first, the idea seems utopian and over simplified but as the movie unfolds; it gradually catches on and affects the lives of hundreds of people.

It is vitally important we develop a sense of care and respect for all things in life, big or small. Just think, we can defend ourselves against the forces of nature, wild animals, and even bullets and bombs, but we find it hard to protect ourselves from germs that are one hundredth the size of a grain of sand.

That's amazing, isn't it? Let us not be fooled into thinking that small things are not as important as big things. In the grand design of life, all things, big and small, have their purpose. And as people who aspire to be great, it is our job to realize that all things count even when we don't really know or understand how.

*Belief #4: There are no desperate situations, only desperate people."*There are no desperate situations, only desperate people," said Shimon Peres, the former prime minister of Israel and a Nobel Laureate, when he was asked whethera the conflict between the Israeli's and the Palestinians was beyond hope. This is a priceless piece of wisdom. Knowing that people make situations, rather than situations making people is a fundamental core belief that all great people posses. To them, there is no such thing as "no way" and they consider no situation to be lost or beyond repair.

Whenever we attempt to accomplish something, we are bound to run into obstacles. We talked about this inevitability in chapter 4. Obstacles and problems are a natural part of life. The question is, "How are we going to deal with them?"

Hannibal's march into Italy through the perilous Alps is legendary. The Romans were sure there was no way for Hannibal to cross the Rhone with thousands of men and war elephants. But Hannibal was committed. He slipped northward, avoiding Roman sentries and attempted to cross the river on pontoons and by swimming. But the crossing appeared treacherous; not only was the river in spring flood, but if he were to be discovered by the Romans during the crossing, his army would have been destroyed on the spot.

Standing on the banks of the river, Hannibal realized an even greater challenge. The river was too deep for the elephants to wade, and no pontoon bridge would hold them. Without the elephants, his army would lose most of its supply and would not be able to sustain the lengthy Italian campaign. But Hannibal was determined. The elephants had to reach the other side of the river. After much contemplation, he finally found the solution. He ordered bladders to be filled with air and attached to the elephants, thus creating elephant water wings. Then, miraculously he floated them across the river.

"We will either find a way or make one"

~ Hannibal ~

It is tempting to give up on a problem and deem it "unsolvable," especially if we have tried several different solutions that didn't work out. Great people believe a solution always exists. They believe that we as human beings would not have been given problems to which there are no solutions. Sure, sometimes the right solutions might be hard to find or require extra effort but nevertheless, they are always out there.

Sobibor was a well constructed death factory, a part of Hitler's final solution plan to exterminate Jews and other minorities in Europe. More than 250,000 people found their graves at the camp either by firing squads or by gassing.

In 1943, the prisoners at Sobibor faced a desperate situation. The word was out that the entire camp work force was about to be replaced which for them meant certain death. They felt helpless. In fact, they felt so helpless that they began to turn on each other. Riots began to break out within the barracks, prisoners began to steal food and clothes from one another and chaos slowly took over as the prisoners felt the end drawing near.

One day, a transport of Polish Jews from a nearby town arrived at Sobibor. They brought the stunning news of the Warsaw ghetto uprising. The news spread through the camp like prairie fire. An uprising? An escape? Was that even a possibility? Hundreds of guards patrolled the perimeter armed with automatic assault rifles and dogs. The camp was surrounded by two rows of barbed wire fences and fearsome watch towers loaded with heavy machine guns. On top of that, the Nazis also planted mine fields outside the camp which made an all out mass escape unfathomable.

Determined to seize the day, a small, committed nucleus began to form around Leon Feldhendler, a Polish Jew from a local village and Alexander (Sasha) Pechersky, a soviet POW. The main problem the two leaders faced was how to free the entire camp without alerting the guards or moving through the mine fields. The first plan was to dig a tunnel underneath the camp, beyond the mine fields and into the woods. But Sasha objected. He believed the hours of the night were not sufficient to allow the entire camp population of 600 to crawl through the tunnel and fights were likely to flare-up between prisoners waiting to crawl through. The two leaders debated for several days until finally, they decided to abandon the plan entirely due to heavy rains and the upcoming winter.

Time was running out. It was becoming clearer every day that the only way to escape safely from Sobibor was by passing through the main gates of the camp. A three phase plan was quickly conceived. In the first phase, members of the underground who had access to the warehouses and sorting sheds were told to deliver knives and small axes to the conspirator's command post.

The second phase included the placement of six combat groups, of three people each, in preparation for the secret killing of the Nazi officers. According to the plan, the SS commanders would be individually lured to various workshops around the camp to pick up finished products like boots, uniforms, or leather coats, and once there, the combat teams would move into action and assassinate them. It was important that the SS commanders did not cry out while being killed lest any of the guards were alerted that something unusual was happening. At the same time, two electricians were to pretend to fix phone lines which were to be cut so that the escapees would have several hours in which to flee under the cover of darkness, before back-up could be called.

In the third phase, all the prisoners would report as usual to the roll call square and then walk together in regular formation towards the front gate. The idea was that the guards would think it was a German order for some work assignment; this would allow the prisoners to come as close as possible to the main gate without arousing suspicion. Then the members of the underground, who took up position in the front rows, would take the gate by storm and overpower the guards.

At the end of the day, more than 320 prisoners escaped the death camp of Sobibor in what has become the most epic revolt of the Second World War. The uprising succeeded against immeasurable odds due to the relentless commitment and brave leadership of Sasha and Leon to find a way out of the camp. In 1987, the story was finally made into a truly inspirational movie entitled *The Escape from Sobibor*, which I warmly recommend you watch.

Remember, there is always a way out. There are no unsolvable problems and there are no unconquerable challenges. It doesn't matter how dark and desperate a certain situation might seem, if you are committed to finding a way out, you eventually will.

Belief #5: The past does not dictate the future. The person responsible for shaping the psychological paradigm we have today for dealing with our past is none other then Dr. Sigmund Freud. Freud's brilliance was in identifying the impact of childhood events on the psychological functioning of adults. He was the first one to point out that many of the personal and behavioral problems we may experience as adults can be traced back to particular childhood experiences that our brain has repressed in order to help us deal with the world. Therefore, he concluded, most of our adult behavior is driven by unconscious motives and emotions deeply rooted in our childhood.

To a certain extent, Freud's observations were accurate. And I'm sure you've noticed similar patterns as well. The little boy who was poor develops an unquenchable thirst to become wealthy. The little girl who didn't experience enough affection grows up looking for love in all the wrong places. The little boy who was abused grows up to become an abuser himself. When I was working at the "Pines," I worked with about 35 adolescents, all convicted as sex offenders. While looking through their files, it was hard to ignore the fact that as a child, each and every one had been a victim of sexual abuse. Obviously, there's a powerful pattern in action here.

For years we have been told by psychologists that the experiences we have in our childhood determine how our lives will turn out. Research and statistics have proven over and over again that if we had alcoholic parents, we will probably grow to become alcoholics ourselves. If we had a broken home, we will probably become home wreckers ourselves. If we have been abused, we will probably turn into abusers ourselves. In essence, we have been taught that we are nothing more than an amplified projection of the experiences we have as children and that there's not much we can do about it.

The truth is that it's easy to believe that we are a product of our past. It is a relief to know that we are controlled by unconscious forces we can't grasp and that it's not really our fault we are the way we are. But that's really a cop out. By developing an awareness of the forces that drive us, like our identity, our emotions and our beliefs, we can easily take charge of our lives and determine where we want to go and what we want to do, regardless of our past.

In previous chapters we learned that we are not helpless victims drifting along with the currents of life. But we can be, if we are not careful. When we allow limiting beliefs and past events to dictate to us what we can and can not do, we destroy our chances of improving our lives because we don't have a compelling future to drive towards. It's like trying to drive a car forward using the rear view mirror.

Great people know the past may influence the present. It

may influence how they think and feel about certain things, but it does not *dictate* who they are or what they are capable of doing at any point in time. While most people use their past as a reference source for their future, great people treat their past as a lesson.

"Those who cannot learn from history are doomed to repeat it"

~ George Santayana ~

Great people realize that every life experience has something to teach them. They know that the past is not a reliable reference for their characters and abilities but rather, an indication of a particular strategy or behavior they used which has yielded a certain outcome. It may not be the outcome they were looking for but nevertheless, it is still an outcome. For example, when I started my first business, my partner and I had great dreams of success but we ended up losing money and had to cut our endeavors short after only a year. I could have concluded that I'm a lousy businessman and that from then on, I shouldn't go into business again because I'm just not good at it. But that would have been ridiculous. When we had a close look at what went wrong, both my partner and I discovered that a small mistake in the marketing of our product had actually cost us our entire business. Had we been more aware and knowledgeable at the time, this mistake would have surely been avoided. So you see, we didn't fail, we learned. It might have been an expensive lesson but it was a lesson which I'm sure neither of us will ever forget.

Great people understand the essence of what Heraclitus said in 543 B.C. "You cannot step twice into the same river." This aphorism means that it is not only us who change, but the world around us constantly changes as well. Many times, something that doesn't work today may work tomorrow, not because of us, but because the world is different today than it was yesterday.

An important part of learning from our past is looking at ourselves as dynamic evolving and growing beings and not as structured artifacts that either "work" or "don't work." We are not machines. We don't have a fixed design or an instruction manual. We evolve. We grow. And in my opinion, it is never too late to learn from our past, even after ten, twenty, or even thirty years. I'm not saying it's easy, but I'm saying that as people who strive to be great, we must be able to find a lesson in everything that happens to us.

Let me share with you the story of Mark Hughes. Mark Hughes was born on the tough side of Los Angeles to a single mother. As a teen, he got hooked on drugs but managed to escape. He became so passionate about helping other kids beat drug addiction that he became a fundraiser and an activist in his community. However, when he was eighteen, his mother died from an accidental overdose of prescription diet pills. Mark was devastated. His mother was all he had. He refused to accept the fact that losing weight could be so dangerous. There had to be an easier way. So he began researching. He traveled all across the country and even made trips to China until he finally came up with the Herbalife formula. But there was a problem. Mark was broke. He could not advertise or promote his ingenuity so he began selling it to his relatives from the trunk of his car.

Since then, Mark dedicated his life to helping people lose weight and improve their health safely and effectively. In February 1980, he launched Herbalife International, which is now a multi-national nutrition company with sales of over $1 billion a year. How about that? Did Mark let the past dictate his future? He sure didn't. Could he have used his life predicament as an excuse for failing? I'm sure he could have. But he didn't. He chose to learn from it and turn his personal tragedies into opportunities.

Not letting the past dictate the future is also an important belief we must adopt in our global affairs. Many people are negative and fatalistic about the future of human beings. They believe that we haven't learned anything from our past and that we keep on making the same mistakes over and over again. But in my opinion, that's just needless pessimism.

The truth is that we have gotten better. Even though the 20th century has seen two devastating world wars, numerous genocides, a great economic depression, the AIDS virus and the apocalyptic threat of a nuclear war, in the 21st century we have already achieved significant improvement. The AIDS virus, although still spreading, is discussed and educated against in seminars, lectures and classes in most high schools and universities around the world. Polio has been eradicated almost entirely. Global awareness of the necessity for the health and well being of the planet has become a serious issue on the international daily agenda. Europe has a single currency. The internet has turned the world into a global village allowing for cooperation and knowledge sharing worldwide. NASA has made tremendous strides with the landings of the Spirit and Opportunity Rovers on Mars in January 2004, and much significant legislation has passed to increase the rights of minorities.

You and I have a personal responsibility not to live in the past. We have come too far, overcome too many challenges and suffered too much pain in order to give up on what's to come. By living for the future, by letting our dreams and visions guide us instead of our fears and doubts, we honor our history and shape our destiny, not only for us, but for generations to come as well.

Belief #6: Change happens instantly. All along we have been talking about the power of change. We learned that in order for us to be successful, achieve the things we want and live a great life, we must be able to change and change fast.

In our culture, we are raised to believe that personal change is something difficult that happens very slowly, if at all. We struggle daily with habits like smoking, over-eating, drinking, and self sabotage. We spend years in counseling and therapy with high hopes of eventually feeling good about ourselves and one day enjoying our life. Most of us think we need to do something special in order to change, but the truth is that we really don't.

There are several reasons why people don't change and we talked about them in depth in chapter two, but let's revisit two of them quickly. First, most people don't believe it's possible to change. They try to shape a behavior or a personality characteristic with sheer will power and they fail over and over. Therefore they conclude that they simply don't have enough will power to create a change.

The second reason people don't change instantly is because they don't know how. Unlike a new stereo system, we don't come equipped with an instruction manual. As human beings, we have to discover how we function on our own. In the past, strategies and techniques for creating personal change have been the exclusive domain of psychologists and psychiatrists and have been regarded as arcane knowledge, the kind that is kept in ivory towers by old men with white beards who know more about us than we do.

We have been conditioned to believe that the human mind is so complex, that only after years of training and laborious study can one begin to understand how it works. But nothing could be further from the truth. The last 20 years have pioneered unique breakthroughs in the field of personal development. Today, any person can walk into a library and read about new personal change technologies such as neuro-linguistic programming or neuro-associative conditioning and change almost anything about themselves within less than 20 minutes. That's just a fact. Any person can learn the fundamentals of change, if he is interested.

The reality is that most people who become great do not

count on psychologists or psychiatrists when they want to change. They simply "become the change they want to have," as Gandhi put it. They know that most conventionally trained psychologists and psychiatrists work with outmoded theories and models of human development and they realize that the responsibility to learn how their brain operates is theirs. It's a part of knowing who they are.

Let me give you some basic fundamentals of dynamics of change. First of all, change is a bio-emotional process. It's not a thinking process; you can't think yourself into a change. Our entire nervous system must be involved in the process, both physically and emotionally. When people pick up a cigarette, they don't begin to think about the pros and cons of smoking, they simply feel an urge to smoke and they do it. They are driven by an emotion.

The secret to creating an effective change of any kind is to control the source of a particular emotion, or in other words, in changing the belief that controls that emotion. Remember that beliefs act like safety valves for emotions. They control the amount of neurotransmitters our brain releases into our body. When we take control over a belief, we take control over the emotion. If we want to create an effective change, we must create an intense emotional experience that alters the emotional connections within our nervous system. Any changes that does not have an impact on our nervous system, will not last for long.

One of the best places to create a quick change is at a live seminar. We use our live seminars as a platform to allow people to create those intense experiences where they can change their beliefs by themselves, and thus create any change they wish to create. We use every tool at our disposal, from thundering music to dynamic exercises and atmosphere transitions in order to create a powerful experience that allows people to shape and mold their future, and as a result, boost the sense of control they have over their lives.

Belief #7: Life is a team sport. In our culture, we are brought up to be individualists. Most of the cultural icons we grew up with are solitary figures like the Lone Cowboy, Superman, Spiderman, and of course, Rambo and Rocky. Those icons teach us that we can take the world on our own. They teach us that one person can do it all. But is that really true?

If you think about the most successful business endeavors of the 21st century you'll discover that the vast majority of them are the result of successful partnerships. Think of Bill Gates and Paul Allen with Microsoft, Larry Page and Sergey Brin with Google, Ben Cohen and Jerry Greenfield with Ben & Jerry's Ice cream, Jason and Matthew Olim with CDNow, Bill Hewlett and Dave Packard from HP, and Larry Ellison ,Bob Miner and Edward Oates, the founders of Oracle.

For the majority of my life I believed that working with other people was the most difficult thing in the world. I believed people are just too different to get along. In school projects, on the job and even with neighbors, there always seemed to be some sort of friction present at all times. So I concluded that living solo was the only way of living without conflicts. I think all of us wish we were left alone every now and then. We all have been hurt or offended by lovers, roommates, strangers, and even teachers and family members. We have experienced disagreements, conflicts, arguments and fights. Sometimes, it seems easier to just shut the world out.

However, the best things in life are things we achieve when we are a part of a team. Sure, we have our own personal victories; graduating from college, getting a promotion, landing an important contract. But if we don't have anybody to share those personal victories with, they quickly lose their value.

Think for a minute about all the things that make you feel good. If you are like me, then it's probably things like good music, movies, sporting events, family gatherings and parties. Let me ask you a question, what's common to all these things? The obvious answer is: lots of other people!

I'm sure you realize that whatever it is you enjoy in life, other people are always involved in it. That's because when people are coming together and are emotionally involved, they create what is known as "synergy." Synergy is an interaction that creates a whole that's greater than the sum of its parts. When people come together while compensating for each others weaknesses and magnifying each others strengths, they create a unique and powerful dynamic that creates a powerful feeling of unity and bond.

Synergy is everywhere around us. Look at nature for a second. If you plant two plants close together, the roots co-mingle and improve the quality of soil so that both plants will grow better than if they were separated. If you put two pieces of wood together, they will hold much more weight than the total weight they can hold separately. When effective synergy is created, one plus one doesn't add up to two, but three, or four or five and even more. Do you remember how the Chicago Bulls played during the 95/96 championship season? Now that's synergy. The Bulls were led by their coach Phil Jackson and the terrorizing three, Michael Jordan, Scotty Pippen and Dennis Rodman. This powerful line up propelled the Bulls to set an NBA record by winning 72 regular-season games and losing only 10, as well as stringing an eighteen game winning streak.

But you don't have to bring megastars together in order to achieve great results. Just consider the Florida Marlins for a moment. No one gave them a chance at the beginning of the 2003 season. In fact, they made a managerial change when the team hit a low point early in the season. They fought back to win the National League wildcard, then defeated the San Francisco Giants, then overcame the Chicago Cubs when they were down 3-1 in the National League Championship Series. In the World Series, though trailing again the Marlins defeated the mighty New York Yankees to win the World Series!

Synergy simply means that it's better to work with people than against them. It is a team concept. Just like a well oiled steam engine with all its parts working in perfect harmony. In fact, let's use that as an example. Imagine how each and every component, both big and small, performs to its designed potential. But each part can only work as part of a whole thus creating a powerful locomotion that eventually can thrust even the heaviest freight trains.

If there is one skill that will catapult your life to the next level it is learning how to work effectively with other people. Or in other words, becoming a team player.

"Coming together is a beginning, staying together is progress, and working together is success"

~ Henry Ford ~

If you are alive, then you are playing on a team. Your family is a team. In school, you belong to a team. In the work environment, you belong to a team. You also belong to a community, a city, a state, a country, and eventually a planet, all representing different teams. Every time you enroll in a particular social circle, system, or program, you represent that particular entity, whether it's with your permission or without. So you're already part of a team. The only question is what type of player are you?

Once you begin to look at your life as a collection of team memberships, two options become available. The first is to seek only your own personal interest, which will eventually make you a lousy team player and cause the other team members to see you as selfish. The second option is to realize that by serving the team and catering to the members' needs, you are actually serving yourself long-term. Here's how. A team or a community is like a hangar full of tools and resources. Each team member has skills, talents and personal resources which he loans to team. And in return, he gets to draw from the team's collective pool of resources. The more a member contributes to a team, the more resources he gets to draw in return. Simple reciprocity. That's the way it works in families, companies, sports teams and rock bands. Those that contribute the most to the other members, get more in return.

You and I probably play on very different teams but there is one team we play for together. I'm talking about the "human" team. We entered this team on the day we were born without being asked. And the way I see it, it's really up to you to determine what role you want play in it. We can either spend our life feeling isolated and alone and caring only for our own needs or we can realize that we are all in this adventure together, for better or for worse. And even though we didn't get to choose our teammates, we can still choose how we want to play the game. Life is a team sport. Anywhere you want to go and anything you want to be or do, there's somebody out there that can help you get there faster than you can on your own. But if you don't find a way to meet his needs, he won't meet yours.

Are there more empowering beliefs you can adopt other than the seven I shared with you? Of course. And the more of them you can come up with, the better you will be. In this chapter, we covered only seven basic beliefs and it's my conviction that they will serve you very well, just as they have served me. Again, my suggestion is: give those beliefs a try. Implement them in your life for a while and then observe the difference. If you think they need refinement, go ahead and refine. If you think they totally contradict your experience so far, then ask yourself some of the questions we talked about in the previous chapter and try to figure out why there's a contradiction. Whatever you choose to do with them, I hope you will continue to search for empowering beliefs that will make a difference in your life as well as the life of others.

I'm sure you have noticed that gradually, we are beginning to gain a comprehensive awareness of what it takes to become great. We discussed the power of identity. We learned about happiness and emotions. We looked at how beliefs work and we discovered the tremendous impact of beliefs, both to create and to destroy.

The first section of Being Great is behind us. In the next section, we are going to talk about a subject that most people consider a taboo. Why taboo? Because for most people, this subject is a cause for much pain. But after reading the next two chapters, I'm sure you'll be able to heal your...

Answer Key

Give yourself 5 points If you circled "true" on statements: 1, 2, 4, 5, 7, 8, 11, 15, 17, 18. If you circled "false" on any of those statements, give 0.

Give yourself 5 points If you circled "false" on statements: 3, 6, 9, 10, 12, 13, 14, 16, 19, 20. If you circled "true" on any of those statements, give 0.

What your score means:

0-15 Very strong external locus of control
20-35 External locus of control
40-60 Both external and internal locus of control
65-80 Internal locus of control
85-100 Very strong internal locus of control

Section II.
Personal Finances

Chapter VII

Wealth Wounds:
Why Isn't Everybody Rich?

"It is said that wealth is like a viper which is harmless if a man know how to take hold of it; but, if he does not, it will twine around his hand and bite him"

~ *Frank K. Houston* ~

Everybody wants to be wealthy but very few people are. Did you ever wonder why? I sure have. If you are like me, you have thought about wealth on more than one occasion. Not in the greedy sense of the word, but from learning perspective. What does it really take to be wealthy and does wealth have anything to do with greatness? After all, we already learned in chapter 1 that being great doesn't necessarily mean being rich. Some of the world's greatest people were poorer than average and yet, their influence and legacy far outweighed their income. Mahatma Gandhi owned a single pair of walking shoes and sewed his own clothes. Mozart lived and died in poverty. At age 69, penniless, Ralph Waldo Emerson had to borrow money from friends, neighbors and relatives after his house burned down.

While it's obvious you don't need to make billions of dollars to be great and have an exciting life, you also don't need to suffer from financial pressure or lack of resources. I believe that your ability to attract wealth should reflect your understanding of your ability to create things of value and to contribute to the market place. Fair and square.

I don't believe in instant cash formulas or quick profit schemes so don't expect to find those in this chapter. People who strike gold overnight are as rare as flying pigs. And if that's what you are looking for, you better go play the lottery. The road to wealth is long and it can get tedious and uncomfortable. And while you are not going to become an overnight millionaire after reading the next two chapters, you are going to have the fundamental understandings of what wealth is, who has it, how it is distributed, and obviously, how to obtain it.

Before we begin, let me ask you, what do you think makes wealth so attractive and beguiling? How is it that in order to get more money, people are willing to sacrifice time with their family and friends, push themselves to exhaustion, travel hundreds and sometimes thousands of miles and even expose their innermost secrets to the public on T.V.?

Regardless of how we choose to look at it, the facts speak for themselves. Money is one of the biggest motivators in our society, if not the primary one. And there is no doubt that money has a remarkable appeal today, probably more than ever before. But when we say we want to be wealthy, do we really mean that we want more money? After all, you and I know that money (which can also take the form of stocks, bonds, treasury bills, electronic credit, property value, checks, credit, money orders, insurance policies, will's, antiques and valuables,) is nothing but a green piece of paper, right? It has no significant value in and of itself. Just think about it, if I'd given you suitcases and suitcases of outdated hundred dollar bills, would you be wealthy? Of course you wouldn't. The most you could do with them is to start a fire.

The appeal of money is in what it can get us, and if you remember what we talked about in chapter 3, then you know that the appeal is emotional. The power of money lies in the emotions it symbolizes. It is synonymous with feelings of power, security, freedom, fun, lavishness, social status, fame, excitement. It can also symbolize greed, envy and corruption.

"Money will buy you a bed, but not a good night's sleep, a house but not a home, a companion but not a friend"

~ Zig Ziglar ~

Wealth, therefore, is not a bank account figure; it's an emotion, a feeling of abundance. For some people, this feeling comes from owning four cars (one for each season), a 15- bedroom Victorian mansion, an Olympic size pool, a tropical garden with a bubbling waterfall, a 50-foot yacht and a tennis court while for others it comes from providing for their family, going on vacation twice a year and building a studio in the basement. Some people have lavish life styles that require constant spending of millions of dollars while for others, an income of $60,000 a year is more than enough.

The truth is that wealth and abundance have nothing to do with how much you own or how much you have in your bank account. If you don't feel wealthy right now, if you are not convinced beyond a shadow of a doubt that you have everything you could possibly need in order to make your dreams materialize, no amount of money or possessions can change that.

Just by being alive today you already have access to more resources, more opportunities, more knowledge and more wealth than the greatest kings of medieval times. Every bit of information that was ever gathered and written about is available for free, on-line and in libraries. Music has become (almost) free and recordings are of better quality than ever before. Higher education, which was once the commodity of the rich and noble, is within reach of everybody, even the penniless and destitute. If that's not wealth, than I don't know what is.

Money can only give you financial security. And while that is extremely important, it won't make you feel wealthy and abundant in the truest sense of the word.

Most people generate more money in their life times than both their parents put together but still they never allow themselves to feel wealthy. That's because most people still operate from a scarcity mentality. They believe we live in a reality where food, land, oil, money, quality homes, opportunities and even love are limited. As a result, they always have a gnawing sense of lack- as though something is always missing. How many times have we seen people who tried to fill the holes in their souls with money and failed? Much too often. Remember Elvis? Marilyn Monroe? John Belushi?

"I've never been poor, only broke. Being poor is a frame of mind. Being broke is only a temporary situation"

~ Mike Todd ~

The truth is that everything you and I need in order to survive exists in unparalleled abundance. There is enough oxygen for all 1.5 million different species that inhibit the earth. And it's free. Food is also plentiful. According to the Institution for Food and Development Policy, "Abundance, not scarcity, best describes the world's food supply. Enough wheat, rice and other grains are produced to provide every human being with 3,500 calories a day. That doesn't even count many other commonly eaten foods-vegetables, beans, nuts, root crops, fruits, grass-fed meats, and fish. Enough food is available to provide at least 4.3 pounds of food per person a day worldwide: two and half pounds of grain, beans and nuts, about a pound of fruits and vegetables, and nearly another pound of meat, milk and eggs- enough to make most people fat! Even most "hungry countries" have enough food for all their people right now. Many are net exporters of food and other agricultural products." For example, in 1995 India, where some 200 million people live in hunger, exported $625 million worth of wheat and $1.3 billion worth of rice. In Brazil, approximately 70 million people are considered poor but the average yearly food export is about $13 billion.

Money is also bountiful. According to the CIA, the United States general national product (G.N.P) for 2003 was approximately $10.99 trillion, which means that the production power of each individual is about $37,800. That's the highest in the world.

So how come we still hear about people starving? According to the US Bureau of Labor Statistics, during 2000, 31 million people lived below the official poverty line. Amongst those, 6.4 million were classified as "working poor." And that's in the richest country in the world!

Even though we are living in the richest time in the history of the world, most people reach the age of 65 after 30 or 40 years of work with empty pockets. There is absolutely no guarantee that even with all the technology, education and resources available to each of us, that we will become wealthier than our predecessors. A recent study by the American Council of Life Insurance found that for every 100 people starting their careers and retiring by age 65:

- 25 have died

- 20 have an annual incomes under $6,000

- 51 have annual incomes between $6,000 and $35,000

- Only 4 have incomes over $35,000

How can this be? How is it possible that so few manage to reach retiring age with comfortable incomes? How is it, that even though we have more resources and opportunities than

ever before, most people end up living under significant financial pressure? Part of the answer to these questions lies in understanding how wealth is distributed in our society.

The Distribution of Wealth:
The Pareto Principle

In the 18th century, Italian economist Vilfredo Pareto noticed that in Italy, 80 percent of the land, property and live-
stock was owned by approximately 20 percent of the people.
What he didn't know was that that ratio was applicable everywhere.

The Pareto principle can be observed in almost every aspect
of life. 20 percent of Americans have 80 percent of the college
degrees. In almost any company or sales force, 80 percent of
the money is earned by 20 percent of the people. And this goes
further and deeper. Of the top 20 percent that's making 80 percent of the money, 80 percent of that money is made by 20
percent of that group of people. We are now down to 4
percent. Among that 4 percent, once again 80 percent of the
money is made by 20 percent of the people in this group. Now
we're down to almost 1 percent of the people, making 51.2 percent of the total wealth. That's 256 times more than the 80 percent on the bottom.

How close does the Pareto Principle come to real life? Very
close. While the theory predicts that about 51.2 percent of the
wealth is earned by one percent of the people, the Economic
Policy Institute indicates that 50.4 percent of the national income is earned by the top 1 percent. That's very close. The
United Nations, by their income distribution data of 1999, found
that the world's top 20 percent receives 83 percent of all income. That's also very close. According to the Pareto Principle,
4 percent of American households should be millionaires. In
reality, about 3.5 percent are millionaires.

It was once said that if all the wealth in the world was collected and divided equally among all people, within five years every penny would return to its original owners. And I believe that's absolutely true. Being wealthy is first and foremost a mind set. Even though many people think that wealthy people have something special going for them; that they are better or smarter or just luckier than most people, current research shows otherwise.

"He who knows that enough is enough will always have enough"

~ Lao Tsu ~

Who are the Wealthy?

So who are the 20 percent? What signifies them? And what can you and I learn from them?

Unlike what we see on television, the vast majority of those who's net worth are $1 million or more are quite ordinary people. You won't see them on television and you won't be able to tell they're wealthy if they sit next to you in the doctor's office. In their classic *The Millionaire Next Door*, Dr. Stanley and Dr. Danko have meticulously researched the characteristics of millionaires in order to discover who they really are. They created a long detailed list of the most common traits that typify the average millionaire. I strongly recommend you read it, but what follows is the gist of their findings which I'm sure you'll find interesting, if not surprising.

- Less than 1 percent of all millionaires are entertainers or athletes.

- About two-thirds of those that work are self-employed (Interestingly, self-employed people make up less than 20 percent of the workers in America but account for two-thirds of the millionaires.)

- Many of the types of businesses millionaires own could be classified as dull/normal. They are welding contractors, auctioneers, rice farmers, owners of mobile-home parks, pest controllers, coin and stamp dealers, and paving contractors.

- Most of them never received inheritance and about 80 percent are first generation millionaires.

- Less than 10 percent of all millionaires drive Mercedes, BMW's or Jaguars. The rest drive American made cars such as Ford F-150 or Explorer.

- Most live in homes valued at $320,000 in average.

- Only about one in five is not a college graduate. 18 percent have master's degrees, 8 percent law degrees, 6 percent medical degrees, and 6 percent Ph.D's.

- On average, millionaires live on less than 7 percent of their income, well below their means.

Personally, I don't believe that most people's bank account balance is a true reflection of their level of intelligence or ability. I think the reason most people greatly underachieve in financial terms is *not* because they don't have the talent to do well. On the contrary, most people have more education and talent than they actually need. However, they let limiting perceptions and lack of financial knowledge handicap their ability to convert their talents into wealth.

"One of the reasons the rich get richer, the poor get poorer

and the middle class struggles in debt is because the subject of money is taught at home, not at school"

~ Robert Kiyosaki ~

The main reason why most people never master wealth is because they never develop a financial plan. Most people have only a vague idea about what it really means to be wealthy. They want to make a lot of money and live abundantly but they never take the time to learn what wealth is or how to generate it. They don't know what the price-tag for their current life style is, and have no conception of what it takes to have the life style they wish to achieve. They live above their means, they spend more than they earn and they purchase liabilities without considering long term value depreciation or maintenance expenses. Plus, they don't invest because they think it's too complex and risky which only decreases the value of the little they manage to save. They get caught in the cultural chase to "keep up with the Joneses" and as a result, lose sight of the things that matter to them most. Do you think 96 percent of the population plans to reach the age of 65 with less the $35,000 in annual income? Of course not. People don't plan to fail, they simply fail to plan.

The goal of a financial plan is to help to create wealth by increasing your *assets* and decreasing your *liabilities*. In financial terminology, an asset is anything that generates income. Your job is an asset. The check you got on your birthday is an asset. Any saving plans or trust funds you have are also considered assets. Other forms of assets are stocks, bonds, real estate, or anything else you that can generate a cash flow.

On the other hand, a liability is considered to be anything that takes money away from you. Liabilities are things like your bills, taxes, debts, car insurance, rent, leisure and entertainment expenses; anything that drains your account.

The gap between your assets and liabilities is your wealth, also known as your net worth. Let's assume your monthly assets are $5,000 and your monthly liabilities are $4,500. After you subtract your liabilities from your asset you are left with $500. That's your net worth.

One of the biggest mistakes people make is that they confuse between assets and liabilities and as a results, they are always in debt. They treat monthly leftovers as spending money and are quick to depart with it, usually by buying a fancy appliance or a toy that ends up as a liability. In the next chapter, I will introduce you to the "Four buckets," which is a practical financial plan that will show how to manage your savings and monthly leftovers in a productive and effective way.

One of the financial goals I believe you should have is to become *financially independent* as fast as you possibly can. What is financial independence? It's the ability to live from the income of your own personal assets. In other words, when you are financially independent, you don't have to work for a living. You might be working for fun, for pleasure, for productivity, but at that point in your life, no one is going to have any financial claims on you.

"Being rich is having money; being wealthy is having time"

~ Stephen Swid ~

The second reason most people aren't wealthy is because they have mixed emotional associations about what it takes to make more money. On one hand, making more money may mean more freedom, more opportunities, more fun, better life style, better vacations and less pressure but on the other hand, it may also mean working a lot harder, sleeping less, giving up quality time with family and friends, neglecting hobbies, and even appearing greedy. Which one is right? In chapter 3, we learned that all human action is driven by emotions, therefore, when we experience contradicting emotions, our emotions cancel each other out and we end up rationalizing ourselves into stagnation.

Other than having mixed emotions about making more money, people also have limiting beliefs about wealth. I like to call those "Wealth wounds." Those limiting beliefs are based on myths and half truths regarding wealth which results in negative emotional associations and prevents people from unleashing their full economic potential. Let's heal eight of those wounds right here and now.

Myth#1: It takes money to make money. This was true 50 years ago when the driving force behind the market was retail and mass manufacturing. Back then, if you didn't have inventory, you had nothing to sell. And having inventory demanded money. But today, what you really need in order to make money are ideas and ingenuity.

Ever had a piece of Kentucky Fried Chicken? Do you know how Colonel Sanders managed to build a multimillion dollar fast food franchise from scratch? Let me tell you how. When the Colonel began to actively franchise his chicken business, he had nothing more then a $105 from his social security check and a chicken recipe. When the Colonel was 40 years old he began to cook for travelers who stopped at his service station. However, just as things seemed to be finally working out for the Colonel, the main highway leading to his restaurant was rerouted, sending his restaurant down the drain. It wasn't long before the Colonel went broke and had to retire from business.

The Colonel could not just sit home, unemployed, and quietly watch the years go by. The man who since the age of 12 had worked as a streetcar conductor, a solider, a railroad fireman, a law student, a steamboat ferry operator, and even a tire salesmen, decided to give himself one more chance. He decided to take his special chicken recipe and travel across the country by car from restaurant to restaurant, cooking chicken for restaurant owners and their employees. Alone, and sleeping in his car, the Colonel was rejected more than a thousand times before someone was finally willing to back him up and take a chance on his recipe. And that's all he needed. Today, the Colonel's fried chicken is available in approximately 80 countries around the world. Not bad for an old man with no money, right?

Even though the Colonel did not have money or investors when he first started out, he had something far more powerful than money. He had ambition, ingenuity, perseverance, endurance, commitment, belief, and conviction. Would a handful of green Franklins have helped Colonel Sanders? I'm sure it would have. But, he knew that having money was not a precondition to making money. Remember that next time you eat a piece of fried chicken at the Colonel's Place.

Myth #2: Money isn't everything. Money isn't everything in life, but it ranks right up there with oxygen. Robert Louis Stevenson, the Scottish novelist who wrote *Treasure Island* and *The Strange Case of Dr. Jekyll and Mr. Hyde*, once said that "Money alone is only a means; it presupposes a man to use it. The rich man can go where he pleases, but perhaps please himself nowhere. His purse may be full and the heart empty." Money can buy you a house but it won't buy you a home. It can buy you a companion but not a loving relationship. There are many things that are far more important than money like health, growth, personal fulfillment, satisfaction, happiness, and love.

Is having more money a guarantee that you won't have any problems and that your life will turn into a surreal paradise? It sure isn't. However, being wealthy will give you access to the best tools and services when problems do arise.

We live in times where you can't even get a band aid without paying for it. Health care costs money. Good nutrition costs money. Quality education costs money. Entertainment costs money. Vacations cost money. Playing sports costs money. Electricity, sewage, water and gas, phone lines and cable cost money. Transportation and travel cost money. Even parking costs money. Other then oxygen, nothing on our planet is free.

From the moment you wake up in the morning till the moment you close your eyes at night, your financial meter is running. So while money is not everything in life, it is pretty damn important, would you agree? So give money the appropriate value it deserves, but not an inch more. And always keep in mind that your *ultimate* purpose is not to make money but to live well and enjoy yourself.

Myth #3: It takes hard work to be wealthy. The truth is that it takes smart work to be wealthy. Not hard work. Here's a silly example. You can chop a tree down with a hammer in about 30 days, that's hard work. But, if you exchange the hammer for an axe, or a saw, you can do it in about 30 minutes. That's smart work. Many times, things that appear extremely difficult and complex only appear that way because we don't know how they are done. I remember when I first saw somebody using PowerPoint back in 1996, I was very impressed. I thought it took hours and hours of training to make the words swirl and move up and down. I thought I had to be a computer geek just to get things going. However, once somebody explained to me how the program works, my apprehension dissipated. It turned out to be one of the easiest things I had ever learned. It's the same with wealth. Don't get fazed by mega millionaires and enormous business empires. Observe them carefully. Watch for the kind of "axe" they are using. Most wealthy people do not work more than 40 or 50 hours a week and some work considerably less. Whereas in the past, manual labor and overtime were the keys to wealth, today, as I said before, those keys are ideas and ingenuity.

Myth #4: I don't need a lot of money anyway. Austerity is probably the most common excuse to justify financial mediocrity. In a sense, none of us needs more than shelter, food, warm clothes and some education. But we be satisfied with plain survival?

Being wealthy doesn't mean you have to live extravagantly. You can maintain an austere life style even with billions of dollars to your name. Warren Buffet, the world's greatest stock market investor and the second wealthiest man in the world lives in a house he bought for $31,500. He does his own taxes, drives himself to work in an old Taurus, and drinks coca cola every day. Does Warren need billions of dollars to his name? He sure doesn't. However, his financial success allows him to advance the worthy causes and special interests he has that otherwise he wouldn't be able to support.

If you don't need much than that's great, there will be more you'll be able to share with others. Remember that it's selfish to limit your contribution just because you think you don't need much in life. There are many worthy causes that could use a financial boost, from education to scholarships to upcoming bands and artists. So whenever you hear somebody justifying not doing well financially because he "doesn't need much," hit him over the head and remind him that being wealthy is not about him, it's about other people.

Myth #5: I don't have enough time. Abstract Expressionist William De Kooning once said that "The trouble with being poor is that it takes up all your time." That's an astute observation. Most people spend their time making a living instead of designing a life. They focus on survival instead of greatness.

You and I have been given the same amount of hours in a day as Bill Clinton, Mahatma Gandhi, and Bill Gates. And we should find this comforting. Time is the only resource we have all been given in equal amount. If you think you don't have enough time to improve your financial future it's only because you let what's urgent override what's important in your life. You live in reaction to your environment rather than executing your own will.

Are we taught how to manage time? Are we taught how to shape our life force? Are we taught how to string together the seconds and minutes and allocate them effectively so we won't feel like time escapes us? Are we taught how to create a design for our lives and set priorities? We sure aren't. And that's a grave tragedy.

Time mastery is what makes the difference between the wealthy and the poor, and not only in financial terms. When I say time management, I don't mean having To-Do lists and being punctual, although those are a good start. I'm talking about controlling your life force. I'm talking about using your time, your existence, purposefully, with a design in mind so everyday you invest your time on what brings you the most amounts of joy and happiness. I'm talking about not being a slave to a clock, but to your own will and wishes.

We are going to discuss time mastery and all its aspects in chapter 14 and we will discover the distinctions that allow a person like Arnold Bennet to write more than eighty books, while most people never find the time to write one. I warmly suggest you check it out his *How To Live On 24 Hours a Day*. If that one is a bit old for your senses then try listening to *The Time Of Your Life* by Anthony Robbins or reading *First Things First* by Stephen Covey. Those should help you make better use of your time instantly.

Myth #6: Wealthy people are ruthless and greedy and are inconsiderate of other people's needs and emotions. Indeed, there are many wealthy individuals who are cruel, vicious and and deceitful (Enron executives come to mind.) Such power abusers have done irreparable damages to the reputation of high-earning CEO's of big corporations across the nation. They epitomized greed and vanity with their behaviors. But nevertheless, there are many wealth owners who care, love and cherish their employees and are truly committed to social well being.

Remember Mark Hughes of Herbalife? What do you think drove him to make $2 billion a year in sales? Was it greed? Was it vanity? Not really. By making $2 billion, Mark was able to support the D.A.R.E (drug abuse resistance education) program with millions as well as advance scientific research through the Mark Hughes Cellular & Molecular Nutrition Lab at UCLA.

And Mark is far from rare. According to a December 1, 2003 article in *Business Week*, between 1999 and 2003 alone, Bill Gates, George Soros, Michael Dell, Ted Turner and the Walton family have collectively donated more than $27 billion dollars for such causes as health education, children's health care, and the environment. Obviously, the list doesn't end here. There are many other philanthropists who use their wealth for the greater good but in many cases, their actions are overshadowed by stories about corruption, fraud and financial dishonesty.

Myth #7: If I become wealthy, people will change their attitudes towards me. You know you can't control what other people think and feel about you. When it comes to dealing with other people's attitudes, I always ask myself two questions. The first is "if I could do better financially, should I?" and the second is "Am I going to let other people's opinions stop me from doing better?"

Like it or not, money is an emotional issue. It brings the best and the worst out of people. When a person ups his socioeconomic status, the people around him may respond with jealousy. Actor Vic Oliver summed it best when he said, "If a man runs after money, he's money-mad; if he keeps it, he's a capitalist; if he spends it, he's a playboy; if he doesn't get it, he's a never-do-well; if he doesn't try to get it, he lacks ambition. If he gets it without working for it, he's a parasite; and if he accumulates it after a lifetime of hard work, people call him a fool who never got anything out of life."

When we become wealthy, some people will turn green with envy, others will hate you, and the rest won't care at all. The people that truly care and love you will love you regardless of the size of your bank account. To them, your socioeconomic status is as irrelevant as the color of your underwear. At its worst, becoming wealthy will reveal who is a true friend and who isn't. That's the worst that can happen. As long as you are true to yourself and to your goals, you have absolutely nothing to worry about.

Don't ever lower your standards for yourself and what you can do just so others will approve your behavior. Remember that your first commitment is to greatness and excellence, to unleashing your potential; not to making sure others don't feel bad because of their own incompetence. If you can do better financially, then you must.

Myth #8 Money is the root of all evil. It tears families apart and it destroys relationships. Let's make a small correction here- it's the *love* of money that is the root of all evil, not money by itself. Money is just a piece of paper. French critic and novelist, Remy de Gourmont said that "Money is nothing; its power is purely symbolical. Money is the sign of liberty. To curse money is to curse liberty, to curse life, which is nothing, if it be not free." The truth is that the roots of evil are poverty and scarcity, not wealth. According to many studies, there is a strong correlation between poverty and crime, poverty and drug abuse, poverty and illiteracy and poverty and stunted growth. There is nothing good or beautiful about being poor.

How about relationships? Is the presence of wealth the main reason for family breakdowns? Nope. The main reason many families fall apart is not the existence of wealth but the improper management of it. Stephen Pollan, the author of *Die Broke*, says that "by inserting economic self interest into emotional decisions, family members can damage family relationships. Suddenly, a son views his father buying a new sail boat not as a fulfillment of a life long dream but as money coming out of his own pocket. Then, the father begins to suspect the motivations behind his daughters visit during the holidays: does she really want to see me or is she just worried about maintaining her share?" Pollan believes that even traditional inheritance is a mistake: "There's even evidence that inheritance hurts the person who receives it. Studies show that the expectation of an inheritance erodes the drive and motivation to work."

Are there any families that enjoy wealth and abundance without being torn apart? Sure there are. But we never get to hear about them. Newspapers, magazines and tabloids focus on disasters and drama because it sells much better than success.

Today, everybody wants to become wealthy overnight. But very few people actually take the time to learn what being wealthy really means. The wealth wounds we learned about in this chapter cause many people to spend their life in financial frustration and struggle. The real enemy to wealth is our own limited concept of what is possible and what is not. If you and I allow television and magazines to shape our perceptions of wealth, we are going to suffer disastrous consequences. But if we take charge of our own financial awareness and cultivate the principles of wealth by using the advantages that the 21st century economy has to offer, we will ultimately achieve a level of abundance far greater than we experienced as children. Unfortunately, many of the financial principles you and I have been taught by our parents (if you have been taught any at all,) relate to the economies of the 80's and the early 90's. Many of those principles, like how to approach the job market, how to become more valuable, and how to protect your niche, do not work in today's economy. In the last 20 years, technology has turned the job market upside down. Wireless communication has changed the pace at which we do transactions, globalization has created new opportunities, (as well as new threats,) and immigration has significantly increased competition. While our parents had the privileges of union protection, seniority standings and limited competition, for us Gen-Xer's the market place has become a real jungle.

But don't worry. Even though the 21st century may appear to be a scary place, with the right mind set, you'll find it to be a goldmine. While in this chapter we talked about the theoretical aspects of wealth, in the next chapter I'm going to give you several guidelines which you'll be able to apply to your finances instantly. So let's not waste another moment. Let's flip the page over and learn about the business of...

CHAPTER VIII

Swimming with the Sharks:
Thriving in a Chaotic Economy

"To become financially independent you must turn part of your income into capital; turn capital into enterprise; turn enterprise into profit; turn profit into investment; and turn investment into financial independence"

~ Jim Rohn ~

"Teen Stock Whiz Nailed," was the front page headline of *The Daily News* on a bright summer day in May of 2000. It was the incredible story of, Jonathan Lebed who by the age of 14 was making hundreds of thousands of dollars manipulating stocks online. Between September 1999 and February 2000, Jonathan's take from online trading had been nearly $800,000. The feisty 14 year-old managed to build a powerful reputation and had people calling for investment advice around the clock.

A short while after his 11th birthday, Jonathan opened an Internet account with America Online. He first built a Web site dedicated to the greater glory of Stone Cold Steve Austin. But about the same time, he began to develop a unique fascination for the world of economics.

His father, Greg, who in his 30-plus years of working for Amtrak had worked his way up to middle management, had also accumulated $12,000 of blue-chip stocks. And as he watched the market's daily leaps and jerks, Jonathan would join him, staring transfixed at the numbers running on the screen.

Soon, Jonathan began reading everything he could lay his hands on that dealt with the stock market. He used to watch the market ticker on CNBC for hours at a time, learning every daily movement with pure awe and fascination. At the age of 12, Jonathan declared he wanted to own a stock. A savings bond his parents gave him at birth had just matured releasing $8,000 which Jonathan immediately got his father to invest for him in the stock market.

From that day on, Jonathan woke up everyday at 5a.m. to read market reports, economics books, and investment strategies. He learned to find information about companies through the Internet. When he couldn't find what he was looking for on-line, he made his mother drive him to corporate headquarters to make sure they existed.

During the following 18-months, Jonathan turned his $8,000 savings bond into $28,000. He learned so much about trading stocks on-line that he began running a website offering amateur stock market analysis to investors. A couple of months later, Jonathan found himself in the middle of a network of people who spent every waking hour trading stocks on the Internet. At its peak, Jonathan's website generated more than 1,500 visits a day, many of whom were by professional stock traders and large capital investors.

We live in a "Brave New World," as Aldous Huxley's famous classic suggests. Ours is a world of Xbox's and instant messaging, a world of virtual markets and on-line dating. Techno-logy has influenced every aspect of our lives from how we earn, shop and entertain ourselves to how we communicate and travel. Our economy has changed considerably. Many of the leading companies today are not industry mill manufactures but online communication giants who offer virtual services like Google (who went public for more than $30 billion in August of 2004) and eBay.

Our dreams have also changed. In his book *The Guerilla Way* author Jay Levison writes "Originally, the dream meant having enough food and protection from the weather. Cave dwellers dreamt of hunting enough game or gathering an abundance of nuts and berries. The dream changed, replaced by the hope of earning enough money to feed a hungry family. The Industrial Revolution took care of that and eventually gave birth to the American Dream: a house, a job, and financial security. Entrepreneurs of the twentieth century were motivated by a slightly different version of the American Dream. In place of a house, a job, and financial security, they sought fortune, security, and power. But that journey was characterized by workaholism, sacrifice, and greed."

So what do we dream about today? Today, we dream of freedom and balance. We want to be financially free without risking our underwear. We want to lead the field and be respected by our peers without letting work dominate our lives. We want our work to be challenging and meaningful and not just improve the company's bottom line. We want to make a difference, love what we do, and be well compensated at the same time. We want to able to go to the Caribbean at a moment's notice without having to worry about our job. Is our dream possible? It sure is. But you won't achieve it by climbing the corporate ladder. You'll achieve it by owning the corporation.

Think about Jonathan for a minute. He came from an ordinary middle class family. He was an average student, and he didn't excel at sports. And yet, by taking advantage of the minimal resources he had, he was able to compete and take names on one of the toughest markets in the world. His story is a great example of the amazing opportunities the 21st century has in store for us, that is, if we are willing to play the game of entrepreneurship.

In the last chapter, we learned that most people do poorly

with money not because they don't have the intellect, the ideas, or the talent; on the contrary, they usually have more then enough. It's just that they might be operating from a scarcity model of the world or that they fail to understand the financial climate in which we live. While we live in a capitalistic society, most people do not behave like capitalists. This can make it very difficult for them to win the financial game. It's as if they are trying to win at basketball by using football rules. It just can't be done.

So in this chapter, I want to talk to you about what I believe it takes to live the dream and win the financial game in our current economic climate. Once you understand that, I'm going to equip you with some of the key distinctions that will help you to take immediate advantage of the opportunities you already have around you. By the time you reach the end of this chapter, you'll have a crystal clear picture about how to position yourself in the market and how to focus on creating wealth rather than just earning a living. So let's go, we have a lot of ground to cover.

A Snapshot of the Present

The high-tech bubble of the late 90's and the rapid rise of the telecommunications and biotechnology industries have led to massive hiring throughout the western world. Professions such as computer programming, web development, and data management have become top trades, pushing retail, sales and engineering to the background. But as the bubble burst and the market began to cool off, a new reality was slowly unfolding. Massive layoffs caused hundreds of thousands of young, well-trained people to find themselves falling from an economic Eden of company cars, paid vacations, and fat bonuses into an abyss of complete economic uncertainty.

Another factor that has tremendously influenced our economy is the movement towards globalization. The opening of global markets has increased competition as more countries see themselves fit to vie for a piece of the pie. As a result, many large companies have been gradually transferring jobs into foreign markets where labor is cheaper. Wages have been slashed, raises have become a rarity and large corporations have begun to adopt a "pay-for-performance" policy as they struggle to minimize expenses and stay ahead in the economic race. In fact, competition has intensified to such a point where the only thing that matters today is the bottom line. Employers no longer feel obligated to train and develop the upcoming workforce. Training is no longer viewed as an investment in the future of the company. Long gone are seniority statuses, protective corporate cultures, and even network politics. Most jobs have become shaky social environments with little security and few opportunities for meaningful growth. In fact, it is estimated that the average 22-year-old will change jobs approximately 8 times in order to keep a career growing.

The current economic reality is especially difficult for young people and graduates fresh out of college. When in the past, a college degree almost guaranteed a well paying secure job, today, college diplomas have become common commodity; everybody has them. Last year, hiring of new college graduates dropped 36.4 percent while and according to a May 2, 2004 issue of *ABCNews.com*, "around 42 percent of employers surveyed by the National Association of Colleges and Employers, say they expect to cut college hiring this year." And to add insult to injury, Daniel Kadlec who writes for *Time* magazine informs us that, "the salary median has been progressively declining since 2001 and the average job search has stretched to a 19-year high of nearly five months."

I think that Beth Kobliner, the author of *Get a Financial Life*, and a writer for *Money Magazine* expressed our collective feeling when she wrote that "Most Americans 25 to 34 years old today have incomes that are about 20 percent less on average than those of our 1970's counterparts. It's not surprising that many of us are convinced we'll never be able to afford the homes we grew up in or the lifestyles we became accustomed to as kids."

The situation sounds gloomy, doesn't it? But have no fear. In the upcoming decades, more people are going to become millionaires and billionaires than at any other time in history; not by climbing the corporate ladder, but by intelligently developing their passions and entrepreneurial talents. In *The Millionaire Next Door*, Thomas Stanley and William Danko discovered that two thirds of the millionaires in America are self employed entrepreneurs while most others are self employed professionals, such as doctors, lawyers and accountants.

Unfortunately, as I suggested earlier, most of us have not been trained to take advantage of the opportunities we have available to us. We have been guided to specialize in one particular area, usually to be determined in college, and we build on that as our ticket to success. Worse than that, we have been trained to be professional automatons that come to work at 9, do as we're told until 5 o'clock, and then go home. And even worse, we've been taught to aim for early retirement, despite the fact that every psychological study done on the topic concludes that doing a meaningful job, working in a team environment and being creative and productive are crucial factors in determining one's emotional and psychological well being.

We've never been told to be proactive self-starters and calculated risk takers. We've never been taught how to collaborate with people from different countries who have different customs and beliefs. We've never been coached to be task oriented and goal directed. We've never been disciplined in the arts of negotiation and influential communication. We've never been shown how to scout our environment for potential needs or problems. We've never learned how to take an idea, refine it, test it, market it, and manage the profits. What I'm trying to say here is that we've never really been guided in taking an active role in the economic game; we were never taught to be entrepreneurs. And that saddens me.

Entrepreneurship is the lifeblood of our economy. It's a growth catalyst woven into the fabric of our everyday interaction. Entrepreneurs are the people that make things happen, the movers and shakers. They lead the field, stimulate the market, create jobs, and determine our quality of life through the development of products and services. Without entrepreneurs, things like Windows, Xbox, Armani clothing or Mercedes automobiles would not be possible. In fact, everything around you, from the tiny screw that holds your sunglasses together to a Tequila shot glass in your local bar, is the result of someone's entrepreneurial initiative. And today, that initiative is available to all of us.

Why do people become entrepreneurs? Obviously, there's the monetary aspect, the chance of making a handsome profit. But that's not the real reasons people become entrepreneurs. If money was the only motivator, then the only thing entrepreneurs would be interested in would be the highest-profit-lowest-risk enterprises. But instead, you can see them opening bars, running on-line record stores, designing computer games, operating health clubs or doing artistic landscaping for high risk, hard work, and meager profits.

I believe that people become entrepreneurs because they want to enjoy what they do to make a living. They want to control their own destinies while doing what they like to do. That's why I became an entrepreneur. I just love to take an idea, refine it, improve it, test it, and then stand back and watch it make someone's life better. To me, that's the real profit.

The Age of the Entrepreneur

While in the past only the affluent and business savvy could engage in business and commerce, today, entrepreneurship is within reach for all of us. David Gumpert who writes for *Business Week*, explains that "Up until the mid-1990s, the conventional wisdom among business-school academics was that those who waited until their early 30's to start a business were most likely to succeed. By that age, according to the then-current reasoning, individuals would have enough meaningful work experience to improve the odds of achieving success. Moreover, it would be early enough in their family lives for still-modest lifestyle demands to handle pressures of meeting the challenge. The proliferation of highly successful students and twenty-something entrepreneurs who emerged during the Internet boom tore a big hole in that model. Today, students taking entrepreneurship courses are encouraged by many of those same academics to think in terms of launching their own businesses while still in school or shortly after graduating."

Today, any kid in baggy jeans can build a towering economic empire. Take Paul Orfalea for example. While he was still a student at USC, Paul took a $5,000 loan from the bank and opened a small print shop in a former hamburger joint in Isla Vista, California. Word has it that the shop was so tiny that when a customer wanted to make copies on his copy machine, Paul had to push the machine out of store and park it on the sidewalk. Funny enough, Orfalea decided to name the business after his own nickname, which sprung from his funky spring like curls- Kinko's.

What makes entrepreneurship more relevant and appealing today than any other time in history? The answer comes in two parts: freedom of information and effortless communication. Today, anyone can hop on-line and learn anything from web design, stock trade and 3D-animation to real-estate investments, medicine, accounting, film production and law. Not only that, today you can easily collaborate with people from all around the world and share ideas and knowledge without any cost. The internet has erased all geographic barriers and redefined innovation and ingenuity. Ideas don't need a passport or a visa; they can be communicated on-line, in real time, with an enormous number of people from every part of the globe and in any language. This was not possible 10 years ago.

Today, the playing field is wide open. Anyone who has enough guts and wits and who is willing to learn can compete with the big dogs. George Kozmetsky, the founder of IC2 Institute, a research center in entrepreneurship at the University of Texas, affirms that "Today, everything is up for grabs. No Matter what field you are talk about- electronics, education, entertainment, or anything else- it opens up more opportunities than I've ever seen in my entire life." This was not the case 10 years ago. So what are you waiting for? The time to get off the bench and step onto the playing field is the now.

The first step you must take if you want to join the game of entrepreneurship is to:

Find Your Passion

Have you ever known anybody who has become wealthy by doing something they hate? I sure haven't. When you truly love what you do, you are bound to do it better then something you merely tolerate. You will compete harder, be more creative, handle more frustrations, and hold yourself to a higher standard of performance. That's just human nature. When we care, when we are emotionally invested, we perform better.

Dr. Mark Albion, a former Harvard Business School professor, made a 20-year study of business school graduates. He found that students who chose careers that tapped into their passion upon graduation made significantly more money than those students who chose to make money first and postpone their passionate work to a later date. Research has shown that people who choose their passion first are more likely to become millionaires than those who choose jobs based on financial concerns. In fact, 40 percent of the 255 students who chose their passionate work first became millionaires. Only one of the 1,245 students who chose a career based on financial concerns became a millionaire.

Entrepreneurs have a special fire burning in the heart. You find them working from an expensive office in a skyscraper, a tiny living room, or a murky basement (which is where I started out). But regardless of where they work, they are always professional, competitive, focused, energetic, hard-working, goal directed and fair. That's because they are driven by pure passion. They do what they love and love what they do and that's all that matters to them.

Kevin Smith always had a passion for movies. But he had a hard time dealing with authority. He attended the New School for Social Research's creative writing program but dropped out after administrators caught him launching water balloons out of his dormitory window. He subsequently enrolled in the Vancouver Film School but after four months decided he was better off using his tuition to pursue his passion on his own. After raising $27,000 from parents, credit-card advances, and the sale of his beloved comic book collection, he shot *Clerks*, a hilariously scabrous flick about consumer culture inspired by his experiences behind the cash register of a local convenience store.

Shooting each night in the same convenience store where he worked by day, Smith completed production in just three weeks and began promoting the feature on the festival circuit. In 1994, *Clerks* debuted at the Sundance Film Festival, becoming the hit of the event which lead to a distribution deal with Miramax who invested $100,000 to spruce up the film's picture and sound. After winning a court battle to replace the often-vulgar NC-17 rating with a more commercially palatable "R," *Clerks* hit the Art house circuit, where it generated over $3-million achieving cult status in legions of fans' video collections. Not bad for something that only cost $27,000 and a few sleepless nights. Smith used the profits to buy back his beloved comic book collection and make more movies such as Mallrats, *Chasing Amy* and *Dogma*, as well as opening his own chain of comic-book shops called *Jay and Silent Bob's Secret Stash*.

"When you are making a success of something, it's not work. It's a way of life. You enjoy yourself because you are making your contribution to the world"

~ Andy Grantelli ~

But maybe movie making is not your passion. How about walking then? Seth Kamil and Ed O'Donnell were just two urban history graduate students strapped for some cash when they started giving walking history tours in New York. Today, Big Onion Walking Tours conducts more than 700 walking tours each year and draws as many as 500 participants a day who pay $15 a pop. Conclusion: Passion can pay off, big time.

So what's your passion? Is it music? Writing? Sports? Video games? Cooking? Gardening? Surfing? Traveling? Teaching? Designing web sites? Fashion? Dancing? One of my girlfriend's passions is helping women succeed. I have a childhood friend who's passionate about flying and airplanes. What are you passionate about? What gets your juices flowing?

I submit to you that if you are motivated by anything other than your own dreams and passions, you should take a long hard look at yourself and do a bit of soul searching. Success, especially in business, is a marathon, not a sprint. Winning may not come easily or quickly. And if you don't have a strong passion to fuel you when times get rough, you'll probably quit before you have a chance to taste victory. This brings me to the second step:

Prepare to Struggle

Many times, we make the mistake of looking up at successful entrepreneurs and the empires they built with awe and reverence and we can't help but feel small and incompetent. We think, "How can I ever compete with a corporation like Microsoft or Nike?" But we forget that most of those empires were once nothing more than an idea inside the head of a penniless, timid, and failure struck entrepreneur. Bill Gates was a college dropout. Michael Dell used to deliver news papers and sell custom built computers from his dorm room. Ray Kroc used to travel across the country selling milkshake machines before he acquired the McDonald's franchise from the McDonald brothers and turned it into an international empire. Ben Cohen, Co-Founder Of Ben & Jerry's Ice Cream, held a wide assortment of dead-end jobs including cashier at McDonald's, Pinkerton guard at the Saratoga Raceway, night cleaner at Jamesway, an assistant superintendent at Gaslight Square Apartments and a school cook before teaming up with his childhood friend, Jerry Greenfield, and using their combined life savings of $8,000 to convert an old abandoned gas station in Burlington, Vermont, into an ice cream shop. All beginnings are humble.

Although I'm a huge advocate of entrepreneurship, I must also give you an honest reality check: entrepreneurship is a tough climb. Trust me, I know it first hand. My first attempt at business was an abysmal failure, and so was my second. According to a report by Paul Reynolds, a professor at Marquette University, at any given time, approximately 7.2 million Americans are attempting to start a business. After two years, only about 10 percent survive. The remaining ninety percent do not make it for a variety of reasons (poor capital management, weak leadership, destructive in-house politics etc,).

It's rare to strike gold on a first entrepreneurial venture. Upon reviewing its listing of the top 500 businesses, *Inc.* magazine discovered that the average number of previous start-ups for each company's founder was 1.9. Unfortunately, there is no fail-safe recipe for success in business. Sometimes entrepreneurs fail because of a mistake they make personally, like misjudging a marketing budget or missing a dead line, while at other times they may go down because of something completely beyond their control like a new technology that renders their business obsolete.

In business, you are almost guaranteed to experience hard times, especially during the first years. It's just a natural part of the game. So don't panic when things don't fall immediately into place. You have to hang in there. Soichiro Honda was only 16 when he relocated from his birth town Konyo, to Tokyo to become an apprentice mechanic in a shop that sold and maintained vehicles. He soon came to realize that he'd never get wealthy working with his hands and that manufacturing auto parts would be much more profitable. He borrowed enough money to start a small company that made piston rings but unfortunately, his enthusiasm was greater than his business and technical knowledge and the company was soon in deep financial trouble. He decided to attend Shizuoka University where he had an opportunity to sharpen his business skills as well as learn the rudiments of alloying. Armed with new knowledge, he decided to give his piston ring factory a second try. This time, things seem to click into place and it wasn't long before the factory was doing business. However, Honda's luck was about to run out again. At the beginning of World War II, his factory was marked as a strategic military target by the Allied Forces and it wasn't long before American bombers leveled his factory to the ground. But Honda refused to be broken.

Only a year after World War II ended, Honda took to business one more time and established a small company that repaired and refurbished small gasoline engines. However, at that time, the economic and industrial infrastructure of Japan was in a shambles. Business was slow. At times, Honda had to make repair parts from scratch because the supply market was virtually nonexistent. Nevertheless, he managed to keep his small factory in business believing that better days were to come.

Interestingly, the primary choice for personal transportation in Japan after the war was the bicycle. It was better than walking and cheaper than an automobile although it had its own disadvantages, especially when the rain season hit. Honda was quick to realize the shortcomings of bicycles as a means of transportation and decided to purchase a small number of tiny, war surplus, two-stroke engines. He figured that that if he could somehow attach the two stroke engine to a bicycle, he would have a fast, inexpensive, fuel conserving and relatively safe means of transportation that everyone could afford. Honda and his then twenty employees launched themselves into motor history with the three-horsepower, two-speed transmission "D" model. The motorcycle was aptly named the "Dream D" after jubilant employees allegedly shouted "It's like a dream!" upon its completion. And a dream it was. The overwhelming success of the "D" model and the later "E" model helped Honda build a reputation for quality and design supremacy, even when an early-1950s economic depression threatened to dim the company's shining star. And the rest, well, you know the rest. Today, millions of people around the world enjoy Honda's selection of Accords, Civics, Prelude's, Passports, Acuras, and Odysseys that bear the Honda seal of safety and excellence and forever remind us of Soichiro Honda's resilience and persistence.

I think there are several things we can all learn from Honda. Number one, if you want to survive in business, make sure you know how to play the game. Honda's first attempt at business fell short simply because he was not knowledgeable enough about what it takes to run a business. It was only after he learned how to manage marketing and sales, conduct inventory listings, manage time and control a payroll that Honda's business began to grow. Number two, patience and persistence ultimately win the day. Stick to your guns, follow your dream, and just like Rocky, always keep coming back for one more round. Number three, keep a sharp eye on the market and try to...

Find an Opening

Earlier on, we talked about the importance of finding your passion and doing something you like. I strongly believe that's an essential building block for a successful business career.

However, I also believe that doing what you love is not enough. If you want to be successful, other people, a lot of other people, must be willing to pay for it. For an entrepreneur, the market place is a playing field governed by two primary forces: supply and demand. That's basic business sense. If you create something but nobody needs it or is willing to pay for it, you're not going to make a profit. On the other hand, if you identify a need that can be fulfilled but you don't have the means to meet it, you won't make a profit either. A successful entrepreneur understands that profitable business is essentially an intricate relationship; a meeting point between what he can and likes to do and what the market (other people) needs or wants.

Doing what you like, on one hand, and having people who are willing to pay you for it on the other, is known as a "Market opening." Put differently, a market opening is an opportunity to fulfill a need or improve the way a certain need is currently being fulfilled. Bill Gates identified a need for a simple, manageable operation system that would allow people to utilize the power of a computer without knowing too much about its hardware. Pierre Omidyar realized that people have a need to buy and sell used items after his wife, an avid Pez collector, told him how great it would be if she could interact with other Pez collectors over the Internet and purchase their collections. So he decided to create eBay.

How do you find a market opening? My advice is simple: become abnormally curious. Learn about other people. Inquire about their needs, dreams, pleasures, hobbies, and desires. Take a look around your neighborhood. Talk to your friends. Talk to your family. Try to find out what could make their lives better or what they need in order to make their lives better. Talk to young mothers. Talk to the elderly. Listen to their concerns and see if you can respond.

While in college, I got involved in community volunteer work. After talking with several of the less fortunate people we were working with, I realized that many were dissatisfied with the steep pricing of high quality food that was sold in their area. They simply could not afford to buy it. So I started selling coupon booklets that offered discounts on high quality, organic food products. That went well. Then, when the MP3 download craze began, I sold customized music CD's and commissioned research papers. Later on, I offered speed reading classes to freshmen and sophomores. Remember that in order to find a market opening; you don't have to do something spectacular. You don't have to invent an octagon shaped burger or discover a new way to treat acne. It can be a landscaping business during the summer or snow shoveling in the winter. It can be teaching, tutoring, braiding hair, or even offering massage therapy. It can be something you already do in your leisure time such as painting, writing, designing crafts, woodworking, upgrading computers or cooking.

Once you find a market opening, it's important to consider timing. People often use the term "window of opportunity" to describe a time period during which a market opening must be seized or lost. The notion of a window that opens for a while and then closes highlights the fleeting nature of opportunities, where timing is everything. When I was in college, I used to work for University Instructors, a company that specialized in supplemental education services. In the early nineties, its founder, Jim Popp identified a need for professionally trained tutors that could support teachers and students and help them achieve the lofty educational objectives set by President George Bush Sr. However, when the "No Child Left Behind" act was passed, the market demand for supplemental education exploded and the company went from employing fifteen on call tutors to more then a thousand. How's that for timing?

When a new idea hits, there's a great temptation to run with it to the end zone without checking out the playing field first. This can be fatal, even for a great idea. In *What Losing Taught Me about Winning*, successful entrepreneur and former star quarterback Fran Tarkenton shares a heartfelt story about one of his ambitious entrepreneurial ventures that went sour. Apparently, at 28, while still playing for the New York Giants, Fran decided to jump into the fast-food business. He envisioned a place called *Scrambler's Village* that would offer chicken and fish and veggies, much like the Boston Market. He believed it would spread across the country faster than prairie fire. Along with his lawyer and partner, he purchased an expensive real estate property in Piedmont Road, Atlanta, before even developing a menu, let alone testing it. He also did not bother to design a production process or a training manual and did not invest funds in developing market awareness. Sure enough, *Scrambler's Village* did not survive and Fran ended up taking a considerable financial blow. The lesson: Don't rush, even if you feel your idea is a bull's-eye hit.

On the other hand, consider Sandie Ledray who started making her own soap because her skin was too sensitive to most soap in the market. When her friends began buying all her private stock, Sandie and a friend decided to pitch in $300 each and start Brookside Soap Inc. Today, the business grosses $200,000 a year and offers different kinds of natural herbal soap. But pay close attention: between the initial $600 investment and the $200,000 gross, Sandie invested three years of market and competition research as well as package design before the first product was available for sale. In an interview to *Entreprenuer.com* she confidently says: "Slow and steady wins the race. We are trying to get a really broad base underneath us, instead of going straight up with this thing. I want to be okay in case one of our private labels decides to do something else instead of making soap next year. No matter what, our company will be around, and be safe and healthy."

Business, as I said before, is a marathon, not a sprint. If you want to succeed, you must be thoroughly prepared for a war of attrition. You must outlast the wind, the sun, the rain, as well as the competition. This can be tough. That's why I never recommend to anyone to rush into business full time before the business has proven to be a positive income generator. When you begin your first entrepreneurship enterprise, don't invest more than a few hours. By all means, hold on to your job. There is no point in putting yourself in a financial hole before you're guaranteed income. Use this time to test your product or service and establish a working routine. Begin creating a customer base. You can do this by giving free services or samples. Start searching for a potential partner. There's only so much you can do on your own. A partner will allow you to increase both your client base as well as your gross income. From that point on, you'll need more than I can offer you in this chapter. Just don't forget to have fun, especially in the early stages where insecurity and hesitation are in the air. Remember to enjoy yourself and don't forget why you embarked on this road to begin with.

In the last chapter we learned that one of the primary reasons people aren't wealthy is because they do not have a financial plan. Making money is not their problem. Keeping it is. Let me share with you a wealth management philosophy that has been put to the test countless of times by both business people and 9-to-5 employees, and which has proven reliable in either case.

The Bucket System

An important aspect of successful living is wealth management. All wealthy people manage their finances according to a plan. They use a certain formula that allows them to routinely diversify and manage their income in ways that maximize the advantages that the free enterprise system has to offer. The percentages of allocation may shift and vary according to the level of risk they are willing to take but nevertheless, the basic principles are always the same.

I found that the wealth management system that works best for me is "The Bucket System." The bucket system is a strategic, financial allocation plan that allows you to spread your income across four buckets, each representing a different financial category. Every bucket has a different purpose that's designed to help you take maximum advantage of our current economic reality. The system is logical, easy to implement and most importantly, it works. According to the system, every dollar you make is broken down into four buckets in the following way:

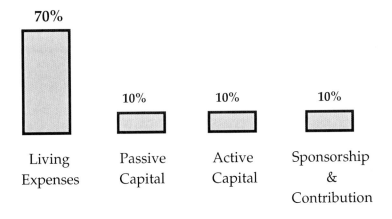

70%	10%	10%	10%
Living Expenses	Passive Capital	Active Capital	Sponsorship & Contribution

The first bucket, which represents 70 percent of your income, is the fundamental building block of your entire wealth management strategy. Manage this bucket and the other buckets will be a piece of cake. This bucket stands for your living expenses. The rule of thumb here is simple: live on 70 percent of your income or less. If you do not make enough at the moment and need to live on 85 percent of your income, that's fine too, but make sure you adjust the other buckets accordingly.

The second bucket represents 10 percent of your income in the form of passive capital which is just another term for low risk savings and investments. This is money you put aside for security, college for the kids, medical emergencies etc. I like to call this a "Go-to-Hell" fund. The third bucket represents 10 percent of your income in the form of active capital. This is money you set aside for entrepreneurial projects and investments you are directly involved in. The fourth bucket also rep-

resents 10 percent of your income. This is the charity and sponsorship bucket. Why charity? I'll explain later. Let's talk about
the first bucket.

Bucket I -70%
Living Expenses

The cornerstone of wealth management is expenditure control. In simpler words, it's about learning to live on a budget.
Why does every successful business organization, sports team,
theatrical show or movie production have a budget? It's kind
of obvious, isn't it? The budget tells them how much they can
spend within a certain period of time. However, common sense
as it may seem, most people don't live on a budget. I think there's
nothing worse than reaching the end of the month and getting
that billing statement and realizing that you have absolutely
no idea where and when you spent all that money. Do you
agree?

Budgeting is fail safe strategy to make sure you stay within
your economic boundaries and don't run the expenditure out
of control. Other than being one of the fundamental habits of
the wealthy, budgeting is also a proven counter-measure against
overdraft and empty pockets. Learning to live on a budget is
also your ticket out of debt. It's the fastest way to take charge of
your expenditures and control your finances.

We live in a society where all you have to do in order to get
several thousand dollars worth of credit is a signature. It's just
too easy to get cash these days. Most people find themselves in
a constant financial deficit because they fall victim to
"Parkinson's law." This law simply states that our expenses
tend to rise to meet our income, even when it comes from credit
cards. The more we have, the more we tend to spend. Just think,
what that did you do the last time you got a raise or a bonus?
Did you save it, or did you spend it all?

Just think, how many times have you gone into Wal-Mart determined to get just one thing, but ended up finding yourself loading dozen plastic bags into your car? I know I've been guilty of this in the past. Walking the aisles, every pair of jeans and DVD seems to be on sale, and you get the feeling that if you don't buy them now, you'll be missing out on a great bargain. This is known as "buyer's impulse."

I believe most people are impulsive buyers not because they are unintelligent or because they have too much money, they fall victim to sophisticated marketers and advertisers who are doing an excellent job selling us everything from 3-minute weight loss programs to heart attack hamburgers. There's no doubt in my mind that advertising works. And not only does it work, it works very well. Most people greatly underestimate the power of marketing and advertising, dismissing it by saying things like "that stuff doesn't affect me." But, if you look at the clothes those people wear, the foods they eat and the products they use, you'll notice popular tags and big brand names only. Marketing directors pour millions of dollars into ad campaigns and T.V. commercials because they are absolutely worth it. It's estimated that::

- The average child sees more than 20,000 commercials every year, that works out to at least 55 commercials per day.

- Advertisers spend an average of $2,300 per year to reach one household.

- In 2001 alone, U.S. advertising expenditures topped $230 billion, more than doubling the $105.97 billion spent in 1980.

So advertising works. And it affects you and me whether we like it or not. Just imagine that there are people working night and day to try and capture your attention and influence you to buy their product, which you don't necessarily need. Advertisers associate their product with attractive feelings and use the most advanced persuasion strategies and psychological instruments to convince you that if you buy their product, your life will be fulfilled.

This is where budgeting comes in handy. It's going to help protect your pockets from the advertiser's long reaching arm as well as from your own desire for instant gratification. It's going to give you more control and plug the financial leaks you have been experiencing.

The first step you need to take in order to control your expenditure is very easy and straight forward and yet most, people won't do it. They dismiss it as too simplistic. Personally, I don't care much if something is considered simple or complex, I only care if it works or not. And this one does so let me give it to you:

Write down everything you buy and every dollar you spend

Listen, what would you be willing to do to become a millionaire? Quite a lot, right? But what if I told you that by writing your expenses and living on a budget you could be a millionaire, would you do it? I sure hope so. Almost every self made millionaire I have met has begun his journey to fortune by writing down his expenses. Needless to say, they all live on a budget.

By writing down what you buy and how much you spend, you will immediately raise your financial awareness and begin to notice just how much money actually travels through your pockets. Writing your transactions will also work as a monitoring system as you will begin to think about the necessity of each expense. Guilt plays an important factor here. There is just something about seeing your expenses on paper that will force you to ask yourself, "Was that really necessary? Do I really need that?"

So get a notebook, a palm pilot, a notepad, or a financial management software like Quicken. Doesn't really matter what. The important thing is that you begin to write down what goes through your pockets. Trust me, this action alone will be enough to kick the impulsive buying habit and get you on the road to wealth.

Once you get into the habit of writing things down, you will need to learn how to design your budget, or in economic terminology, how to fill in a financial statement. That's the ultimate expenditure control instrument. We said before that living is a business. Everything costs money, from the water we use to the clothes we wear. Quality of life has a high price tag. Remember that before you ever posses wealth of any sort, you must first learn how to manage effectively what you currently have, even if it's not much.

An efficient monthly expense organizer should have at least seven categories of expenditures:

1) **Utilities + rent**: Gas, water, electricity, swage, DSL, cell phone, long distance calls, beeper, cleaning products, laundry detergent, etc.

2) **Transportation**: Car payments, insurance, gasoline, bus tickets, taxis, subways and air fares.

3) **Food/Groceries**: Eating out, pizzas, home cooking, candy, sodas, and anything else that comes through the mouth.

4) **Entertainment:** Movies, clubs, parties, Bush Gardens, Disneyland, DVD rentals, magazines, paintball, video games, renting ski jets, etc.

5) **Personal:** Clothes, books, office supplies, beauty care, hair cuts, health club membership, the money you lent to your cousin, etc.

6) **Miscellaneous:** Everything that you buy and don't really need like a Porcelain statue of liberty, a stuffed Shreck puppet, thigh buster, fake flowers, etc.

7) **P. savings:** at least 10 percent. Extra cash for you put aside for future personal expenses such as concerts, big dinners, birthday gifts, airfares, or anything else that needs immediate cash, etc.

Obviously you can include many more columns of expenses like, pets, health and fitness, dry cleaning, credit card debt, and medical expenses. But for the sake simplicity, I have decided to minimize everything to seven major categories that are easy to monitor.

The expense organizer on the next page represents a person with a monthly income of $2,857. The expenditure budget is already set 30 percent lower than the total monthly income in order to fit the 70 percent bucket model.

MONTHLY EXPENSE ORGANIZER
(Based on a monthly income of $2875)

	Budget	Jan	Feb	Mar	Apr	May	Jun	Jul	Aug	Sep	Oct	Nov	Dec
70 % Monthly income after deductions	$2,000	$2,000	$2,000	$2,000	$2,000	$2,000	$2,000	$2,000	$2,000	$2,000	$2,000	$2,000	$2,000
Expense category	Budget												
Utilities+Rent	$700	$710	$712	$701	$695	$720	$721	$725	$727	$705	$708	$700	$704
Transportation	$170	$180	$162	$150	$181	$172	$171	$163	$169	$184	$300	$163	$174
Food/Groceries	$300	$320	$310	$313	$300	$305	$340	$323	$6,303	$290	$320	$307	$302
Entertainment	$50	$40	$50	$80	$15	$53	$55	$45	$38	$19	$50	$42	$35
Personal	$150	$151	$147	$158	$120	$108	$144	$100	$112	$160	$154	$132	$154
Misc.	$100	$20	$10	$80	$25	$27	$10	$86	$58	$95	$29	$55	$76
P.savings	$200	$200	$200	$200	$200	$200	$200	$200	$200	$200	$200	$200	$200
Total Monthly Expenses	$1,670	$1,621	$1,531	$1,682	$1,709	$1,585	$1,641	$1,642	$1,607	$1,653	$1,761	$1,599	$1,645
Monthly Balance	$330	$379	$409	$318	$291	$415	$359	$358	$393	$347	$239	$401	$355

This expense sheet reflects very moderate and controlled expenditure habits. Most rises in expenditures can be traced to unforeseen circumstances, such as car accidents and repairs, household maintenance and repairs, heating during winter time etc. We can see a commitment for steady "P. savings" which is very effective, since each month, $200 is set aside towards future "personal," "miscellaneous," or "entertainment" expenses that allow for considerable financial flexibility.

The category that could cause you the most amount of damage is the "miscellaneous" category. These are those things you buy that you don't necessarily need like neck massagers, AB-rollers, discount DVD's (better rent it, get it from the library for free, or download it from the net,) or anything else that you surely wouldn't buy if you gave yourself a second chance to think about it.

I 'm sure your budget will look different then the one I gave you. Maybe your rent is lower or your transportation expenses are higher. It doesn't really matter. Once you plug in all your numbers, you'll have a clear picture of how much everything costs. Your goal, as we learned before, is very simple: to keep your expenses well below your income. Never, ever, max out your budget. Obviously there are some things you can't play with like your rent or your car payments, but everything else, from your utility bills to your grocery shopping, can be significantly decreased. Remember that the fastest way to improve the quality of your life is to create a gap between what you earn and what you spend, even if it means lowering your current quality of life. Cut down on eating out, give up the candy, and skip the soda machines. Reassess your cell-phone plan. Do you really need it? Do you need a cell-phone at all at this point in your life? Or rather, do you need a landline?

How often should you go over your budget? I recommend at least once a month. Although most paycheck cycles run on two week intervals, loans, interests and utility billings are collected on a monthly basis. By aligning your budget with your bills, and not with your checks, you will be able to get a clearer, more realistic picture of how much money you can afford to spend each and every month.

Surely, a budget will help keep you focused on your financial goals. And you should always remember that your job as a businessperson in the business of life is to show profit, that is, increase the gap between your income and your expenses. Don't be seduced by Parkinson's Law. Stay frugal. Remember that what makes you wealthy is not how much you earn, but how much you get to keep.

Bucket II-10%
Passive Capital

Passive capital refers to money that you set aside to work for you indirectly. I'm talking about investments. Investing is the most powerful financial instrument you have at your disposal. To put it differently, if you are not investing, or if you are afraid of investing, or you don't know enough about investing in order to invest, you are forfeiting your chances for wealth and you render yourself forever poor.

Most of us have been taught to stockpile our resources and hold on to them for as long as we can, especially when it comes to money. We learn that we need to "protect" our money from banks, creditors, and other financial vultures. But that's absurd. Money can't be stockpiled, and it sure won't keep its value if you stuff it in your mattress. That's because the biggest threat to your wealth is not the banks or the creditors or even the advertisers, it is something much more subtle and clandestine. Obviously, I'm talking about inflation.

Inflation always eats at your fortune. Currently, our inflation rate is about 2.9 percent. This means that an automobile that last year cost $10,000 will cost today $10,290. Same car, same make, same everything- just more expensive.

Let's say you went to your mattress and you dug out the $1,000 you stashed in it last year. Do you have the same purchasing power with the $1,000 today that you had a year ago? You sure don't. The inflation rate has depreciated your purchasing power by 2.9 percent, or $29 which means that now, the $1,000 you had a year ago can only buy you $971 worth of goods.

Investing is the key to beating inflation. Even if all you want to do is protect the value of your money from the inflation rate-you must invest. When it comes to increasing the value of your money and letting it work for you, you shouldn't let your bank take care of it. Remember that banks are in business too. Proactively investing is the only way to beat inflation and creating an increasingly positive rate of return for your money-that is the beginning to wealth. Check out the historical rates of return for the past 50 years:

Your Mattress: 0 %
Checking Accounts: 2%
Savings Accounts: 3%
Money Market Accounts: 3%
U.S. Treasury Bills: 4%
Government Bonds: 5%
Large Company Stocks: 11%

Evidently, stocks have proven themselves most profitable throughout the years. Are stocks risky? Sure they are. There's always risk involved in investing, but I think that today, you can't afford not to take that risk.

During the past two hundred years, the stock market has crashed several times. Billions of dollars were lost. People lost their entire life savings and committed suicide as a result. And that's usually the news that makes the headlines. But did you know that during the past two hundred years, every time the stock market has crashed, it has always come back up to set new records?

First of all, understand that investing is nothing more than a vote of trust. Trust in the market, in companies, in products and services, and mostly, trust in the free enterprise system. When you choose to invest your money in a company or in a mutual fund, you indirectly say "I believe in you, in your products, and in your people. Here is my money, use it wisely and make us all a fortune."

Our entire economy is based on ordinary people trusting each other in business. The best example I can give you about people trusting each other in business and in products is eBay. There is nothing easier than cheating your customers on eBay. But it's not worth it. People have discovered that when it comes to business, being honest and truthful pays better long term than being deceitful and dishonest.

"Honesty pays dividends both in dollars and in peace of mind"

~ B. C. Forbes ~

One of the most important keys to successful investing is time and patience. When Stanley and Danko did their research for *The Millionaire Next Door*, they weren't amazed to discover that 95 percent of all millionaires own stocks. However, they were surprised to learn that those millionaires don't actively trade stocks. They don't call their broker every morning and they don't follow the ups and downs of the market with great frequency. In fact, Dank and Stanley learned that "42 percent of the millionaires we interviewed for our latest survey had made no trade whatsoever in their stock portfolios in the year prior to the interview."

Do you know what makes long term investing so powerful?

I'm sure you've heard it before, but if you haven't then here it is: compounding. Let me show you the power of compounding. Let's say I was a Genie that could give you the honor of choosing one of two wishes, a million dollar in cash right here right now or a magical penny that doubles itself everyday for 45 days? What would you pick?

Nine out of ten people would pick the million dollars in cash. And I would have done the same- before I understood the power of compounding. Let's see what happens to the magical penny over the course of 45 days. Well, the first days are somewhat discouraging. On day 2, you would have 2c, on day 3, 4c on day 4, 8c and on day 5 you would have 16c. No fortune yet. By day 15 you would have $163.84. By day 20 you would have $5,242.88. Still no fortune. But by day 28, your magical penny will have turned itself into $1,342,177. By day 38, you would have more than a $1 billion. And by day 45 you would have more than a $1 trillion (do know how many zeros are in a trillion? 12!)

The point I'm trying to make is simple: It takes patience to unleash the power of compounding. In the first several years, growth will be slow. But if you reinvest profits continually, you will make a terrific fortune.

Here is another example to drive my point home. The Gardner brothers (The Motley Fools) tell the story of Anne Scheiber who at the age of thirty-eight decided to invest her life savings in the stock market. Anne's brother promised to manage her investment with care but when his brokerage company went bankrupt Anne went broke. But she did not give up. Twelve years later she managed to save $5,000 and placed it back in the stock market, this time under her own supervision. By the time she died, Anne was a hundred and one years old and her meager $5,000 had grown to an amazing $22 million.

Remember, delayed gratification pays off big time. It doesn't mean you have to wait until you die to enjoy your fortune, not at all. But if you truly want to reap the rewards of long term investing you need to start investing now! You don't even have to use real money to begin with. Just go on line, open a virtual portfolio on yahoo and start getting familiar with ins and outs of investing.

I also want you to think about other less conventional venues for investments. Consider industries you are familiar with, such as the movie industry or the music industry. Have you seen the movie *My Big Fat Greek Wedding*? The production costs for that movie were $5 million. Within one year, it grossed $241 million in the United States and $354 million world wide. An impressive return, isn't it?

Another big profit movie was *The Blair Witch Project*, which cost only $35,000 to make and grossed $140 million in the United States and $248 million worldwide. Can you imagine what would have happened if you had committed let's say, a $1,000 or $2,000 to the production cost?

Other than movies, you can also invest in music bands; start up projects, theatrical productions, scientific research, and just about everything else that has the potential of generating profits.

One last thing about investing. The key to being a great investor lies in knowing everything you can possibly know about your investment. And when I mean "know," I don't mean to be familiar with it; I mean knowing everything you can possibly know about it. Become an expert. Don't just have blind faith in a broker or a good friend who had a lucky streak. When you choose to invest, get down and dirty with your investment. Learn about the company. Call for their prospectus. Get familiar with their performance. Research their history. Get to know the people who work there. Use their products and services.

Remember that investing is the most powerful economic tool you have at your disposal. Instead of working for your money, you can let your money work for you. Don't be like most people who don't invest simply because they don't take the time to educate themselves about it. Make investing a study. The amount of literature available about wealth and investments is absolutely spectacular. Just walk into any library and go to the business section and you will be dazzled by the books they have to offer. From real estate acquisitions strategies, to private ownership and entrepreneurship manuals, to stock market analysis, long term financial planning, and international market trends, it's all there, free for the taking. Also, check out the following books: *The Warren Buffet Way, The Roaring 2000s Investor, One Up On Wall Street, The Best Salesmen In The World, The Richest Man in Babylon,* or any of Robert Kiyosaki's *Rich Dad Poor Dad* releases. This should give you a decent start.

Bucket III-10%
Active Capital

This is my favorite bucket. Aside from your primary source of income, (bucket I,) the active capital bucket finances any side projects or business endeavors that you will be directly involved in, be it through management or production. This bucket is primarily about generating extra income through active entrepreneurship. Since we already discussed the basic mental skills that successful entrepreneurship requires, let's devote a few a few lines to some technical aspects.

Fundamentally, there are three ways to begin a business. You can start your own, purchase an existing business or invest in a franchise operation. Most people start their own business because of the (usually) small initial investment that's required in comparison to purchasing or franchising. People who start their own business can either sell products such as soap bars or cars or offer a service such as plumbing, accounting, or copy editing.

Now, let's say you've managed to set aside a bit of money to go into business, you've zeroed in on your passion, you're prepared to struggle, and you've found a market opening. Wonderful. But what's next? How do we take an idea and transform it into a profit generating entity? It begins with a business plan.

Like a wise general who strategically plans his battles, you will also need a plan of action that will serve you as a map and allow you to anticipate problems. A business plan is a detailed description of what you intend to do, how you intend to do it and by when. A business plan has three primary objectives: First, to define your business. Second, to identify your market. And third, to determine your operations. Let's talk a little about the first objective.

Defining your business is the process of transforming your idea into a clear explanation of what you are trying to do. Ask yourself questions like: "What type of business will I operate? "What's unique about my products or services?" For example, wanting to open a car service shop is a good idea, but simply stating: "I want to own a repair shop" is a little vague. Compare that with: "I'm going to build an automobile repair business, specializing in Porsche that will gain a reputation for outstanding service and will, first and foremost, always be responsive to customer's needs." Now that's clarity.

Next, you'll need to **identify your market**. In order to identify your market, ask yourself:

1) What industry will I belong to?

2) How big is the market?

3) Who will be my ideal customers?

4) What's the competition like?

5) What services will most appeal to my clients?

6) Why does the market choose one particular service/ product over another?

7) What can I offer that no one else offers?

Keep in mind that knowing your market is extremely important because unless you can fulfill or improve a market need, you will not have any customers/clients. So you need to know what's going on out there. Opening a computer repair store in your local neighborhood may sound like a great idea but what if there are already three computer stores all struggling for business? Better do your research.

Lastly, you'll need to **determine your operations**, that is, how you are going to run your business. Here you'll consider questions like:

1) How will I generate revenues?

2) Am I going to need office space?

3) How will I advertise and promote my products and services?

4) Will I need a sales strategy?

5) Will I have inventory?

6) How will I manage the business?

7) Will I need employees?

8) Will I need a partner?

9) How will the business run if I'm sick or on vacation?

10) What are my financial goals for the next 6 months, one year, and three years?

11) How am I going to expand?

With a basic plan in hand, you'll be able to communicate your idea with clarity, and when required, show it to potential investors. Now, there are literally hundreds of books and thousands of websites that can give you clear guidance on how to create a business plan. A few of them are: www.score.org, www.sba.gov, *The Small Business Advisor* by *The Entrepreneur* magazine, Bob Adams' *Complete Business Plan*, and David Kintrler's *Independent Consulting: Your Comprehensive Guide to Building Your own Consulting Business.*

Bucket IV-10% Contribution/ Sponsorship

Contribution is an odd concept, especially among young people like you and me. Most people don't consider contribution until they are well off financially and they want to know that their fortune can be put to good use to improving the lives of other people. But monetary contribution has a far greater aspect to it. When you are contributing, you are communicating a powerful message to your brain that says "I have more than enough." This is a message of abundance, wealth, and power that lets your brain know that you are able to go beyond your immediate needs and reach out to help others.

The goal in saving 10 percent towards contribution is to be able to support worthy causes and to help others, who are less fortunate, succeed and grow. This is not about the amount of money that's given, it's about the concept. Just think, how would you feel if you had sponsored a science competition in your elementary school where the winner would get $200? Or how about creating a creativity scholarship in your alma mater (high school or college) for those who display promising artistic talents?

You can sponsor independent film projects, young recording artists and performers, youth chess competitions, cook-outs, fund raisers, social research projects, clubs, organizations, and just about anything else. There is tremendous power in knowing that you can support not only yourself, but other people and other causes as well.

"No man can become rich without himself enriching others"

~ Andrew Carnegie ~

While I was in college, I volunteered at Saint Mary's home for the physically disabled children. Saint Mary's is a unique place. It hosts 88 children whose lives are far less fortunate then yours and mine. As you walk through the thick metal doors you can immediately feel that this is not an ordinary hospital. Instead of the noise and vivaciousness you would expect from kids ranging from 3-18, you are confronted with an uncomfortable silence. That's because, out of the 88 children that live at Saint Mary's, only about eight have the physical capacity to communicate. About the same number can consume food through their mouth. The rest have to be fed thorough an abdominal tube. None of the children is strong enough to walk by themselves and most are incapable of sitting in a chair. All the children suffer from severe neuro-motor dysfunction. Some are cortically blind, others only respond to touch while others are so medically fragile that they have to be constantly medicated just to be able to breathe independently.

How do children get to live in Saint Mary's? Well, some have been born with severe neuromuscular complications. Others have been involved in awful accidents and the rest have been horribly abused as infants. I remember going through the charts one day and learning that Brian, a beautifully green-eyed 10-year-old with a well developed body, was repeatedly bashed against a concrete wall at the age of 3 by his drunken father, rendering him a vegetable for life. "What a waste," I remember thinking to myself, shaking my head in disbelief.

Despite the silence and the tragic stories, Saint Mary's has a lovely serenity to it. The kids are lucky to have what I consider to be the best staff in the world. They participate in daily physical therapy sessions, they attend classes, and they go on field trips as often as the weather permits. The nurses and the teaching staff are doing everything humanly possible in order to give those children a normal life, something they would probably not experience anywhere else.

I'm sharing this story with you not to get you sentimental or mushy about those children. Not at all. However, I do want you to realize that what makes a human being truly wealthy is his ability to reach out and improve the quality of life for those around him. Some people don't have enough strength to survive independently, like the children at Saint Mary's. Others struggle to provide for themselves and their families, while others have the means of supporting hundreds and sometimes even thousands of people. Your wealth is measured by the size of your contribution to life, not only in monetary terms but also in knowledge, skills, inspiration, support and the opportunities you create. The challenge to become wealthy is the challenge to be able to support and strengthen as much of the force of life as you possibly can. And when I say the force of life, I mean all living creatures, not only human beings. Take a trip to your local dog pound. Inhale the atmosphere. Put yourself in the skin of a stray dog. Imagine being born on the streets, scrapping for food, being beaten, spat on, cursed, chased, and eventually caught and put in cage that is half your size. That's not much of a life. Maybe even not worth living at all. Now ask yourself, is there something you could do to ease the agony and suffering? Maybe you could volunteer your time, or clean up some cages, or maybe even take some of the dogs for a walk every now and then?

Remember Loren Eiseley's story about the starfish thrower? A traveler was walking along a beach when he saw a young woman scooping up starfish off the sand and tossing them into the waves. Curious, he asked her what she was doing. The woman replied "When the tide goes out it leaves these starfish stranded on the beach. They will dry up before the tide comes back in, so I am throwing them back into the sea where they can live". The traveler then asked her "But this beach is miles long and there are hundreds of stranded starfish, do you really think throwing back a few starfish is going to make a difference?" The woman picked up a starfish and looked at it, and then she threw it into the waves and said "It makes a difference to this one." Be a star thrower. Make a difference. Remember that when you choose to contribute or sponsor someone or something, you are first of all contributing to yourself. The more you give, the more you allow yourself to receive.

Should you wait until you are making thousands of dollars in order to start the contribution habit? Absolutely not. Tell me, what's easier, giving $1 out of $10 or $100,000 out of $1 million? The answer is obvious. If you postpone contributing, you will never do it. You will always find some way to rationalize yourself out of it. So take charge and start doing it now, even if it is very little.

Remember that the essence of sponsorship and contribution is in the message it sends to your brain, not in the amount of money you choose to give. Learn to put that 10 percent aside and every couple of months, find a worthy cause and support it. The sense of satisfaction you will feel will be unmatched by any amount of money you will ever make.

Oh, and don't forget to **have some fun with your money** as well. I know we haven't talked about it much but I'm sure you already know all about that. A lot of people spend their entire lives hording their money, as if they can take with them to the after life. Enjoy your money. Buy a friend a gift. Surprise your soul mate. Buy your nephews a computer game. Take them to Disneyland. Remember that wealth is an emotion, and that the purpose of money is to allow you to feel and experience great things. Don't horde it, and please don't be stingy. There's nothing great in being the richest man in the graveyard.

Alright, we covered a lot in this chapter. I hope you will take everything we talked about, refine it to fit your dreams, and then put it into action. Know that the road to wealth is strewn with rocks and cracks, not roses. Along the way, you will encounter obstacles and problems that will require extraordinarily creative solutions. In fact, much of your success will depend upon how you deal with the obstacles that will come up.

Have you noticed that some people have an uncanny creative ability to solve problems? Ever wondered how they do it? Is it sheer luck? An inborn talent? The result of training? Let's find out.

Section III.
Creativity

Chapter IX

Breaking Out of the Box

"The world is but a canvas to the imagination"

~ Henry David Thoreau ~

He was surrounded by nothingness. Not empty space, since even empty space is something. Not darkness, because there was nothing that could be dark. Just nothingness, awaiting transformation.

He gives orders: "let there be space." but what kind of space? Three dimensional? Multidimensional? Crooked?

He makes his choice.

Another order, and a sliver painted liquid begins to flow and spread throughout causing vortexes and turbulences to occur. He paints the space in blue and than adds white stream-lines to expose the motion patterns.

Another order and a small, red ball, appears in the fluid. The ball stands on the surface, motionless, as if untouched by the fluid. It's waiting for an order. He shrinks himself to a hundredth of his normal size and jumps on top of the ball as if to see the sea of vast spaces from the bird's eye.

They begin to float together. Every few seconds or so, he sends a green marker along the fluid to document the route he has been taking. With each touch, the green markers begin to blossom like a desert cactus after the rain. Each green marker is quickly covered by pictures, numbers and symbols. Another order and the ball now begins to expand and as it does so, the pictures, numbers and symbols on the green markers begin to change rapidly.

Since he is dissatisfied with the trail of green markers, he orders the ball along an upward stream. They now resemble a ski elevator, only there is no end to their climb. He looks down and he understands that they are moving further and further away from the plane he had created. He orders the ball to stop. He snaps his fingers twice and suddenly; tens of thousands of balls begin to surface from down under. They float towards him like helium balloons set free.

The balls stop once they reach his surface. Another order and the balls begin to stack up, one on top of the other to create crates, mountains, and canyons. He decides that is not enough and he begins to wave his arms like a symphony conductor. He arranges, re-arranges, deletes, colors and erases and until, with utter exhaustion, he slowly begins to fall back towards the silver plain he created earlier.

He is now between the plains and falling slowly. Another order, and the picture freezes. Another order: "Save A̲s... title: the chaos phenomenon in four dimensions."

When Ian Stewart, one of the most prominent scientific philosophers of our time, wants to be creative, he closes his eyes and dives into an imaginary world where natural laws such as gravity do not apply. Then, when he feels he is done playing, he opens his eyes and tries to translate his experience into numbers. The paragraph above, taken from the opening page of *Nature's Numbers: the unreal reality of mathematics*, gives us a unique insight into Ian's world of visual mathematics with all its wonder, peculiarity and creative freedom.

There is much confusion and mystery surrounding the concept of creativity. Much like the blowing wind, we usually don't see the writer writing, the composer composing, or the peacemaker negotiating. All we see is the end result. Therefore, like the blowing wind, we don't understand the inner workings of creativity. But nevertheless, we know it's there. We know that some people have an incredible ability to teach, create business, paint, invent, write music, play sports and dance in ways so compelling and innovative that they allow us to understand and enjoy life from a totally fresh perspective.

What is creativity? Is it an innate talent that only few individuals, such as the likes of Picasso, Da Vinci, Mozart and Spielberg possess, or is it a skill that can be attained by each and every one of us?

Plainly speaking, creativity is the ability to come up with something new, be it an idea, a concept, or a method. To be creative implies bringing new meaning or purpose to a task, finding new uses, solving existing problems or adding beauty or value.

During the last several decades, we have made great strides towards understanding the human mind and its ability to create and conceive new ideas. The pioneering work of people like Tony Buzan, Edward De Bono and Howard Gardner has helped us understand what creativity is and how we can apply it to our everyday life. Today we know that creativity is not the blissful revelations of the few, but the commodity of the many. It's a capacity we are all born with, yet fail to cultivate effectively throughout our lives.

In the this chapter we are going to talk about creativity. We'll take a look at what creativity is and what hinders us. We are going to learn how to use specific creative thinking strategies to solve problems and improve our lives. So let's begin.

In a rapidly changing world, new challenges in every area of human life are bound to occur. And new challenges require new solutions. Einstein intelligently observed that "the world we have made as a result of the level of thinking we have done thus far creates problems we cannot solve at the same level of thinking at which we created them." That's an astute observation. When we look at the world we have created, we have to ask ourselvs, "Where are we going from here? What products and services will we create?How will we manage worldwide markets? How are we going to preserve the environment, create more jobs, improve our schools, abolish AIDS and end poverty and hunger?" Those are only some of the tough questions we will have to answer in the upcoming years. And the quality of our answers will depend on one thing: our creativity!

It's important to realize that Einstein's observation is not only true for worldly affairs. It is also true for our own personal lives. Whether you are trying to raise a family, resolve conflicts with your spouse, get a promotion, fix the company debt, go back to school or retire and begin your second act, you need a constant flow of new ideas and solutions. In the past, we had to be creative in order to survive. Our ancestors had to invent different ways to keep themselves warm in the winter. They had to design new tools and develop weapons in order to improve their ability to gather food. Today, companies that do not innovate and create new products and services are doomed. Countries that do not allocate large portions of their budgets for military R&D (research and development) are bound to fall behind. The central role technology has taken in our lives during the last hundreds years is a strong proof for the dominance and importance of creativity in our culture. We have learned that to be successful in any field, one must be creative.

"There is no doubt that creativity is the most important human resource of all. Without creativity, there would be no progress, and we would be forever repeating the same patters"

~ Edward de Bono ~

Creative people have an undeniable affect on the people around them. Because they see the world differently, they behave differently. And because they behave differently, they tend to lead unique and fascinating lives. In *Lives of the Artists*, author Kathleen Krull illustrates what it means to live in proximity of a creative individual:

> *"Neighbors of artists have risked ear damage — from enduring the same song blaring one hundred times in a row (Warhol) or early-morning violin serenades issuing from the bathroom (Matisse). Neighbors have dodged paintings hurled from an artist's window (Chagall). But artists have had stones thrown at their windows by neighbors protesting a turbulent lifestyle (Picasso). Neighbors have been mystified by weird shadows radiating from an artist's darkened rooms (Michelangelo), and at their most superstitious, they've suspected an artist of witchcraft (O'Keeffe). Savvy neighbors might have sneered to realize that the more money an artist spends, the less he has (Dali), but savvy artists have thwarted inquisitiveness by buying adjoining lots to keep neighbors at a distance (Kahlo and Rivera). Neighbors have been known to protect artists from Nazi persecution (Kollwitz), but they've also banded together to run an artist out of town (Van Gogh). "*

Our culture is fascinated with creative people, most notably musicians, actors and entertainers. Maybe it's because they are not afraid to be different and take risks and be honest about their feelings and thoughts. David N. Perkins, coordinator of Harvard University's Project Zero, identified six psychological traits that distinguish creative people and make them stand out:

- A drive to find order in a chaotic situation.

- An interest in finding unusual problems as well as solutions.

- The ability to balance idea creation with testing and judgment.

- The desire to push the boundaries of their competence.

- Motivation by the problem or task itself rather than external rewards such as money, grades or recognition.

Do you remember a time when you were creative? A time when you felt incredibly curious about something or somebody? How did you feel? How did you behave? Were you rigid and serious or were you frisky and daring?

When I was in my senior year in college, I conducted a survey where I asked fifty children below the age of nine and 50 adults above the age of 29 to answer the same question: Are you good at (a) singing; (b) poetry; (c) art; (d) dancing. Not surprisingly, for the nine-and-under group, over 90% checked "Yes" for every box. But strangely enough, in the 29-and-up group, over 90% checked "No" for every box.

What does this mean? Do we "forget" how to be creative after the age of 29? Not really. People don't "forget" how to ride a bicycle, even if they haven't ridden one in 20 years. It is only our perception of ourselvs that changes. As children, we are all naturally creative. We are playful, curious, experimental, unconventional, humorous, and mischievous. We have absolutely no problem to create imaginary friends, invent new games, change the rules of existing ones, pretend we are superheroes or snow queens or paint flowers that are bigger than the sun. At that age, we enjoy creating and do our best to show it.

But as we grow up and enter organized social structures, we quickly develop what developmental psychologists call "Social-awareness." We become aware of other peoples opinions and beliefs. And therefor, out of our natural need to feel normal and fit in, we gradually begin to compromise our individuality and match our creations with those of the people around us.In her book *"Mindmapping,"* Joyce Wycoff explains that "the school system that wants order and discipline and the child who complies with the system in order to avoid failure and ridicule jointly establish an environment of mediocrity. The fear of failure begins to dominate the child's natural curiosity." This coercing interaction between our own unique individuality and one-size-fits-all social institutions begins in primary school, continues through high school, becomes stronger in college and carries on into the market place. By the time we are out of the coercing social loop, our creativity and originality of thought has completely drained.

The Power of Patterns

Fear of failure and group pressure play an important role in diminishing our creative abilities. However, the main reason for creativity loss is much more subtle, since it has to do with the way our mind works.

In order to help us deal with the unlimited stimuli around us, our mind sorts and organizes structures, and stores patterns of information. Our mind is basically a pattern making system. What's a pattern? A pattern is a repetitive sequence of any form, object or color. For example, many popular songs such as "Lift me up" by Moby and "Bring me to life" by Evanescence follow a song structure that looks like this:

Intro
Verse
Chorus
Verse
Chorus
Bridge

Chorus
Outro

Our mind recognizes this song structure since it's repetitive, easy to identify and as a result, easy to remember. But our mind can create and identify patterns that are much more complex than the structure of a popular song. Try to identify the patterns in the following sequences.

Which number should come next in this series?

1, 4, 9, 16, 25,

The correct answer is 36 since the pattern progressively increases: +3, +5, +7, +9, +11. Here's one that's a little more difficult. Which number should come next in this series?

3,5,8,13,21,

The right answer is 34 because in order to calculate which number comes next each time you should add together the last two numbers. 3 + 5 = 8, 5 + 8 = 13, 8 + 13 = 21, 13 +21 = **34**. Our mind also has an incredible ability to recognize visual patterns. With this problem, try to recognize the picture that fol-

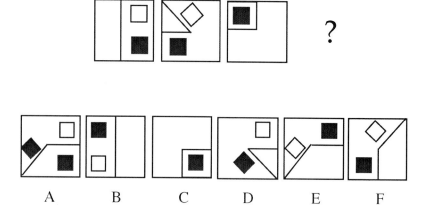

lows logically from one of the six below.

The correct answer is E. Why? Because each figure moves according to a pattern: the block moves clockwise and the square moves anticlockwise while rotating 45 degrees around itself. Half of the line moves 90 degrees clockwise while the other half moves 45 degrees anti-clockwise. Please don't feel bad if you didn't get all three on the first go. I didn't get all of them either. The important thing is that you read the explanations and understand how the different characters relate to one another to form patterns.

Why does our mind create patterns? Because that's the only way it can deal with the enormous influx of information coming through the senses. Without this ability our mind would be overwhelmed.

The amazing thing about our ability to make patterns is that we can learn complex skills like riding a bicycle, playing tennis or doing quantum mechanics with relative ease. With enough attention and repetition, we finally "get it." And once we "get it," we get it for life. Once patterns have been firmly established, we can activate them successfully even after decades of neglect. You never forget how to ride a bicycle or use a stick shift or play ping pong.

We all have patterns of thought in our minds that we have been building all of our lives. For example we learn to recognize and name aspects of experience - both tangible aspects like "car" or "factory" and intangible aspects like "passion" or "development". Those firmly established patterns like "car" or "passion" are called concepts. Concepts are unconscious understandings we have about the world. They operate as mental short cuts that help us deal with new and unfamiliar situations.

As we grow up and learn to cope with new situations effectively, we develop complicated concepts that allow us to understand and perform complex tasks. But with maturity, as new situations occur, we tend to rely on old concepts and understandings instead of creating new ones. We assume that because our patterns of thinking have worked for us in the past, they will also work for us in the future. But that's not true.

Confined by Concepts

Below, you'll find a little exercise that demonstrates the power a familiar concept has in shaping our ability to solve problems. This exercise is taken from William Warren Bartley's: *Werner Erhard: The Transformation Of A Man.* Consider the following nine circles.

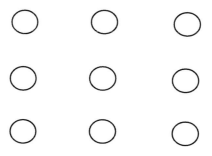

The challenge is simple. Try to connect the circles with four straight lines without lifting your pen from the paper. This challenge is somewhat well known so you may know the answer, but for a person encountering it for the first time, a typical attempt to solve it would look something like this:

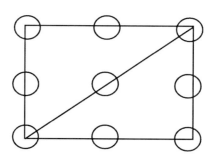

In most cases, the person that produces such a result is willing to swear that it is impossible to connect the circles with less than *five* straight lines. But he would be wrong. The answer is pretty simple and looks like this:

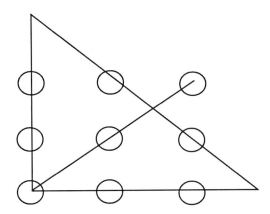

What prevents people from seeing this obvious solution is that they create an invisible barrier around the circles. And they do it because they form a concept about this problem, the concept of a box, which prevents them from solving it creatively.

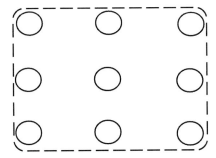

What if we changed the problem a bit? What if I asked you to connect the circles with three lines? Could you do it? Give it a try. If you succeeded, that's great. But if you haven't, than here's the solution:

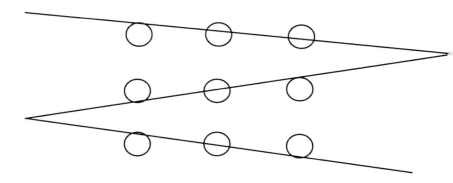

Even people who managed to solve the first problem usually find the second one especially difficult because they have created a different conceptual barrier. They assume that the *circles* are *points*. True enough, it's very hard, if not impossible, to connect nine points with three straight lines. But with circles, it's easy. What if we took this problem to a whole new level? What if I challenged you to connect the circles with only *one* straight line! Sounds impossible? Not really. All you need is a pencil or a brush wide enough to cover all the nine circles at once. After all, nobody said you should use ordinary size pencil to solve the problem, right?

"Creativity requires the courage to let go of certainties"

~ Erich Fromm ~

Consider another example. Imagine there is a $100 bill lying on a plain table. On top of the bill there's a wobbly champagne glass full of water. How would you remove the $100 bill without spilling the water or tipping the glass over? Tricky, isn't it?

This problem could be easily solved by tearing the $100 bill in half. But for various cultural reasons, most people would never consider this option. For starters, we don't usually tear up things of value. And second, we automatically assume that the $100 bill has to stay intact. Would you think about this problem differently if a piece of plain paper was involved?

In this problem, it's clear that the *concept* of the $100 bill acts as a blinder rather than the $100 bill itself. After all, a $100 bill is only a piece of paper with green imprints on it. It has no value of itself. It's the value we attribute to the concept of the $100 that ultimately determines our ability to solve this problem.

Concepts are a double-edged sword. On one hand, they help us make sense of the world but on the other, they considerably limit our ability to "see" the big picture. In our efforts to develop our creative potential, we need to move beyond the conceptual blocks that prevent us from exploring our creative abilities. Most of the barriers we posses are self or culturally imposed and in most cases, they are hidden from our consciousness. I like to call conceptual blocks "Blinders and Blinkers" because they fixate our mind, and as a result our lives, into a narrow tunnel of existence and rob us of the richness and aliveness we should experience.

Blinders & Blinkers

Most of us live routine and redundant lives. Not because we want to, but because we have limited concepts of possibility, much like a race horse who sees nothing but the track. This lack of awareness for possibility diminishes our creativity and turns us into blind automatons. It affects every aspect of our lives, from our ability to overcome challenges and solve problems, to our ability to create new ideas in business and enjoy our leisure time.

There are two primary types of conceptual blocks that hinder our creativity. The first type is blinders. Blinders are acquired when we are exposed to different social and cultural experiences. The second type is called blinkers. Blinkers are limiting beliefs we acquired throughout childhood. They channel our awareness into a narrow passageway and thus, limit our creative potential. Let me give you a few examples.

We'll start with blinders. Please read the following riddle by mathematician Douglas Hofstader. A father and his son are driving to a football game. They begin to cross a railroad crossing and, when they are halfway across, the car stalls. Hearing a train coming in the distance the father desperately tries to get the engine started again. He is unsuccessful and the train hits the car. The father is killed instantly, but the son survives and is rushed to the hospital for brain surgery. The surgeon, on entering the operation room, turns white and says, "I cannot operate on this boy. He is my son."

What's the relation between the boy and the surgeon? Take a minute to think about it before you look at the answer, which is written in reverse: ɹǝɥʇoɯ s,ʎoq ǝɥʇ sɐʍ uoǝƃɹns ǝɥʇ

If you had a hard time finding the answer, it's probably because it was hidden behind a common stereotype in our culture, that surgeons tend to be males and not females. But don't feel bad, I fell for it as well. It is important to note that in and of themselves, stereotypes are neutral. They are neither good nor bad. Stereotypes are just a mental device we use to classify different groups according to personal opinion, preconceived ideas, or bias. And as long as you can remember that, you should have no problem working around it next time.

Here's another riddle, this one taken from James Adams' *Conceptual Blockbusting*. Let's assume that a steel pipe is embedded in the concrete floor of a bare room. The inside diameter is 0.6" larger than the diameter of a ping-pong ball (1.50") which is resting gently at the bottom of the pipe. You are one of a group of six people in the room, along with the following objects:

100' clothesline
A carpenter's hammer
A chisel
An empty box of Frosted Flakes
A file
A wire coat hanger
A monkey wrench
A light bulb

List as many ways you can think of (in five minutes) to get the ball out of the pipe without damaging the ball, tube, or floor.

There are plenty of possible solutions and I'm sure that with minimal effort, you'll come up with some that are highly original. One solution would be to fold the wire coat hanger in two and make large tweezers to retrieve the ball. Another would be to smash the handle of the hammer with the monkey wrench and use the splinters to retrieve the ball. That's pretty creative. If you managed to do something with the light bulb and the Frosted Flakes box, then you are definitely in a league of your own. But let me ask you, did you think about having your group urinate in the pipe? If you haven't, why haven't you? You probably haven't thought about this solution because in our culture, urinating is considered a private matter and urinating in public is considered *taboo.*

The significance of this answer is not that urinating in the pipe is necessarily the best solution, (although it is certainly a good one), but rather that cultural taboos can prevent us from seeing practical and efficient solutions to problems.

"Man's mind stretched to a new idea never goes back to its original dimensions"
~ Gerald Holton ~

Blinkers are very common because of the analytic training

most of us receive in school. In our efforts to be logical and rational we have created fixed concepts of reality that not only determine what is possible and what is not, but also what feelings, emotions and pleasures we are allowed to feel. Blinkers originally stem from our puritan heritage and our technology-based culture that relies on order and precise data in order to predict outcomes and achieve results. Here are a few examples:

There is Only One Right Answer. Most of our lives we have been trained to solve problems by finding one particular answer. Mathematics would probably be the best example for this internal blinder. When required to solve a mathematical equation such as 5+5 we get points for reaching a final conclusive answer as in:

$$5+5=10$$

But we forget that 5+5 also equals 100-90 which equal (-50)+60 which equals (5x10)-10(6-2). Although all answers are equal, such creativity is seldom encouraged. In fact, we usually get penalized for it. But what would happen if math teachers would start posing challenges such as "find the most creative ways to represent the number 10"? We may end up having little geniuses running around. Obviously, there is no such thing as a "one right answer," not even in mathematics.

That's Not My Area. Many times we think that we shouldn't have anything to do with a specific subject because we are not experts. But that's ridiculous. Some of the world's greatest discoveries have occurred because someone was "messing around" in a new area. It 1928, Alexander Fleming accidentally put a bacterial growth plate in the refrigerator next to some mushrooms. By morning time, he had noticed that the bacteria were all gone. That's how penicillin was discovered.

Have you ever used Post-It notes? Wonder how they came about? In 1968, Dr. Spence Silver was trying to improve the glue that 3M used on its tapes. But all he could come up with was a weak adhesive that did not stick very well when it was applied to paper. It wasn't until Art Fry came along looking for a way to keep his scrap paper bookmarks from falling out of his choir hymnal that the potential of posted notes was finally realized and turned into a house hold commodity.

Always Follow the Rules. I believe that rules are important, especially when they are designed to protect us. But not all rules are created equal. Rules are man made principles that are designed to regulate behavior. They are not designed to regulate thoughts or imagination. When operating in the real world and functioning in society, you should play by the rules, otherwise you'll suffer. But for the sake of creativity, you must allow your imagination to transcend "the rules." Here's what I mean. During my junior year in college, I wrote a term paper comparing the anti-social attributes of different serial killers. I was always intrigued by the creepy personas of serial killers and always wondered what made them so different than you and I (assuming you are not a serial killer, of course.) So in order to understand the mind of a serial killer better, I tried to visualize how I would plan my killing spree. The end result was not very creative and somewhat pathetic. I planned to run over people with a black Mac truck but quickly abandoned it since I figured the cops would be on to me in no time.

Obviously, I'm not suited to serial killing. But that's not the point. The point is that I allowed my thoughts to travel far beyond their conventional boundaries. By allowing my mind (but not my body) to break the rules and ethics of society, I could envision life from a criminal point of view without risking any harmful consequences.

"Creativity is a central source of meaning in our lives... and when we are involved in it, we feel that we are living more fully than during the rest of life"

~ Mihaly Csikszentmihalyi ~

Once the blinders are lifted and people become aware of their creativity they tend to be independent, self-confident, resourceful, risk-taking, energetic, enthusiastic, spontaneous, adventurous, curious, fun and child-like. They begin to paint, sculpt, invent, play, joke around, express their emotions and try new things.

Open the Floodgates

The first step you need to take in order to unleash your creative potential is to open your mind to new experiences. Now, with the blinders and blinkers off, you can begin to add spice and flavor to your life without worrying about preconceived judgments and opinions. Many times, we miss out new and exciting adventures because we allow too much rational and logical thinking to dominate our behavior.

Step out of your comfort zone. Every week, do at least once thing you've never done before. Go to the opera. Draw a picture. Ride a horse. Go bungee jump. Attend a Salsa class. Go fishing. Visit the animal shelter. Ride a roller coaster. Eat a new dish at your favorite restaurant. Join the neighbor's cookout. It doesn't have to be something big or important or even serious. You can do something as silly as eat yogurt with a fork or fly paper airplanes from a rooftop. The important thing is that you do something new that let's you experience life from a different perspective.

Open your ears. Listen to different types of music. Try to find harmony and significance in pop, rock, heavy metal, rap, hip-hop, reggae, electronics, classical, swing, jazz, country and R&B. I'm a huge soundtracks fan. I have hundreds of soundtracks in my audio library which I constantly try to refresh and keep up to date. I find soundtracks intriguing because they make movies come alive. They also include different genres and styles of music that create exciting mood swings.

Open your eyes. The cinema is a great place to stimulate your creativity. Today, there is a large assortment of high quality foreign movies in the market. There's no need to live on the diet Hollywood feeds us. These movies portray different cultures and represent different cinematic interpretations than what most of us are used to. I'm sure you'll find foreign movies unique and refreshing.

Visit the local museum. Let yourself be drawn to painting and sculptures. Instead of judging what you see, try to feel what the artist attempts to express. Try to see the painting or the sculpture from his point of view. Ask yourself questions like, "Why did he paint this picture?" "What influenced him?" "How long did it take him?" and "Is he satisfied with his creation?" Remember that the purpose of art is to challenge your perception of reality and rattle your perspective of the world. Yes, art can be entertaining, but there's usually a hidden meaning behind an artist's work, as in the case of riddles and puzzles. Whatever you do, don't allow yourself to leave the museum feeling indifferent. If you do, you might as well ask your money back. Get curious. Challenge yourself. Find the hidden meanings. Don't be afraid to ask questions. And always remember to enjoy yourself.

We are ready to move on. With the floodgates open and creativity flowing free, it's time to equip your mind with new, state-of-the-art problem solving tools. In the next chapter, you are going to be given the keys to...

Chapter X

Keys to Creation:
Strategies and Devices for Deliberate Creativity

"Sometimes the situation is only a problem because it is looked at in a certain way. Looked at in another way, the right course of action may be so obvious that the problem no longer exists"

~ *Edward de bono* ~

Many years ago in a glorious kingdom lived a young and beautiful princess who was greatly admired by the men in her kingdom. Once the princess grew old enough to be married, the king and queen sent messages throughout the kingdom inviting young men to try and win their daughter's hand.

During the first several weeks, hundreds of wealthy, handsome and eligible young men answered with eagerness and enthusiasm. But the king and queen were not impressed by any of the prospects. Then, on the day where the king and queen were about to renounce their invitation, two aristocratic young men arrived from the outskirts of the kingdom. Their names were Jack Ruttger and David Youngblood. This time, the king and queen were very impressed. After a scrupulous evaluation, they determined that both equally deserved to marry their daughter. But how would they choose? A contest was devised. In order to prove who was superior, Jack and David would have to reach the top of the northern tower where the princess would wait for them in a locked room. They figured that the northern tower would be perfect for the contest since it had two entrances and separate sets of stairs. Also, each floor was guarded by the most gruesome warriors and monsters in the kingdom.

And so, the king and queen summoned Jack and David and told them that even though they did not want to send them into danger, it was necessary to determine who was braver, more resilient and more creative since the one who would get to the princess first would not only marry her but one day would also become king. As soon as the king finished giving his instructions, Jack raced towards the northern tower screaming "Don't worry, I'll get there first." David on the other hand, decided to take his time and organize his backpack since the tower seemed particularly tall, therefore, he figured, it would probably take him several days to get to the top.

Sure enough, Jack got to the tower first. He had much confidence in his fighting skills and was unmoved by the king's warnings about the dangers that lurked in the tower. He kicked down the door to the first room and stepped inside fearlessly. There, in the darkness, a pair of blazing red eyes stared at him. It was a giant black tiger with fangs as long as a human forearm. The tiger slowly moved to the center of the room while licking its chops. Jack drew his sword and prepared for battle...

Meanwhile, David was outside the tower questioning the guards: "How many floors are in the tower?" "Who's guarding the first floor?" The guards answered as best as they could and when David felt he knew enough, he headed towards the entrance. He peeked through the key whole and saw a giant Cyclops sleeping in the middle of a corridor. He knew that Cyclops were not particularly smart. So he looked in his bag and found an apple. He opened the door slightly and threw the apple at the Cyclops. Bull's-eye. Bang on the head. The Cyclops woke up languidly. He muttered and grunted but to David's relief, he did not get angry. Instead, he put down his club, picked up the apple and began to munch it. David smiled to himself. His device worked. Now was the perfect time to attack...

Jack was breathing heavily. His strength was slowly fading. He had already fought a tiger and two trolls but was only on the fourth floor. He had several deep cuts on his left arm and his back was badly bruised. But he refused to rest. He took a deep breath, straightened his armor and kicked down the door to the fourth floor. But this time, his enemy was more than ready for him. Apparently, the evil ghoul that was guarding the fourth floor had heard the battle cries of the troll that Jack had slain several minutes ago and was prepared for his arrival. As the door came down, he pounced on Jack and dug his long, razor-sharp nails into his neck. The sudden attack worked. Within moments, Jack collapsed to the floor and breathed his last.

In the meantime, David was making slow yet steady strides towards the top. He carefully plotted his moves before each and every floor, diligently choosing his weapons and saving his energy whenever possible. At last, after four days of relentless fighting, he finally reached the last floor. Tired, hurt and crawling on his knees, David slowly approached the room where the princess was kept. He got up on his feet and picked the lock with no difficulty. He gently opened the door but the room was....empty! Somebody had gotten to the princess before him.

Now, I know very few people who like problems. That's why when most of us face problems, our natural tendency is to pick the first solution that comes to mind and run with it. But the disadvantage of this approach is that we may end up running off a cliff or into a worse problem than the one we started with. In the last chapter, we talked about creativity in all its different aspects. We uncovered the different traits of creative people, we learned that our mind organizes and structures information into patterns and then stores them in the form of concepts, and we talked about the way concepts affect our creativity. In this chapter, I want to build on what we learned earlier and show you how to use specific creative thinking tools that will take your ability to solve problems to a whole new level. What's so great about the tools I'm going to share with you is that you'll be able to apply them immediately to any area of your life, from your personal relationships to your professional career. Not only that, but they are also simple to understand and easy to apply; that's why I hope you'll pass them on to your friends and relatives. But before we dive into the details, let me tell you how our story ended.

David couldn't believe it. How this could be, he thought to himself. He knew Jack had died since he had seen his body on the way up. Suddenly, he heard bells tolling. He approached the window and to his amazement, a grand wedding ceremony was taking place in the royal palace. Shocked and chagrined he rushed down the stairs. By the time he reached the first floor, the ceremony was over and the guests were slowly dispersing. He approached the newly wed prince and said: "I have to know what happened. How did you reach the princess before me?"

"Ah, my brave friend," answered the new prince. "My name is John Kalimdore and I arrived at the king's court a day after you and Jack left for the northern tower. The king said I was too late and told me to go back home. But I refused. I begged and pleaded until finally, he allowed me to participate under one condition, that I would carry no weapons and no armor. Reluctantly, I agreed. I knew that beating the two of you to the top of the tower would be impossible. First, because the two of you already began your climb, which gave you a significant head start. Second, I had no weapons and third, I'm not much of a warrior.

"At first, I became anxious. I carefully reviewed the king's instructions. He said that the first contestant to reach to the princess who was locked at the top of the northern tower would win her hand. But I noticed he didn't say we had to climb the tower or even enter it. Maybe I could get to the princess without actually having to fight my way through the tower."

"And so," John paused again and took and inhaled deeply, "I examined my alternatives. Climbing the tower walls proved to be a bad idea because the moment I approached the tower walls, the king's archers threatened to shoot me. Then I thought, 'If I can't get to the princess, maybe the princess could come to me.'

"So I had one of the guards fire an arrow into the princess's room with a beautiful love letter attached to it. In the evening, while the sound of your clanging sword was filling the castle, my words were wrapping the princess in a warm blanket of passion. The next day I did the same, only now I promised to sleep under her window throughout the night. By the third day, we were exchanging love letters as though we had known each other for years. On that day, I gathered as many leaves as I could and formed a huge hill under her window. Then, I told her that you two were on your way and would be there shortly. And finally, I told her that the only way we could ever be together was if she could muster enough courage to jump out of the window. And so, she jumped."

In most dictionaries, a problem is defined as a state of difficulty that needs to be resolved. Personally, I like Edward de Bono's definition much better. He defined a problem as the difference between where you are and where you want to be. The definition we use for the word "problem" is extremely important because it determines our conceptual framework not only for this chapter, but also for other areas in our lives. When we begin to think about our relationships or professional problems as roads to be traveled or a destination to be reached, we unconsciously shift our attention from the difficulties of the situation to the possibility of finding a resolution. It's an important distinction that's going to serve us well as chart our way through this chapter.

"The vertical thinker says: 'I know what I am looking for.' The lateral thinker says: 'I am looking but I won't know what I am looking for until I have found it"

~*Edward de Bono*~

We can solve problems by using three different strategies. These strategies can be used separately yet they do not overshadow each other and operate best when combined.

The first problem solving strategy is called the "Bulldozer." This strategy involves the use of persistence, determination and strength in order to bulldoze through resistance and difficulty. Bulldozers don't care much for listening to instructions or planning because all their mental energy is directed towards breaking through barriers and overpowering the opposition. If you think back to our opening story, you'll realize that Jack was a classic bulldozer in his approach. As soon as the king finished reading the instructions, he took off without thinking too much about what lay ahead of him. He was so self-assured and confident in his strength and combat skills that he could not imagine failing. Of course, he was wrong.

However, the fact that Jack died doesn't mean the *strategy* is bad or wrong. There are many situations where an effective solution can only be reached by applying the bulldozer strategy. Unfortunately, this just wasn't one of them.

The bulldozer strategy is extremely effective in cases where the problem is clear, obvious and measurable. It is also highly effective *after* you have tried to employ the tactician or the magician strategies. If you know exactly what's ahead of you and you know you can bulldoze your way through safely then by all means, do so. But if you're not sure it's better to evaluate the odds and research a little bit first.

The second problem solving strategy is called the "Tactician." In our story, David represents the tactician. The tactician uses logic, reason and rationale to solve his problems. For example, let's say you are having a hard time finding the local Fed-Ex office. How would you solve this situation? You'd probably go online and look up the exact address or you'd ask someone for directions. That's the logical thing to do: if you are missing important information then stop trying to solve your problem and go get it. What would a bulldozer do in this situation? Probably drive around for hours and hours without asking anybody or even looking at a map.

The tactician strategy is most effective when applied to the routine problems we face daily like finding a babysitter, cooking a meal or writing a final paper. That's because these types of problems usually require more information in order to be solved. Most of us are tacticians to a lesser or greater degree. That's because we have been trained in school and at home to deal with problems from within a logical frame work that relies on analysis and a rationale.

What does a tactician do when he faces a challenge or a difficult task? First, he gathers information. He learns as much as he can about the subject by asking, reading, and observing. Then, after he feels he knows enough about the subject, he tries to foresee any unexpected circumstances that may arise. Then he devises a plan of action and if he is particularly sophisticated, he devises a backup plan as well and finally, he executes. That's exactly what David did, right? And deservingly, he got to the top of tower. But he still didn't win the competition.

The tactician strategy is extremely ineffective in cases where there is too little information to create a logical step-by-step solution. Let me show you what I mean. Imagine you are Sherlock Holmes and trying to solve the following accident. A man lived in a house for two months. Nobody came to visit him and he never went out. At the end of the two months, he became deranged and decided to leave. One night he got up, put out the fire, turned the lights off, and walked out of the house. He was never seen or heard from again. As a direct result from his action, more than 90 people died. What happened?

Let's try to be logical about this problem and find our more information by asking a few questions.

Q: Is what he did after leaving the house relevant?
A: No.

Q: Could he have left the house earlier?
A: Yes.

Q: Was it an ordinary sort of house?
A: No.

Q: Did he perform some function or duty within the house?
A: Yes.

Q: Was the cessation of this function or duty the cause of
   the deaths?
A: No.

This is a tough one. Obviously, we have limited information. We are missing some important details and the questions aren't helping much. Want to take a guess at it? Go ahead, I'll bet you a Slurpee. But in case you're not into guessing, here's the solution. The man was a lighthouse keeper and the house in which he lived was on a remote and outcrop island. When he left the place and turned the lights off, there was no signal to warn passing ships and as a result, a shipwreck occurred.

Many of the problems we face in life cannot be solved with analysis and rational thinking. Sometimes, more information is not available and we have to make things up in order to connect the dots. Let's say you are an excellent car salesman but there is one car you just can't seem to sell. You know that the car is slightly overpriced but you have a quota to fill, plus you gave your word to the distributor promising to sell it fast. What are you going to do? You could go back on your word and return the car, but that wouldn't look good. Researching for more information won't help since you already know everything there is to know about the car. The only way out for you in this situation is to get creative. Maybe you could rent or lease the car? Maybe you could even buy it yourself? That way, you may be overpaying but your distributor would be extremely happy. What if you donated the car to a local charity? What would happen then? What would happen if you put a sign on the car that read "This is the most expensive car in the parking lot"? Would that draw attention to it?

My point is that in a dead-end situation like trying to sell a car that's overpriced, the tactician strategy won't be very helpful. In order to solve such a problem effectively, you must be able to conceptualize beyond the logical boundaries of your problem. And this is where the third strategy comes in.

The third problem solving strategy is called the "Magician." The magician strategy is a creative thinking tool. It is based on rearranging existing patterns of information in order to reach new solutions. In our story, John represents the "magician." Remember what he did? First, he blocked the possibility of beating Jack or David to the top of the tower by conventional means. Then, he reviewed the king's instructions and started tweaking and twisting them until he found a plausible configuration that he thought could work. The magician strategy is particularly effective in situations where there is a considerable lack of information or resources or in situations where logical thinking is no longer effective.

Both strategies, the tactician and the magician, are effective yet they significantly differ in several ways. The tactician's thinking process involves judgment and selection while the magician's thinking process is judgment free and provocative- there is no wrong or right. For example, let's say you are driving along the highway and suddenly, one of your tires goes out. You carefully stop by the side of the road and you notice a huge nail has torn into your tire several inches deep. Luckily, you have a spare. You begin to unscrew the flat tire but as soon as you do, the four wheel-nuts accidentally slip from your hand and fall into the sewage tunnel, irretrievable. How would you solve this?

Well, the tactician would probably call a tow truck or a friend. That would be the logical and reasonable thing to do. But the magician, (after getting resourceful and using a "zoom in" process which I'll explain in a little bit,) would probably solve this problem by "borrowing" one wheel-nut from each of the remaining tires. Then he would drive to the nearest shop and buy another set of wheel-nuts. You could argue that driving with only three wheel-nuts is not safe, and that would be true enough. But what if you were on your way to an extremely important meeting?

Another distinctive difference between the two strategies is that the tactician strategy is based on linear, logical and rational thinking while the magician strategy is primarily based on non-linear, irrational and illogical thought process. For example, when the Wright brothers set out to build a flying machine, many intelligent people assured them that their project was a fool's errand. Everybody knew that a machine that was heavier than air could not fly. It's just wasn't logical. But that didn't bother the Wright brothers at all. When Marconi tried to transmit a radio signal from England to Canada, the experts scoffed at the idea of sending radio waves around the curved surface of the Earth. It just didn't make sense. But Marconi didn't need it to make sense. A tactician would be more concerned with analyzing a situation in order to understand the patterns and connections involved and hopefully refining them. A magician, on the other hand, would try to spin, flip, rotate, and squeeze an existing pattern in order to create as many alternatives as he possibly could.

In order to be effective, the magician strategy relies on the brain's ability to shift perspectives and create new points of view, as illustrated in the picture below.

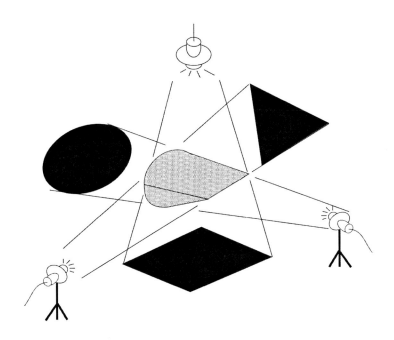

By viewing situations from different perspectives, old patterns are jumbled up and new patterns are created. This allows us to generate an abundance of solutions, which is the secret behind the magician's ability to solve problems effectively. Abundance of alternatives is also known as "Equifinality." **Equifinality** is a term we borrow from systems theory. It means that the system that has the greatest number of ways of reaching the same outcome is the most powerful. It's like the difference between a car with only one speed and a car with a five-speed gearbox system. Which one is going to have an easier time handling a difficult road?

"The way we see the problem is the problem"

~ Stephen R.Covey ~

Flexibility is power. And perspectives make us flexible. The more perspectives we have, the clearer we see of the problem. And the clearer we see the problem, the better the solutions we can generate. That is the essence of the magician's strategy. And once you master the ability to shift perspectives, no situation will ever prove unsolvable.

So how do we create new perspectives? How can we begin to think like John Kalimdore, the Wright brothers or Marconi? Let me show you.

The magician strategy has five thinking processes, or devices, that can be applied in order to solve a problem. When faced with a problem, you can either use all of them in any sequence or just one, depending on how many solutions you would like to come up with. When used, these devices will stimulate your imagination and create a flow of new solutions to even the most difficult of situations.

Device 1:
Concept Isolation

Over and over we have been stressing the power that patterns, beliefs and concepts have in shaping our perception of reality. Just as a reminder, remember the definition of a concept: a concept is an understanding we have about the world. It operates as a mental short cut that helps us deal with new and unfamiliar situations. When attempting to solve problems, our ability to think creatively depends on our ability to identify and isolate the concept of the problem. This is an important process most of us tend ignore because of our urgency to grab the first solution that comes to mind, but as we will soon see, isolating the concept could save us a lot time, money and frustration.

In *Breaking out of the Box*, Piers Dudgeon explains how "Once, there was a problem designing a pen for astronauts because in the weightless environment of outer space, traditional biros and pens simply do not work; you need gravity to enable ink feed. So £ 2 million (that's more than $3 million) was spent in R&D by the Fischer organization to produce a space pen for NASA- a ballpoint with pressurized nitrogen forcing the ink down. The Russian space program had the same problem, but they went back to the operating concept- *'We want something that writes upside down in a weightless environment'* – and delivered it with an idea that cost virtually nothing- a pencil. "This story is absolutely mind blowing. $3 million dollars is a serious amount of money that could have easily been saved if only the scientists would have taken the time to carefully isolate the concept. Here's how to do it. There are three steps to the process.

I. **Conceptualize the problem by answering the following four questions on a sheet of paper:**

1. What's going on in the situation?

2. Who is it affected by what's happening?

3. What is my outcome?

4. What prevents me from achieving it?

II. **Circle the concept.**

III. **Write down the isolated concept on a separate sheet of paper.** Keep in mind that the isolated concept has to be as simplified and concise as possible. This is not the time for elaborative metaphors or a rich vocabulary. Keep it short (two lines at most) and simple. The isolated concept has to state either what you want to achieve, what would you like to happen or prevent from happening, or what you want to overcome.

At this point, you should have two sheets of paper, one containing the problem and the other, the isolated concept. With the concept isolated, you now have a clear view of the situation you are trying to solve. This process by itself can bring about creative solutions but it is most effective when combined together with the third, fourth, or fifth device.

Device 2:
Get Resourceful

The quality of the solutions we can come up with directly depends on the resources we have available. But resources are something we tend to overlook. Many times when we attempt to solve a problem, we forget to check what mental, emotional and physical resources we have to work with. Often, the solution to a problem may be right under our noses but unless we get resourceful, as the next story illustrates, we'll miss it.

A few years ago, I was returning from a west coast trip with my teammates when a snowstorm completely covered the airport parking lot. The locks on our van froze. Everybody was trying to warm the locks so the ice would melt but that proved to be very difficult since the temperature was very low and the ice was very thick. Everybody tried to scratch the locks and get the ice off but that didn't prove useful. It wasn't until we did an inventory check that it occurred to us that the duty-free Merlo we bought would easily do the trick.

When we deliberately shift our attention to our resources, our mind begins to organize and structure them into patterns that eventually can become creative solutions. That's why we must take the time and get resourceful. Here's an inventory list you can easily go through whenever you feel stuck.

- What skills and abilities do I have that can be useful in this situation?

- What knowledge do I have that may be useful in this situation?

- What emotions can be useful in this situation?

- What people do I know that could be of assistance?

- What objects, items, instruments, or devices do I have around me?

- How can I use my environment to solve the problem?

- What can I purchase, trade or give away in order to solve the problem?

- What could I say in order to solve the problem?

Device 3:
The "Flipper"

We already know that our mind creates patterns which then become concepts. But patterns are usually formed by thinking in a certain direction. What would happen if we flip the direction? Would the concept change?

If you recall, in the previous chapter I gave you a sequence of five numbers 1, 4, 9, 16, 25, and asked you what should be the sixth. In order to find the answer, you tried to identify a particular sequence in order to find the missing number.

However, what if I asked you the same question in a different form, such as: Which of the following sequences does the number 36 belong to?

1) 0,7, 21,36,24...
2) 29,20,39,30...

   3) 10,20,45,30...
   4) 1, 4, 9, 16, 25,...

Obviously, you already know the answer. But let's assume you didn't. How would you solve this? You would probably position the number 36 at the end of each series and then try to discover a certain pattern, right?

In both questions, the one in chapter 9 and this one, you had to find a pattern in order to discover the right answer. But whereas in the first question, you were trying to find a pattern in order to find a number; in the second question you were trying to *use* a number in order to find a pattern. It's the same components, only used differently.

By the nature of its formation, every concept must have two opposing sides. A wave must have a crest and a trough. A house must have a floor and a ceiling. A coin must have both "heads" and "tails." Carl Jung was well aware of the principle of duality when he commented on the concept of happiness: "There are as many nights as days, and the one is just as long as the other in the year's course. Even a happy life cannot be without a measure of darkness and the word 'happy' would lose its meaning if it were not balanced by sadness."

The flipper is a method of turning the concept of a problem upside down in order to expose an opposite pattern that may lead to new solutions. It can be unpredictably useful in many everyday situations such as the next one.

A truck got stuck under a low bridge. It could not be moved forward or back without severely damaging its roof. The truck driver was perplexed. He called the police and the fire department saying, "I can't get through because the bridge is too low." Soon, there was a big commotion going on and everyone was thinking of ways to solve the problem. Suddenly, a little girl came rolling by on her three-wheeler. She whispered a few words into the truck driver's ear and within minutes, he was on his way again, driving his truck.

Q: Was the girl's idea easy to implement and without any special equipment?
A: Yes.

Q: Were the bridge and the truck normal?
A: Yes.

Q: Could the bridge raised?
A: No.

Did you get it? In case you haven't here is the solution. The little girl told the driver to let some air out of the truck's tires. Pretty simply, isn't it?

When the driver explained to the rescue forces that he could not get through because the bridge was too low, he immediately created an operating concept. And because of that, when the rescue forces arrived, the only solution they were trying achieve was how to raise the bridge. When the little girl arrived at the scene, she unconsciously formed an opposite operating concept. For her, it wasn't that the bridge was too low but rather, that the truck was too high. So while everybody was thinking about ways to raise the bridge, which was nearly impossible, she was thinking about ways to lower the truck.

The key to applying the Flipper is remembering that every concept has two sides. And many times, it's the flip side, the one that nobody thinks about, that's going to give you the most effective solution.

Device 4: "Zoom In"

When using a camera, we "zoom in" to enlarge an image in order to see it more clearly. As a problem solving instrument, the "zoom in" device is designed to help you focus on specific parts of an isolated concept and by doing so, reveal the patterns that form it. Once the patterns are revealed, they can be flipped or tweaked with ease, thus creating new patterns that breed new solutions. Here's how it works.

In 1997, the cleaning crews at Schiphol's airport in Amsterdam faced a problem. The tile under the urinals was getting extremely dirty and malodorous because urine was spilling to the ground. Apparently, the new porcelain urinals purchased that year were not very effective in preventing urine from splashing. The obvious solution would be to replace the urinals with new ones. But the manufacturer insisted that the urinals were very effective in preventing splashes as long as people did not urinate close to the edges.

How would you solve this? Is there a cheap and effective solution that does not require spending large sums of money in order to replace the urinals? Let's apply the Zoom In device.

First, again, let's isolate the concept:

We don't want the tile under the urinals to be dirty.

Remember that the isolated concept has to state what you want or don't want clearly. Second, we are going to zoom in on the concept by using the inquiry word "why" repeatedly until we find a pattern we can identify and change.

Q: Why is the tile under the urinals dirty?
A: Because when people urinate, there's a splash that spills from the urinals to the tile.

Q: Why is there a splash when people urinate?
A: Because people urinate too close to the edges of porcelain. The porcelain is designed to prevent splashes and spills as long as one "aims" for the middle.

Q: Why do people urinate too close to the edges?

A: Because they have no reason to aim for the center of the porcelain. They think its enough just to hit it.

Q: Why don't they have a reason to aim at the center?
A: Because we never gave them any.

Aha! The Dutch team knew they were on to something. They figured that if they could give people something to aim at while they urinate, they may try to hit it, and thus, the splashes would be minimized and the tile wouldn't get dirty. After thinking for a while, they finally came up with an unusual target: a fly. They decided to etch black outlines of flies into each urinal and then see what happens. After several successful trials, Aad Kieboom, the director of Schiphol's building expansion confirmed that spillage was indeed reduced by more than 80 percent. How's that for a cost effective solution?

Device 5:
"P into O"

When we talked about the flipper, we learned that concepts always have two sides. Think back to the situation Jaime Goldman had to face when her legs had to be amputated. Most people would consider that to be a major problem. But for Jaime, it wasn't a problem. It was an opportunity. She managed to take a potentially devastating situation and turn it first into an opportunity, and then, an advantage. But how did she do that mentally? What did she say to herself?

The process of turning problems into opportunities is triggered by a set of four questions.

1) What can I learn from this?

2) How can I grow from this?

3) How can I use this to my advantage?

4) How can this benefit others?

These four questions unconsciously direct your focus and attention towards empowerment by presupposing that there is indeed a benefit, an advantage, or a lesson to be learned from the situation at hand. Linguistically, they are structured to elicit an empowering response. And they can be used effectively in almost every situation. Try to turn the next situation from a P (problem) into an O (oppertunity).

The following letter was written by Brenda Dyck and originally appeared on the Microsoft Teacher Network. Read it, and then try to help out.

Dear Help!
One of my favorite students just found out she will be moving to a new city over the summer. This is a very popular girl, one of those rare kids who is equally well liked by teachers and students. What's more- her family has been a constant presence at our school- I even taught her older brother and sister when they were going through seventh grade. The whole mood of my class has become quite gloomy, and I sense that the kids are looking to me for help in dealing with this pending loss. I'm not sure what to do. Can you help?

The first instinct most of us have is to try to prevent events from happening. We hope that the teacher could convince the parents or that the principal could get involved and prevent the move. But by offering these solutions, we aren't turning the problem into an opportunity. On the contrary, we may be risking a power struggle. Here's how I turned this situation from a problem to an opportunity.

Dear teacher,
You have a unique opportunity to teach your class something

about the transitions of life here. Most of us resist change in our lives, and it is not too early to equip your students with a new concept regarding change. It may be one of the most important things that you teach them this year.

How did I do it? Well, the first thing I did was to focus and isolate the concept. I made sure that even though the teacher is the one asking for help, the children are the one's experiencing the difficult situation. Second, I answered the four questions.

1) What can the children learn from this?

2) How can they grow from this?

3) How can they use this to their advantage?

4) How can this benefit others?

If you noticed, I tweaked the questions slightly to fit the concept. The concept here is revolves around the children, not the teacher, therefore using the word "I" would be inappropriate and would create difficulty in coming up with creative useful solutions.

There is no doubt that throughout your life, you'll have to face many problems and difficult situations. That's just the way life is. And it is my hope that the strategies and devices I have shared with you in this chapter will help you overcome problems now and in the future. I wish I could offer you a fail-safe system of thinking or a strategy that would take care of every difficulty and every resistance you'll ever encounter, but then that wouldn't be creativity, would it? You have plenty of tools at your disposal. Make good use of them.

Greatness is about experiencing life to its full capacity, about striving and pushing the limits. And to do that, we must have energy. The next part of our journey focuses on your physical vitality. Our goal is to be able to achieve...

Section IV.
Physiology

Chapter XI

Unlimited Health:
Six Keys for Maximizing Energy and Minimizing Stress

"A man to busy to take care of his body is like a mechanic too busy to take care of his tools"

~ Spanish Proverb ~

Another sleepless night. It was around 4 A.M. when he called his cousin Billy to see if he wanted to play racquetball. Even though they had been sound asleep, Billy said "sure." It had been raining off and on all evening, and it started up again just as they walked to the racquetball building. Billy said he was sick of the rain, and wished it would stop. "Ain't no problem. I'll take care of it," he said, and as he held up his hands the rain had suddenly stopped. "See, I told you," he declared with a playful spark in his eye that always reminded everybody to take things lightly. "If you've got a little faith, you can stop the rain."

They started playing racquetball, but he got tired quickly. It wasn't long before the game degenerated into a game of dodge ball, with him trying to hit Billy with every shot. Eventually he hit himself on the shin with his own racquet and quit. "Boy that hurts," he said, lifting up his pants leg to reveal an ugly welt. "If it ain't bleedin'," said Billy employing one of his cousin's favorite sayings, "it ain't hurtin'." And they all broke out in a heartfelt laughter.

As they returned to the house, his stepbrother, Ricky, arrived with the first of three packets of prescription drugs, or "attacks," as he called them. Each packet consisted of varying amounts of Seconal, Placidyl, Valmid, Tuinal, Demerol, and an assortment of other depressants and placebos which generally allowed him to get several hours of sleep at a time.

A couple of hours later Ricky brought him his second attack. But when he called down for the third, Ricky had disappeared. His nurse was already gone as well. He had his aunt call his doctor in order to get the third packet which was made up of two Valmids and a Plandyl placebo. He then got up and went into the bathroom to read and that was when his heart gave out.

Elvis Presley died from "cardiac arrhythmia," also known as irregular heartbeats. In his short yet dramatic life he managed to star in 33 films, sell over one billion records and earn gold, platinum and multi-platinum awards for 149 different albums and singles. Among his many awards and accolades were 14 Grammy nominations (3 wins) and the Grammy Lifetime Achievement Award. And he even served in the army. Without a doubt Elvis achieved more in 42 years than most people achieve in a life time. But was his death necessary? Could it have been postponed?

Elvis's death was no accident. Towards the end of his life, his weight was out of control. He appeared bloated in the face and belly due mostly to the meds he was taking for high blood pressure. Glaucoma made his eyes puffy and tears ran down his face as he painfully looked into the bright lights on stage night after night. He drank excessively and he consumed enormous amounts of artery-clogging foods such as glazed donuts, extra large cheeseburgers, frosted brownies, and fried peanut butter and banana sandwiches. Elvis also had a natural disposition towards cardiovascular disease. According to Professor George Davey-Smith, an epidemiologist from Bristol University "Elvis had a very low birth weight, being the survivor of twins, and was raised in abject and grinding poverty." Elvis was playing with fire, and he knew it. Even though the doctors warned and confronted him about his weight and drinking habits, he ignored them and pressed on. But was he ignoring the doctors-or his own body?

Let me ask you something. How do you start your day? Do you jump out of bed with an incredible feeling of vitality, ready to charge into the day? Or do you drag yourself out of bed and gulp down some coffee to get the day going? Do you go through your day with a positive feeling of anticipation? Or are you thinking, "Gee, I can't wait to get home and just crash." At the end of the day are you still full of energy? Are you looking forward to spending some time with your spouse or your friends? Or, come evening, do you barely have enough energy to get dinner down and then collapse on the couch in front of the TV prior to passing out?

If you don't feel energized and vital when you wake up every morning, it's because you have allowed stress and fatigue to throw your body off balance and drain your energy resources. But do not worry. In this chapter, we are going to learn how, by applying simple health principles, you can restore physiological equilibrium and get our body's most important systems (immune, digestive, lymph, adrenal, nerves and musculoskeletal) to function optimally, even in the face of constant demands and pressures from your environment. But before I give you the six keys, let's learn little bit about stress and how it leads to physiological imbalance, fatigue and obesity, so we can understand what we are up against.

"What happens in the mind of man is always reflected in the disease of his body"

~ *René Dubos* ~

Stress today is the greatest threat to our health and energy levels. *Time* magazine's June 6, 1983 cover story called stress "The Epidemic of the Eighties" and referred to it as the leading causes of death, including heart disease, cancer, accidents and suicide. But that was more than twenty years ago. A 1996 *Prevention* magazine survey found that almost 75 percent of us feel "great stress" one day a week with one out of three indicating feeling this way more than twice a week.

But why are we so stressed? Part of the answer lies in our accelerated life style. According to health expert Dr. Georgianna Donadio, "Prior to the early 1970's, the majority of family units were structured as a one wage-earner household where the male worked and the female stayed at home, taking care of the house and family. Driven largely by social and socio-economic factors, all of that has changed. Now, the overwhelming majority of families include both parents working and we find ourselves on a treadmill of more work, more responsibilities, more demands and non-stop scheduling that has many of us in a state of physical and, at times, emotional exhaustion. Another thing that has drastically changed in our culture is the way we eat. In order to fit our busy lifestyle, most of us fuel ourselves on fast food, fries, soft drinks, candy bars, frosted cereals, and many different kinds of condensed and processed foods that we can eat on the go.

Unfortunately, our modern life style does come with a price tag, and in many cases, it's a heavy one. In an article about obesity that came out in a special issue of *Time* magazine on July of 2004, Michael D. Lemonick writes that "fully two-thirds of U.S. adults are officially overweight, and about half of those have graduated to full-blown obesity. Among kids between 6 and 19 years old, 15 percent, or 1 in 6, are overweight, and another 15 percent are headed that way. Even our pets are pudgy: a depressing 25 percent of dogs and cats are heavier than they should be." With our weight going up, we have also become incredibly vulnerable to coronary heart disease which has become number one the health plague of our century. According to an article on the www.americanheart.org, "931,108 Americans died from CVD during the past year alone and more than 5 millions have been directly affected by it." (Try to get you hands on Fast Food Nation by Eric Schlosser for a better understanding of what has happened to the American diet in the last few decades.)

Stress is something we all have to deal with on a regular basis. From the mom who is trying to take care of her career, her kids, husband and aging mother, to the college student who is working, dating and studying overtime so he can get into graduate school, to the struggling actor who is working full time and auditions day in and day out, stress is something we must learn to negotiate and respond to effectively. And that's exactly what we are going to do in this chapter. Stress is a constant threat to our health, energy, happiness and achievement and unless we learn to control how it affects us, we are bound to suffer.

It is important to know that your body reacts unconsciously to situations that you find threatening. Stressful situations activate the "fight or flight" mechanism by causing certain physiological changes to take place. As the stress response is set in motion, your body produces additional adrenaline; your heart begins to beat faster. More blood flows into the larger muscles and your breathing becomes shallow. These and myriad other immediate and automatic responses have been honed over the course of human evolution as life saving measures to facilitate primitive man's ability to deal with physical challenges. However, the nature of stress in modern living is not an occasional confrontation with a saber-toothed tiger or a hostile enemy but rather, a host of emotional threats like getting stuck in traffic, fighting with customers, co-workers or family members, or even being asked to stay overtime. Today, stress tends to be elongated over weeks and sometimes even months, many times with no respite. Unfortunately, your body still reacts to stress with the same, archaic fight-or-flight responses that are no longer useful and also potentially damaging and deadly. Excessive and extended stress causes all basic bodily functions that require significant amounts of energy such as digestion, metabolism, and removal of waste to become subdued.

In the rest of this chapter, I want to give you six keys that will allow you to experience maximum energy levels in spite of the pressures you experience from your environment. These six keys have worked magic in my life for more than three years now, not only in keeping me healthy and allowing me to negotiate greater levels of pressure and stress, but also by helping me to lose weight, get into better shape, sleep less, recover faster from challenging physical activities, and most importantly, feel strong, vibrant and energetic day in and day out. I'm sure that by applying these keys for a period of at least two weeks, you will reap significant results that will greatly improve the way you feel and perform. Feel hesitant? If you do than that's understandable. But what have you got to lose? I suggest you take a chance and put my principles to the test. Then make a decision based on how you feel. So far in *Being Great* we focused on your mind and your wallet. Now it's time to focus on your body and unleash the energy your truly deserve to feel every single day.

First key: harness the power of effective sleep. Sleep is an enigma. Even today, scientists do not have definitive answers as to what happens (and why) when we sleep. But we do know that sleep is essential to our existence. A survey conducted by the American Cancer Society concluded that people who sleep 6 hours or less per night, or who sleep 9 hours or more, had a death rate 30 percent higher than those who regularly slept 7 to 8 hours. Even those who slept 6 hours or less who otherwise had no health problems had death rates 1.8 times higher than those who slept "normal" hours.

I don't want to waste ink talking to you about giving your body enough rest because that's something we all do naturally. However, life can get unpredictable at times and force us to cut back on our sleep time. But that doesn't mean you have to feel tired or fatigued. The jury is still out as to how many hours we should sleep. We are taught that eight hours is what we should aim for, but most leaders, athletes, and key figures in our culture are perfectly fine with six and even five hours of quality sleep. Whether you are a college student or a young parent, I want you to have the awareness and the knowledge of practicing high quality sleep so even when you are forced to cut back on sleep time you'll still feel energized and strong.

"Sleep is the golden chain that ties health and our bodies together"

~ Thomas Dekker ~

First of all, let's examine what makes sleep so essential to our existence. According to the National Institute of Neurological Disorders and Stroke, "Sleep appears necessary for our nervous systems to work properly. Too little sleep leaves us drowsy and unable to concentrate the next day. It also leads to impaired memory and physical performance and reduced ability to carry out math calculations. If sleep deprivation continues, hallucinations and mood swings may develop. Some experts believe sleep gives neurons used while we are awake a chance to shut down and repair themselves. Without sleep, neurons may become so depleted in energy or so polluted with byproducts of normal cellular activities that they begin to malfunction. Sleep also may give the brain a chance to exercise important neuronal connections that might otherwise deteriorate from lack of activity. "

Hormones are responsible for the rejuvenating effect of deep sleep. During deep sleep the production of growth hormone is at its peak. Growth hormone speeds the absorption of nutrients and amino acids into your cells, and aids the healing of tissues throughout your body. The hormone also stimulates your bone marrow, where your immune system cells are born. Melatonin, often called the sleep hormone, is also produced during sleep. This hormone inhibits tumors from growing, prevents viral infections, stimulates your immune system, increases antibodies in your saliva, has antioxidant properties and enhances the quality of sleep.

Researchers at the University of Toronto Centre for Sleep and Chronobiology have lately uncovered important insights about how sleep heals. Dr. Harvey Moldofsky and his colleagues studied the natural rhythm of sleep by interrupting the sleep of a group of medical students. Over several nights, each time the students entered a deep-sleep phase, called the "non-REM" (rapid-eye-movment) or "delta" phase, the researchers would interfere. After a few nights of these disruptions, the students developed the classic symptoms of chronic fatigue syndrome and fibromyalgia.

Moldofsky conducted another study examining how the immune system reacts to sleep deprivation. The study examined natural killer cells — a component of the immune system that attacks bacteria, viruses and tumors. During the study, 23 men slept about eight hours the first four nights. On the fifth night, the researchers woke the men up at 3 a.m., giving them four hours less sleep than usual. This one insult to their sleep pattern caused the activity of the natural killer cells to decrease by more than one-fourth the next day.

Although sleep is such a basic activity in our every day life, many of us struggle to enjoy it properly. The National Commission on Sleep Disorders Research estimates that 40 million Americans suffer from chronic sleep disorders and another 20 to 30 million experience sleep problems intermittently. And since sleep disorders increase with aging, those suffering from chronic sleep disorders are expected to rise to 79 million and those suffering from intermittent problems to increase to 40 million by 2010. The costs of sleep-related problems are staggering. The commission estimated direct costs of sleeplessness at $15.9 billion annually and another $100 billion or more in indirect costs, such as litigation, property destruction, hospitalization and death resulting from sleep disorders and sleep deprivation.

Why so many of us find it difficult to get a good night sleep? For the most part, it's because of the life styles we choose to adopt. Many of us belong to the Internet generation which has shifted the business paradigm in the world from an 8 hour business day into a 24 hour business day. As a result, many service oriented businesses, such as Wal-Mart and Federal Express for example, now offer their services 24 hours a day, 365 days a year. Another influencing factor is our increasing consumption of stimulants such as caffeine, sugar and alcohol. Stimulants increase our blood pressure and stimulate our nervous system to a point where we feel hyper and restless for extended periods of time.

Alright, so we clearly understand the importance of sleep in rejuvenating our bodies. But what happens when we experience a turbulent week? What happens if say, we have a friend in the hospital or the baby is sick and won't fall asleep? Let me show you how you can maximize the power of sleep even during erratic and stressful times.

Hit the sack early (at least twice a week). Make every effort to go to bed at 10 p.m. at least twice a week. Your body works best when it's synchronized with the cycles of nature. This makes the optimal time for sleep between 10 p.m. and 6 a.m. If you're in the habit of staying up much later than 10 p.m., begin getting up progressively earlier by a few minutes each morning, over several days. This will make it easier to go to bed earlier in the evening until you reach your target.

Create a bed time ritual. Establish a regular, relaxing bed-time routine such as soaking in a hot bath, getting a massage from your spouse and then reading a book or listening to soothing music. Many studies suggest that soaking in hot water (such as a hot tub or bath) before retiring to bed can ease the transition into deeper sleep. Exclude from your ritual things like watching television, paying bills, arguing, and exposure to bright lights.

Reduce stimulants. If you find it difficult to get to sleep around 10 p.m., try cutting stimulants out of your diet - particularly refined sugar and caffeine products like coffee, chocolate and black tea - even in the morning. These take a long time to be eliminated from your body, and their effects can linger into the evening. Also, avoid eating at least 2-3 hours before your regular bedtime since it will make your digestive system work harder throughout the night and make you feel fatigue and sluggish in the morning.

Quiet your mind. If your body is tired but your mind is active, try meditation or prayer. But don't make it hard work. Use a simple and gentle form, such as repetition of a thought or phrase, or just focus on following your breath in and out until you feel relaxed. Personally, I use relaxing music and a breathing pattern called 1-4-2 where you inhale for several seconds, hold your breath in for 4 times as long, and then slowly exhale for twice as long. I'm usually out after about 10 of those.

Leave your worries out of bed. Many times I find myself trying to solve my personal and professional problems in bed. The result: long sleepless nights. Keep in mind that your bed is not a laboratory. It is a resting place. If you are troubled then get a notebook and write your worries down before you go to sleep. Get them out of your head. Spill everything out as fast as you can. Don't be gentle with words and don't worry about punctuation or grammar. Just get it out of your head. I use this technique quite often and it works wonders for me. So make sure you give it a shot.

Lastly, take a look at *Wide Awake at 3:00 A.M.* by Richard M. Coleman who's one of the worlds leading sleep researchers. He examines many beliefs and strategies regarding sleep such as how long we should sleep and how we can reset our biological clock in order to minimize jetlag, depression, and irregular work schedule.

Second key: Feast on raw and water rich foods. Cooking has gathered much popularity during the past decades. The culinary arts are reaching new heights, especially due to culture clashes and improved technology that allows greater versatility and creative freedom. Television is flooded with cooking shows for every taste bud and recipes for just about everything are available on line. But is cooking really healthy?

Seventy percent of our planet is covered with water. Seventy percent of our body is made of water. Seventy eight percent of our blood stream is made of water. Our internal organs are practically "floating" inside our body. When we cook food we lose its water content, which is the most essential ingredient for our body. We can last up to fourteen days without food but only about three days without water. Cooking denatures the proteins in our food, rendering them harder to digest and utilize. Cooking usually destroys about 50 percent of the protein in our food. Between 50 and 80 percent of the vitamins and minerals are also destroyed. When heated, Pesticides break down into more toxic compounds, which are more easily assimilated into our bodies. As a result, oxygen is lost and free radicals are produced.

But more importantly, when we cook food, we destroy the enzymes within it. The key to effective digestion lies in our body's ability to break the chemical bonds between the molecules of the foods we consume. The efficiency of these chemical reaction greatly depends on the existence of enzymes. Enzymes are special proteins, shaped by millions of years of trial and error, into effective molecular robots that break down food particles so they can be utilized for energy. How crucial are enzymes to effective digestion? Extremely. Without enzymes, there can be no cellular division, immune system functioning, energy production nor brain activity. No vitamins or hormones can do their work without enzymes. In fact, it is estimated that without enzymes, it would take our body about fifty years to break down an ordinary lunch.

- There are two different types of enzymes in our bodies, metabolic enzymes and digestive enzymes. We produce over 100,000 different enzymes, each doing a unique task.

- The human body makes approximately 22 different digestive enzymes which are capable of digesting carbohydrates, protein and fats.

When raw foods are exposed to temperatures above 118 degrees, the enzymes within them start to rapidly break down and change their structure, just as our bodies would if we had a fever that high. As a result, most of the foods we consume have damaged enzyme content which requires us to make our own enzymes to process food. This process forces our digestive system to work twice as hard in order to process cooked food. (In general, raw food is so much more easily digested that it passes through the digestive tract in 1/2 to 1/3 of the time it takes for cooked food.)

There are two significant problems with enzyme destruction. First, our bodies cannot produce enzymes in the perfect mix to metabolize our food as completely as the food enzymes nature creates. This results in partially digested fats, proteins and starches that clog up the intestinal tract and arteries. The Eskimos are a remarkable example of this. Eskimo means, "One who eats raw." While living for centuries on a diet that consisted primarily of whale or seal blubber, Eskimos developed no arterial sclerosis. They had almost no heart disease or stroke, and no high blood pressure. Interestingly, even raw blubber will digest itself completely if it is not cooked and its enzymes are not destroyed.

Second, it has been demonstrated that our bodies produce a finite lifetime supply of enzymes. Every cooked meal we eat causes enzyme production that draws on our finite reserve. This can help us understand why an 85 year old has only 1/30 the enzyme activity level of an 18 year old. Aging is really nothing more than running out of enzymes. Cells stop dividing, our immune system fails to handle challenges it managed easily when we were younger.

Our enzyme reserve is gradually depleted over a lifetime of eating cooked food. In 1930, Dr. Paul Kouchakoff found that when we eat cooked food, our bodies attack it with leukocytes, the white blood cells that are the cornerstone of our immune system. These cells bring enzymes to the cooked food in an attempt to break it down and get rid of it. Our bodies actually treat cooked food as a foreign invader. This has been confirmed by hundred of researches cited in the prestigious National Academy of Science's National Research Council's book, *Diet, Nutrition and Cancer*, "all cooking quickly generates mutagens and carcinogens in foods.

When you eat cooked carbohydrates, proteins and fats you are eating numerous mutagenic (carcinogenic) products caused by cooking." On the other hand, no leukocytes are produced when living food is eaten. It is a tremendous burden on our body to produce digestive enzymes and leukocytes. It takes ten metabolic enzymes to make one digestive enzyme. The pancreas of humans and domesticated animals is twice the size (as a percentage of body weight,) as mammals in nature. This is a direct result of the overwork we place on it to create digestive enzymes. It's no wonder we feel so tired after eating a cooked meal.

In nature, all mammals live eight to ten times their maturation age. Humans, and our domesticated pets and farm ani-

mals that eat cooked and processed food only live four times
our maturation age. In the famous Pottinger cat study, it was
demonstrated that cooked food diets result in shorter life spans,
congenital abnormalities and eventually, loss of reproductive
capability. It is amazing to see how all animals in nature maximize their enzyme reserve. If you give a squirrel a raw nut, it
will not eat it, but always will bury it. It will only dig it up
when the nut has sprouted. They have found sensors in squir-
rels' noses that can identify a sprouted nut. Raw, unsprouted
nuts have enzyme inhibitors that prevent the nuts' food enzymes from digesting it. Only when it sprouts are these inhibitors deactivated.

When we consume living foods, our entire bio-terrain operates at optimal health. All of our cells, organs and systems are
able to do the jobs they are capable of in perfect balance. A
healthy bio-terrain requires proper enzyme capacity, acid-base
balance and a healthy digestive tract. With a healthy bio-terrain, our bodies manage all health challenges quite effectively.
This is why we rarely see disease in mammals living in nature.
Feasting on raw (living) foods leads to a healthier, more energetic physiology. When we eliminate the burden of digesting
cooked foods we allow our body to focus its resources on cleansing and rebuilding cell tissue.

So what's considered "raw" or "water rich" food? Dried
fruit, sea vegetables, nuts, seeds, grains, legumes/pulses, extra
virgin olive oil, wheat germ, blackstrap molasses, herbs, miso,
tahini, tamari and yeast extract and all fresh fruit and vegetables. Personally, I don't believe in extremes and don't think
you should eliminate all cooked foods from your menu. But I
do think you should go over *The Raw Food Bible* by Leslie Kenton
which offers an interesting program of raw food recipes. She
recommends that 50-75% of the diet should consist of uncooked
raw foods, which I believe is a good starting point, if you don't
want to give up cooked food completely.

Third key: master the art of fasting and caloric restriction.

Fasting has a very long history, dating as far as Biblical times, as a natural means of purifying the body and the mind. It was practiced in cultures as diverse as those of the ancient Greeks and the Native Americans, and was often used as part of a rite or religious exercise.

Today, the Christian tradition teaches that fasting is one of the three ways in which one can atone for his or her sins (along with prayer and almsgiving.) In the Jewish tradition, fasting is held several times a year. The most important fast occurs on the Day of Atonement (Yom Kippur) which signifies the cleansing of the body and the soul from the sins of the previous year. In the Islamic tradition, an entire month (the Ramadan) is dedicated to the practice of a carefully controlled fast in which believers do not eat from dusk till dawn. And in Hindu tradition, fasting is practiced according to Ayurveda, an ancient Indian medical system that sees the basic cause of many diseases as the accumulation of toxic materials in the digestive system. By fasting, Hindus believe, the digestive organs get rest and all body mechanisms are cleansed and corrected. But does fasting and caloric restriction have real physiological value? Let's find out.

Many scientists believe that fasting and caloric restriction (a diet with between 30-40 percent fewer calories than is typical, but which contains all the necessary nutrients and vitamins to support life) are the best natural healing therapy. It is nature's ancient, universal "remedy" for many physiological ailments. For example, Dr. Ralph Cinque, who has experience with full-time therapeutic fasting supervision since 1976, states that "fasting promotes detoxification. As the body breaks down its fat reserves, it mobilizes and eliminates stored toxins. Not only that, consistent fasting also gives the digestive system a much-needed rest. After fasting, both digestion and elimination are invigorated. Fasting promotes the resolution of inflammatory processes, such as in rheumatoid arthritis. Fasting quiets allergic reactions, including asthma and hay fever. Fasting promotes the drying up of abnormal fluid accumulations, such as edema in the ankles and legs and swelling in the abdomen. And most importantly, fasting stimulates both the metabolism and the immune system, thus it promotes healing and renewal."

The positive results of caloric restriction were documented by George Roth of the National Institute of Health, who studied the response of more than 200 monkeys to caloric restriction for almost three years. In his study, monkeys were being fed 30 percent less than they would eat on their own. The results were conclusive. Measures of body temperature, weight, lean mass and fat were below those of free-feeding animals. Biological markers of aging, such as blood pressure, "good" cholesterol and triglyceride levels, were significantly improved. The blood-borne hormone insulin was better able to help metabolize sugar which, according to Roth, suggests that the monkeys were less likely to develop diabetes as they age.

Aging is a serious issue in our culture. In fact, it has become a multibillion dollar industry that offers a vast array of pills, surgeries and alternative treatments in an attempt to reverse our bio-clock or at least slow it down a bit. But let me share a secret with you. For the past decade, there is a vastly growing body of scientific evidence that suggests fasting and caloric restriction carry great health benefits that may not only assist in weight loss, but affect a series of biological mechanisms that can prolong your life.

Several years ago an interesting experiment involving two groups of worms was done at the Zoology Department of the University of Chicago. In the experiment, one group of worms was well fed and as a result, passed through the cycles of growth, reproduction, aging, and death every three to four months. The second group was given just enough food to maintain the worms at a constant size but not enough to make them grow. These worms remained in good condition without becoming appreciably older for the entire duration of the experiment (three years.) The life-span extension of these worms was the equivalent of keeping a man alive for 600 to 700 years. The experiment found that worms, when well-fed, grew old, but by fasting they were literally "made young again."

In a second experiment, a group of worms were fed normally except for one worm which was isolated and alternatively fed and fasted. The isolated worm was alive and energetic after 19 generations of its relatives had lived out their normal lifespan.

Dr. C.M. Childs, who conducted both experiments, observed that "When worms are deprived of food, they do not die of starvation in a few days. They live for months on their own tissues. At such time they become smaller and may be reduced to a fraction of their original size. Then when fed after such a fasting, they show all the physiological traits of young animals. But with continued feeding, they again go through the process of growth and aging."

Can we compare ourselves to worms and monkeys? The answer is a confident "Yes!" according to Dr. Ray Walford, a famous UCLA researcher. In the "Informational News" Section of *Awake*, Ray stated that "Under nutrition is thus far the only method we know of that consistently retards the aging process and extends the maximum life span of warm-blooded animals. These studies are undoubtedly applicable to humans because it works in every species studied thus far."

"Protect your health. Without it you face a serious handicap for success and happiness"

~ Harry F. Banks ~

Fasting is also a great instrument for self-discipline. When fasting, you are giving your mind a massage that you are in control of your instincts and not the other way around. Through regular fasting, you train both mind and body to endure and harden up against all hardships, to persevere under difficulties and not give up. As Luqman (an Arabic mythological sage) the wise once said, "When the stomach is full, the intellect begins to sleep. Wisdom becomes mute and the parts of the body restrain from acts of righteousness."

Probably the most noted historical figure that ever practiced fasting as a life style was Mahatma Gandhi. He used to fast every Sunday and as he became of age, he used fasting as a political tool (Satyagrah) in order to drive the British away from Indian soil and bring unity among Muslims and Hindus.

It's important to remember that when digesting food, your body uses most of its energy to process the nutrients that are in the food. This is why after a large meal people often feel sluggish and fatigued. During a fast, your body can take a break from this process and can more easily fight infection and can then help the body purge toxins that have been stored up in the cells over time. When I was 23, I had several health problems that I was struggling with. The first was my weight. I was about 15 pounds too heavy for my frame and I found it incredibly difficult to go on a diet. Second, I was getting ill quite often and had continuous digestion problems which affected every area of my life. I knew that if I wanted to feel healthy and energetic, I needed a fundamental shift in the way I was feeding my body. It wasn't until I cut my food consumption considerably (by more than 50%) that I began to feel a significant change in my energy levels. I also began fasting one day a week and consumed raw and water rich foods that cleansed my system instead of processed foods that clogged it. As a result, I lost the excess weight in two months and got my health back on track. I also cut down two hours on my nightly sleep and increased my training schedule. So I'm speaking from experience. Fasting and caloric restriction has made a difference for me and I'm sure it will for you as well. And please, don't be afraid of feeling hungry.

New York freelance writer Richard Elixxir, 42, who restricted his diet to 1,200 calories per day for over 20 years, says caloric restriction is easier than it seems as long as it's not approached in a "fundamentalist" manner. "The biggest problem is that most people try it in a way that's not doable in a real-life situation," he says. "You don't have to be a perfectionist; you don't have to hit 100 percent of every nutrient every day." In his yet-to-be-published book, *The Elixxir Program: How to Stay Young, Slim & Healthy*, Elixxir also recommends taking a "day off" every week or two to eat in the old, unrestricted style. "After 20 years of caloric restriction", Elixxir reports, "the benefits are obvious. My blood pressure and cholesterol levels resembles those of a twenty-something and my appearance is considerably younger than average. It's very reinforcing, when you go to a reunion and everyone is amazed because you look so young."

So you don't have to starve yourself in order to enjoy the benefits of caloric restriction and fasting. But you do need to become aware of the fact that you are probably eating more than you really need to. The average person consumes between 2,000 and 2,500 calories per day, when in actuality, our body needs approximately 1,500 calories per day in order to function effectively. Start by cutting down all your meals by 30 percent. If you eat out often than ask the waiter to box half of your dish before he brings it to the table. When you find yourself invited to lunch or dinner, kindly accept the invitation but say that you are on a diet so you won't be eating much. That way, your host won't be offended when you don't clean your plate like everyone else does. Also, make sure you read the nutrition labels on everything you buy. Know how many calories you put into your body.

In addition, start fasting once a month for twenty-four hours and notice how it affects you body. Personally, I fast between 12 o'clock in the afternoon on Sunday until 12 o'clock on Monday. I like to capitalize on the nighttime but I know several people that like to begin their fasts early in the morning. So you need to find the time that's right and comfortable for you. Make sure you drink nothing but water throughout your fast. Avoid food completely. When you feel your stomach growling, be patient with it. Growling and hunger usually last thirty minutes or so and will eventually disappear entirely as you make fasting habitual. Always remember that by fasting, you are not only allowing your body to detoxify, but you are also allowing your digestive system to rest and restore its normal PH level which will make you feel healthy and vital.

Fourth key: watch out for the "Sweetest Poison." Since the beginning of time, dinning has been an effective social lubricant. It is easy to bring people together around a table since everybody has to eat. Plus, eating is fun, and can be a great source of pleasure, especially when talking about sweets. However, many things that taste good in the mouth can turn bitter in the belly; and processed sugar is one of those things.

Most people enjoy sweets. I know I do. I love chocolate, especially M&M's. But behind the innocent, sweet tasting flavor of candy bars and soft drinks hides a substance that has been associated with obesity, tooth decay, diabetes, osteoporosis, bone fractures, calcium deficiency, heart disease, food addictions and eating disorders, neurotransmitter dysfunction, and even violent behavior.

Refined (processed) sugar is a relatively new substance on the market. Our forefathers never attempted to manufacture processed sugar. They used to satisfy their cravings for sweets with honey, sugar canes, and fruit. It wasn't until 500 years ago that we discovered that we could extract sugar from plants and then, by a process of washing, boiling, centrifuging, filtering and drying, refine it even further. That is when refined sugar became a commodity. The only problem was that during the refining process, nearly all of the plant's nutritional elements were lost resulting in an ingredient that was nutritionally insignificant.

Refined sugar can be lethal because it drains the body of precious vitamins and minerals. Sugar consumed every day produces a continuously acidic condition which affects our liver, pancreas, and heart to a different extent. Probably the most significant danger of processed sugar consumption lies in developing insulin resistance, a condition called diabetes type II. Insulin is a hormone that is secreted by groups of cells within the pancreas called Islet cells and is the only hormone that can prevent your blood sugar level from rising to dangerous levels. When the pancreas begins to over produce insulin, our body begins to store sugar in the liver and the muscles. When that happens, the liver cells, fat cells, and muscle cells become sensitive to normal levels of insulin and our body gradually develops resistance to the normal levels of insulin flowing through the blood stream. At its worst, a person suffering from insulin resistance will have to be assisted by either insulin injections or an insulin pump. In other words, diabetes is no fun. People who suffer from diabetes are usually obese. Not only that, they feel lethargic and tired since their body's cells can not access the calories contained in the glucose without the action of insulin.

Tooth decay is another common consequence of consuming refined sugar. In the 1950's, Harvard University did a study funded by the FDA and the American Dental Association to determine which germs were the causes of tooth decay. The study concluded in 1958 and showed that the true cause of tooth decay was white refined sugar. Not brown sugar, not sugar beets, sugar cane, molasses, honey and other sweets but processed sugar cane. Unfortunately, the study has not been publicized. 50 years later, a tooth decay study was conducted by the University of Connecticut Dental School. The UCONN study found that when sucrose was fed to mice, nearly all the mice developed tooth decay. But, when an artificial sweetener of Malto-dextrin was fed to mice, no tooth decay occurred. The conclusion was that it is not sugar but white refined sugar that causes tooth decay. Again, the results of the study have not been publicized. Wonder why? Because refined sugar is a fundamental ingredient for much of the food produced by some of the biggest corporations in the world. It is cheap to make and therefore, has a tremendous return on investment. Plus, it also has addictive qualities. While sugar doesn't have the instantly addictive quality of, say, crack cocaine, recent studies suggest that refined sugar activates opioids, the same brain chemicals that fuel heroin and morphine addiction, with similar results though at a lesser magnitude.

But still, with all the negative effects, we keep consuming refined sugar in alarming quantities. According to the National Soft Drink Association, consumption of soft drinks today is over 600 12-ounce servings (12 oz.) per person per year. Not only that, since the 1960s the industry has increased the single-serving size from a standard 6-½-ounce bottle to a 20- ounce bottle. At movie theaters and at 7-Eleven stores the most popular size is now the 64-ounce "Double Gulp."

My suggestion would be to cut down your consumption of refined sugar. Or even better, eliminate it from your daily diet completely. It's draining your system, and has absolutely no value to someone who wants to experience maximum health and energy. If you do have cravings for sweets (as I somtimes have), simply trade candy bars and cookies for fresh fruit. Also, buy yourself a juicer and substitute soft drinks with natural juices. If you find freshly squeezed juices to be too acidic, then simply add a little mineral water. The juice of one-half grapefruit added to a glass of sparkling water, for example, makes a delicious, refreshing drink. In restaurants, order mineral water and some pieces of fresh lemon or lime. I also suggest you check out *The Pleasure Trap* by Douglas Lisle Ph.D. and Alan Goldhamer D.C., and *The Sugar Busters* by H. Steward if you want to broaden your knowledge about the dangers of sugar and the effect it has on your body.

Fifth key: laugh often and hard. Our culture is much too serious. Or maybe it is that we take ourselves too seriously. We get caught in the success cycle of competing, achieving, striving, finding the perfect mate, making a name for ourselves and trying to be perfect all at the same time. Along the way we tend to forget some of simple joys of life. Joys that cost us nothing, like laughter.

Laughing is something we all love to do. But there's much more to laughter than just pure fun. Laughter is one of the best tools we have against the stress and pressures of modern living. When we laugh, we trigger the release of endorphins, the body's natural painkillers, and produce a general sense of well being. But more important, laughter stimulates our immune system as Dr. Lee Berk and Dr. Stanley Tan of Loma Linda University in California have discovered.

In a fascinating article that was published in the *Humor and Health Journal* back in 1996, Berk and Tan wrote "Research results indicate that, after exposure to humor, there is a general increase in activity within the immune system, including: an increase in the number and activity level of natural killer cells that attack viral infected cells and some types of cancer and tumor cells. An increase in activated T cells (T lymphocytes). There are many T cells that await activation. Laughter appears to tell the immune system to "turn it up a notch." An increase in the antibody IgA (immunoglobulin A), which fights upper respiratory tract insults and infections. An increase in gamma interferon, which tells various components of the immune system to "turn on." An increase in IgB, the immunoglobulin produced in the greatest quantity in body, as well as an increase in Complement 3, which helps antibodies to pierce dysfunctional or infected cells. The increase in both substances was not only present while subjects watched a humor video; there also was a lingering effect that continued to show increased levels the next day."

The results of the study also supported research indicating a general decrease in stress hormones that constrict blood vessels and suppress immune activity. These were shown to decrease in the study group exposed to humor. For example, levels of epinephrine (a.k.a adrenaline) were lower in anticipation of humor and after exposure to humor. Epinephrine levels remained down throughout the experiment. In addition, dopamine charge levels were also decreased. (Dopamine is a neurotransmitter involved in the "fight or flight response" and is associated with elevated blood pressure.) Apparently, this happened because laughing is an aerobic activity that provides a workout for the diaphragm and increases the body's ability to use oxygen and relax.

And there's more scientific evidence. In a study published in the *Journal of Holistic Nursing*, patients were told one-liners after surgery and before painful medication were administered. Those exposed to humor perceived less pain when compared to patients who didn't get a dose of humor as part of their therapy.

But perhaps the most amazing account about the healing virtues of laughter is the story of Norman Cousins. In the mid-1960's, Cousins was diagnosed with Ankylosing Spondylitis (a form of chronic inflammation of the spine and the sacroiliac joints that leads to the breakdown of collagen, the fibrous tissue that binds together the body's cells.) Frustrated with the results of his treatment and almost completely paralyzed, with a few months to live, Cousins ordered himself checked out of the hospital. He moved into a hotel room and began taking extremely high doses of vitamin C while exposing himself to equally high doses of humor.

Slowly, Norman regained use of his limbs. As his condition steadily improved over the following months, he resumed his busy life, eventually returning to work full-time at the *Saturday Review*. But fifteen years later, life would toss Norman another curve ball, this time in the form of a massive coronary.

As he was brought into the hospital on a stretcher following the attack, he sat up and said, "Gentlemen, I want you to know that you're looking at the darnedest healing machine that's ever been wheeled into this hospital." And once again, a laughter squad was brought into the hospital as Norman laughed away at another devastating condition. After recovery, Cousins chronicled his journey in *The Healing Heart: Antidotes to Panic and Helplessness,* (which I highly recommend along with his best-seller *Anatomy of an Illness.*)

Laughter is also therapeutic and can act as catalyst in transforming sadness and grief into happiness. In a June 2000 article that was published in *Psychology Today*, Alison Stein Welner and David Adox shared the following discovery: "Dacher Keltner, Ph.D., associate professor of psychology at the University of California at Berkeley, studied people who had little reason to laugh: people whose spouses had died six months before. Most psychologists consider a period of sadness or anger after such a traumatic event to be normal and healthy, and negative emotions after the death of a spouse to be pathological. But Keltner- who was struck by how little academic literature focuses on the quirks and patterns of positive human emotions- wasn't so sure. He interviewed mourners and noted their tendency to laugh or smile through their sadness just weeks after a loved one's death. He then discovered that those who had displayed more positive emotions showed less depression and anxiety two to four years later. Keltner now speculates that humor can transform the sadness of a tragedy. 'Laughter is a healthy mechanism; it allows you to disassociate yourself from the event so you can engage in more healthful and social emotions.' But, he adds, the power of laughter needs to be fully examined by positive psychology researchers. "

"Laughter is a form of internal jogging. It moves your internal organs around. It enhances respiration. It is an igniter of great expectations"

~ Norman Cousin ~

As we grow older, we tend to laugh less and less. Maybe this is because of the intense friction of modern living or maybe it's because our dreams have been shattered far too many times but there is no doubt that among adults, laughter is considered childish and naive behavior. In fact, adults who laugh often tend to be viewed as juvenile and irresponsible since they don't seem to understand how serious and tragic life is really is. But I find that ridiculous. Life is not tragic. And it's is not a stand up comedy act either. If you look around you'll find both sorrow and happiness coexisting simultaneously. It's just a question of what you want to experience. Just as an old Jewish saying goes, "If you can't find anything funny to laugh about, you will soon find something sad to cry about." It all depends on what you choose to focus on.

I believe that laughter is what keeps us young. It is probably the purest form of communicating joy. It is universal. It brings people together and is understood in every language. But perhaps the biggest benefit of laughter (unlike drugs, alcohol or any other mood altering substance) is that it is free and has no known negative side effects. All you need are a few childhood friends to kickback with and revive some nostalgic moments from the old neighborhood or watch a Ben Stiller movie. That's about it.

So here's my suggestion regarding laughter. First, schedule it and make it a consistent part of your life. Second, make a commitment to indulge in gut-wrenching laughter for 30 minutes at least once week. Doesn't really matter how you do it, be it by watching movies, going to stand up comedy, or kicking it with friends. But make sure you do it. And when I say 30 minutes, I don't mean giggling or smiling. I mean uncontrollable laughter where your belly trembles so you can hardly breathe and your facial muscles are about to cramp. And please do it religiously, regardless of what's going on in your life or how seriously other people expect you to behave.

"You know the world is going crazy when the best rapper is a white guy, the best golfer is a black guy, the tallest guy in the NBA is Chinese, the Swiss hold the America's Cup, France

is accusing the U.S. of arrogance, Germany doesn't want to go to war, and the three most powerful men in America are named 'Bush', 'Dick', and 'Colon.' Need I say more? "

~ Chris Rock ~

Sixth key: make health an on going life study. In life, there are several matters that you should never put solely in the hands of experts, Gurus, or any other authority figure. Those are your spirituality, your finances, your relationships and your health. In our society, the issue of health is still engulfed in a cloud of mystery and vagueness. Many people, including myself at one point, tend to believe that health and nutrition are complex issues and one can only speak about them after years of laborious schooling. But that's ridiculous. If we look at the dieting market today, we will find hundreds of diets which in many cases contradict each other, all endorsed by prominent doctors. One doctor says "eat this and you'll live forever," and the other one says "eat that and you'll die young." So how do you determine what's good for you? How do you know the right diet, the right vitamins, what's good for you, what's bad for, and in what amounts? Very simple. You read about it, learn, and then give it a try, and then you judge by results. That's the ultimate test for anything. Does it get you the results you want or doesn't it? Results determine whether a medication is appropriate for you or whether a certain diet is good for you or not. Now, when I say you should make health an ongoing life study, I'm not saying you should learn how to perform your own root canal or open heart surgery. But I am appealing to your sense of logic in realizing that no one spends more time with your body than you. No machine, no ultrasound, and no E.K.G can sense your body better than you. Plus, I assume you can't hire a full time physician (or maybe you can) that will keep your body in check and make sure you are taking care of yourself. That is why you must take charge by consistently monitoring your blood pressure, cholesterol count, your diet, and your training schedule. It will probably involve all those things.

Another important reason why you must make health an ongoing study is the fact that throughout your life your body will constantly change due to the friction of everyday living. Your physical capabilities will change, the structure and texture of your skin will change, the sound of your voice will change, the efficiency of your liver and the rate your heart beats will change, and you must learn to respect that and adjust your life style accordingly. Your body has different needs at thirty than it does at sixty. And there's nothing wrong with that as long as you are aware of the differences and have enough knowledge in order to take purposeful action.

There's another benefit to studying health, nutrition, physiological and development, blood structure and exercise methodologies. By keeping health on your daily or even weekly agenda, you keep health at the top of your awareness. For example, when I was working on this chapter, I was compelled to recommit to a new training and diet program in order to fine tune my physical performance. I had made a commitment to run my first marathon and that involved changing my diet and my training regimen, and eliminating some important ingredients from my diet. Would I have taken the time to focus on my health during the hustle and bustle of everyday life? Maybe, but not likely. By taking the time to research health and nutrition, I focused my attention on what's good for me and adjusted my life style and diet accordingly. And that's exactly what you should do as well.

The six keys I just shared with you are a result of my own experimentation with many different health habits. Obviously, there is much more you can do to increase your energy levels, but I wanted to give you some foundational building blocks that would help you set design your own health philosophy. Don't be satisfied with the material in this chapter. Keep learning, keep reading, and keep striving until your body becomes a masterpiece you feel proud of.

Take my six keys and put them to the test. Try to live by them for at least one month and then make a few notes of how you feel. Make sure to check your weight as well. I promise you'll like what you see. But whatever you do, please don't say "I'll try it out later," or "now is not a good a time." *Now* is the perfect time to increase your energy levels and "later" is not even on the calendar. Just imagine how you would feel a month from now having actually followed the keys we learned in this chapter. What if at lunch tomorrow instead of a steak or a hamburger, you would have a fresh salad? What if in the morning instead of coffee you would have a glass of freshly squeezed orange juice? What if you gave your body the treatment it deserves, which is the very best, and you did it day in and day out for an entire year? How would you feel then?

Energy is power. It is the fuel that allows us to operate and perform at our best. And in today's world, it is what gives someone the competitive edge, be it a superstar athlete who must keep in top form, a screenwriter who constantly has to come up with new ides, a salesman who wants to increase the amount of prospects he visits in a day, an actor who wants to perform at his very best, or a university professor who wants to take on a few new classes or write a new book. Stick to the principles we covered in this chapter and I guarantee you'll experience more energy and vitality than you ever dreamed of.

I'm sure you'll take my health challenge seriously. But I want to challenge you even further. That's why, in the next chapter we are going to discover how to…

Chapter XII

Fine Tuning the Ultimate Machine

"It is a disgrace for a man to grow old without seeing the beauty and the strength of which his body is capable"

~ Xenophon ~

The Ironman is the ultimate test of endurance. It's a 2.4-mile swim, a 112-mile bike ride, and a 26.2-mile run, all raced end-to-end in one grueling day. Sounds larger than life, doesn't it?

Every year, these awesome events attract athletes of all ages and backgrounds, some competing for time and others just for a chance to finish. Among the finishers you can find school teachers, engineers, students, firemen, businessmen, nurses, retired army veterans, government officials, professional athletes and even handicapped athletes. In order to earn the title of "Ironman," competitors must finish the race in less than seventeen hours otherwise they are disqualified.

I think you would agree that regardless of training or past experience, completing an Ironman is an awesome task. But can you imagine completing it while carrying another person with you?

Dick and Rick Hoyt are a father-and-son team that competed in their first Ironman in 1999. They finished the punishing course in just over fourteen hours, more than eight hours behind the winner, Luc Van Lierde. But to team Hoyt, time was irrelevant. To them, the completing the Ironman was just another victory, one in a long succession of uphill battles against disability, prejudice, exclusion and self limitation.

When Rick was born in 1962, the umbilical cord twisted around his neck and cut off the oxygen supply to his brain. As a result, he became a spastic quadriplegic, cerebral palsied, non-speaking person. The doctors told the Hoyt's that Rick would amount to nothing more than a vegetable and that they should put him in an institution. Fortunately, the Hoyt's ignored the doctors.

The Hoyt's were determined to raise Rick to be as normal as possible. Even though his body was disabled, his mind was strong and sharp which gave them much hope. They taught him the alphabet and when he was ten-years-old, they commissioned a group of engineers from Tufts University to build an interactive computer that would allow Rick to write out his thoughts using the slight head-movements that he could manage.

When Rick was thirteen, he was finally admitted to public school. Two years later, he wanted to participate in a five-mile benefit run for a local lacrosse player who had been paralyzed in an accident. He asked his dad to push him in his wheelchair. Dick, far from being a long-distance runner, agreed, not really knowing his life was about to change forever.

"I don't feel handicapped when we are competing"

~ Rick Hoyt ~

When Dick runs, he pushes Rick in a modified wheelchair. When Dick cycles, Rick is in the seat-pod from his wheelchair, attached to the front of the bike. And when Dick swims, Rick is attached to him in a small but firmly stabilized boat. This formula has allowed the Hoyt's to race in more than 940 races including 6 Ironman competitions and 62 marathons. Once, they even biked and ran across the country, an achievement that took 45 days to complete.

Unsurprisingly, the Hoyt's have never won a race. They have never set a course record or stood on the winner's podium. But they never lost a race either, because for them, racing is an internal victory. It's a way of conquering self limitation and participating in life just like everyone else.

The first time I saw Dick and Rick was during a late-night television coverage of the Hawaii Ironman. I remember staring at the tube, awe struck. At that point in my life, I was twenty five pounds over weight and could barely run three miles. Watching Dick and Rick run really got my blood boiling. I've been a competitive tennis player for more than sixteen years. I even played professionally for several years. I've always took great pride in my physiology and enjoyed working out and looking sharp. But when my tennis days were over, I found it harder and harder to get myself to workout consistently. In the past, I trained with a goal and a purpose. But now, without a competitive goal, I had no real motivation or drive to break a sweat. As a result, within six months, I gained twenty five pounds.

Watching the Hoyt's run reminded me how far I've let my physical condition deteriorate. It was also then that I realized that training and working out was not about looking good or losing weight. It was not about trophies or popularity either. It was about the internal victory; living up to your own standards and challenging yourself to be your best.

I'm sharing the Hoyt's story with you not because I want you to finish an Ironman or run across the country, but because I think it's an inspiring story that can motivate even the laziest among us to get off the sofa and run a few miles a day. And that's exactly what I'm going to ask you to do a little more often from now on: Move a little more, walk a little more, swim a little more and bike a little more.

Keep in mind that this chapter is not about running marathons or setting world records. It's about taking your body, your health and your energy levels to the next level by making physical activity an essential part of your everyday life. I'm going to show you how, by working-out intelligently and consistently, you'll be able to take charge of your physique and determine how you'll look and feel on a daily basis. We'll explore several key distinctions and strategies that will help you to work out in a way that's fun, energizing and healthy. Plus, you'll learn how to tone your body, improve your endurance and strength and lose those last ten pounds around your waist once and for all.

Whether you are eight or eighty, a couch potato or a seasoned athlete trying to improve PR's (personal records), the strategies I'm going to share with you will help you out immensely because they are health oriented rather than fitness oriented. My goal is not for you to have bulging muscles and PR's that qualify for the Olympics (although I don't mind taking credit in case you do) but for you to experience maximum health and energy and really learn to enjoy your body and feel alive every minute of every day because that's what I believe you deserve. Wouldn't you agree?

"I think the real race we're involved in here is the human race. The important thing is not whether you win in San Jose on Saturday, but the process you're going through as an individual- how you develop as a human being."

~Colleen Cannon ~

Now, I know you are an intelligent and self-conscious person that already knows that working out affects practically every aspect of your life, from your ability to fend off disease and reduce stress to digesting and processing oxygen. That's why I'm not going to waste time selling you on the benefits of physical activity. But, as a starting point, I want us to explore why, even though we all know how beneficial working-out is, very few of us do it consistently (the CDC estimates that only about 32% of us take part in daily activities that increase breathing and heart rate for more than twenty minutes.)

The first reason most people do not work out consistently is that they do not clearly identify their goals. People start work-out programs for many reasons. They want to lose weight, look better, get in better shape, participate in the corporate annual marathon, represent their civic group, inspire their family, fit in their high-school jeans, feel better, or they might do it just out of plain boredom. The challenge with these goals is the fact that they are not specific enough to keep you committed for the long haul. They are great for inspiration and wishful thinking but when it comes to physical training, you have to stick to the numbers. Specific goals might be:

1) Burn off 25 pounds of fat (not water content or muscle.)

2) Hit a target weight of 165 pounds.

3) Lose 3 inches off my waist.

4) Stabilize my cholesterol count and stay in the lower ranges consistently.

5) Run 6 miles under an hour an a half three times a week

6) Swim once a week for 45 minutes

Health and energy, like your personal finances, are a matter of specific numbers. That's because numbers are fixed indicators that allow you to measure your progress. Without specific measurement it's very hard to tell how you are doing and whether you are making real progress.

The second reason many of us do not stick to workout programs is the "no pain-no gain" fallacy. Many people believe that the only way to get in shape and lose weight is through painful and exahustive workouts. They hop on the treadmill, crank it up to maximum speed, and stay on it until our heart threatens to explode. This strategy might be good for improving your ability to escape a robbery scene or a hungry tiger but from a medical standpoint, it just traumatizes your body.People who exercise this way reach frustration quickly because they miss out on the main benefits of working out: burning fat, raising energy levels, and having fun.

There is absolutely no reason for health oriented oxygen based workouts to be painful. In fact, the opposite is true. When you train in the zone (which we will talk about shortly) your body releases endorphins which are morphine like substances that are effective in reducing stress and reliving pain. Once endorphins are released, you brain practically swims in morphine and you feel invincible. That's what the "runner's high," a euphoric, calm and clear state of physical and mental elation, is all about. The distinctions and strategies I'll share with you will show you how to hit the runner's high on each and every workout. There's no great mystery to it. It's just intelligent training based on understanding how your body produces and burns energy.

The third reason people don't workout consistently has to do with lousy prioritizing. Committing to a workout program demands time. Not a whole lot of time, but if you can't set aside three to five hours a week for working-out, you shouldn't start a workout program. We all have to struggle with the inevitabilities of life, those unexpected events that just seem to happen out of the blue. For example, when your boss wants you to stay overtime or when your spouse gets sick suddenly or when a distant relative decides to drop by on a moments notice, you have to adjust your schedule. That's understandable. But you can't allow such events to dominate your life. If you missed a workout yesterday, that's not a big deal. Just get up an hour earlier today and do your thing. When the weather is bad, there are plenty of indoor facilities where you can workout free of charge. I once ran up and down a hotel corridor because there was a blizzard outside. I got a lot of weird stares from the other guests but I didn't care as long as I stayed committed to my program. There is always a way to keep your priorities alive even if it demands a little effort on your part. It's absolutely essential that you make time for your workouts in advance; otherwise, you'll most likely go off track.

"Those who think they have not time for bodily exercise will sooner or later have to find time for illness"

~ Edward Robert Bulwer ~

Understanding Energy

Whether it's during a 26 mile marathon run or one explosive movement like a tennis serve, your body is powered by one and only one compound - ATP (adenosine triphosphate). ATP is a molecule that stores and releases energy for work within your body. It's the energy currency of your cells. Without it, the organs of your body cannot function.

Your body must replace ATP on an ongoing basis in order to provide you with continuous energy. And it does so by using two distinct energy producing systems. Understanding the difference between the systems is the primary key for unleashing your body's potential for endurance, vitality, health, strength, and of course, burning fat.

Your body can produce energy either by burning sugar (the anaerobic system) or by burning fat (aerobic system). **The sugar burning system** is designed to fuel your fight-or-flight responses. It's an emergency system designed to provide quick energy bursts in case of urgent situations where your life or someone else's may be at risk. This system creates energy by breaking down carbohydrates (stored sugar) in order to form ATP without the presence of oxygen. **The fat-burning system**, on the other hand, is more relaxed and provides slow burning fuel. It relies on oxygen to be delivered to muscle cells in sufficient quantities to allow the cells to burn fat and create ATP.

Whenever you workout, your body will use the system that is most appropriate for the intensity of the workout you're involved in. Your body can burn either sugar or fat. Does it matter which one your body burns? You bet. Stu Mittleman, author of *Slow Burn*, believes that "while your body can burn either fuel, it is far better off burning fat. Fat is the body's fuel of choice. Fat, not sugar, is our most inexhaustible and healthful energy resource." Even though our sugar-based energy system is very effective in providing strong bursts of energy for short periods of time, it is highly taxing on the body. Here's why. Our body stores approximately 160,000 calories at any given time. Of those, only 2,500 calories come from sugar while 23,000 come from protein and 134,500 come from fat. In addition to being a scarce resource in our body, sugar based energy is very stressful to produce and it leaves toxic by-products such as lactic acid. Ever tried to burn a lollypop? In case you haven't, a lollypop turns into dark slime when burned. It also lets off a rancid odor. Definitely not something you would want churning around inside your body.

When most of us workout, we do it too fast, too soon and too hard. We go out for a run or a swim or a bike ride without warming up, we hit maximum speed after several minutes and we try to maintain it for as long as we can. This forces our body to tap into its emergency sugar stores to provide us with energy. When our sugar levels decline rapidly, our body lets us know about it by making us feel dizzy and lightheaded. Most of us interpret these warnings as signs that our body is running low on energy and needs more fuel. But what really happens is that our emergency fuel supply is about to be depleted and won't be able to support us for much longer. What do most of us do in this situation? We grab a candy bar or a sugary drink in order to get instant energy. But as we learned in chapter 9, consuming sweets causes our blood sugar levels to shoot up quickly and then fall just as fast. This leads to system instability and sugar cravings because our body has a natural inclination to replenish its emergency energy supply.

It's always important to remember that our sugar based energy system is designed to provide our body energy in case of emergency. It's not designed to burn fat or to enhance our cardiovascular performance. In fact, when we rely on this system for energy, we put our body under stress and make it vulnerable to injuries, colds and allergies. I'm not saying you can't get results or lose weight by working-out this way. You can. But it's a painful and unintelligent way of doing so.

When you train your body to burn fat, you promote health throughout your body. For a start, burning fat does not support lactic acid build-up in your muscles. Second, burning fat increases the size and number of mitochondria, which are the actual organelles that burn the fat and produce ATP. Thirdly, Fat-burning also increases insulin sensitivity which reduces the high insulin production and promotes healthy blood pressure levels. Lastly, training your body to burn fat strengths your heart and lowers your resting heart rate. During a Fat-burning aerobic workout, the entire cardiovascular system, which includes the heart, lungs and blood vessels, responds to moderately increased levels of physical activity by increasing the oxygen that is available to your body's working muscles. And since your heart is a muscle, it gradually learns to process oxygen more efficiently and with greater ease.

Oprah Winfrey is probably one of the best advocates for the potential of Fat-burning aerobic workouts. For years, she struggled with her weight, going from as low as 145 to as high as 237. With determination to fit back into her old high school jeans, she tried every possible diet on the market and was fiercely committed a hundred percent every time. She also worked out on occasion, but was unaware of the distinction between burning fat and burning sugar. Consequently, every time she did manage to lose weight, she gained it all back within several months. It wasn't until her collaboration with personal trainer Bob Greene, who transformed her lifestyle completely, that Oprah finally took charge of her physiology and experienced vitality and power on a daily basis.

What was the transformational key? You got it, Fat-burning workouts. And a lot of them. In the beginning, the workouts seemed much too easy and unchallenging to produce any significant results and Oprah considered parting ways with Greene. But after a month of working out almost every day, results began to show. Oprah's body was slowly becoming a Fat-burning machine. Within two years of working with Greene, she went from weighing 237 pounds and having blood pressure of 180/90 to weighing 147 pounds and having her blood pressure at 110/70. Impressive results. But even more impressive is her completion of the Marine Corps marathon.

Since her collaboration with Greene, Oprah has successfully maintained her weight and blood pressure levels and she works out regularly. Could she have gotten the same results by working out anaerobically? Not likely. She tried to do so in the past but to no avail. With her hectic lifestyle, she needed to workout in a way that energized and revitalized her body rather than causing fatigue and pain. And for that purpose, Fat-burning workouts fitted perfectly.

"Our growing softness, our increasing lack of physical fitness, is a menace to our security"

~John F. Kennedy~

Running is my first choice when it comes to Fat-burning

workouts. Running comes very naturally to me and is far more comfortable than biking or swimming. For our purposes, it doesn't matter what your preferred workout method is, be it running, the Stairmaster at the local gym, or cross country skiing up and down Snowball valley. As long as you have a preferred exercise method that works your entire cardiovascular system, you can easily train your body to burn fat. For simplicity's sake, I'll be using running as a default choice.

Let Your Heart Be Your Guide

Your heart is the most important muscle in your body. In a single day, it beats an average of 100,000 times and pumps more than 4,300 gallons of blood throughout your entire body. Pretty amazing little muscle, wouldn't you say? If your heart were to miss just one beat you would be in serious trouble. In fact, heart disease is the leading cause of premature death in our society. This means we have to take good care of the little guy if we want to enjoy the rest of our lives.

When you workout, it's important you let your heart guide you- not a timer or a finish line. It's easy to hop on a treadmill and let it dictate the pace but there is no way for the treadmill to know how you are doing from within. We all have different bodies and distinct physiologies therefore we need individualized workouts that fit our own stature and level of fitness. That's why the guidance has to come from the inside.

Please meet your new friend, and training buddy: the heart rate monitor. Race cars have speedometers and r.p.m. gauges that measure and estimate performance, and we have the heart rate monitor. No, a stop watch won't do. Not even a fancy one. We are not interested in how fast you can cross the finish line. We want to know how your heart is doing at any point in time throughout your workout so we can adjust and stay in the Fat-burning zone. That's what a heart rate monitor is for. A heart rate monitor is what distinguishes an amateur athlete who trains by gut instincts and seldom improves, and a serious athlete who really cares for performance and wants to see measured results. Again, it doesn't matter if you are a competitive athlete or not. If you want to be measured by how you look and feel, you need to take your workout seriously and get a heart rate monitor. Using a heart rate monitor has several important benefits:

- **Safety.** The heart rate is a gauge by which to assess the intensity of your workout to make sure you're not over exerting or overextending yourself. For example, if your heart rate is above your working heart rate range, it's telling you to slow down a little and use fewer arm movements.

- **Effectiveness.** If your heart rate indicates you're not working hard enough, then you can work out a little more vigorously to maximize the effectiveness of your workout.

- **Incentive.** By monitoring your heart rate from week to week as you participate in an aerobic activity, you'll discover that you will be able to exercise at a higher level of intensity, but at the same or lower heart rate. This is the way the heart tells you it is becoming stronger and more efficient. When you see positive results, it will motivate you to strive for even better results.

- **Easy to use**. Most heart monitors have a wrist band display and very few buttons. Others, (like the HEARTalker model which does not have wrist a display) have ear phones that let you listen to your heart rate and get coached through workout. Some fancy watches even come with a calorie monitor and a thermometer.

Using a heart rate monitor literally changed the way I work-out. In the past, I used to workout with no particular aim or purpose. If I felt motivated, I'd work out. If I didn't, I didn't. The heart rate monitor left me with no excuses and allowed me to workout in a challenging way where I could see and feel immediate results. I'm positive it will do the same for you.

So go on, go on-line and get your self a heart rate monitor. It's the best investment you can possibly make for your future health. You should be able to find a trustworthy brand for no more than $60.00. Personally, I've been using a Polar A3 model for quite some time now and it has been serving me faithfully. Other brands you can check out are Fila, Sports Instruments, Acumen, and CardioWatch.

Training in the Zone

Fat-burning workouts are significantly slower and longer than sugar burning workouts. Where sugar burning workouts may last for as long as 30 minutes, Fat-burning workouts are usually 40 minutes to an hour long. Intensity is also a critical issue. Fat-burning workouts are 20 to 30 percent less intense than sugar burning workouts (Workout intensity is always relative to your age and maximum heart rate, or HRmax.)

In order to train in the FB (Fat-burning) zone, or any zone for this matter, you first need to know your HRmax. You can easily find your HRmax by subtracting your age from 220 (226 for women.) For example, if you are a 30 year-old male, your HRmax would be 220-30=190. Every training zone, be it Fat-burning or anaerobic, has an upper and a lower limit. Those are calculated as partial percentages of your HRmax. For example, your heart rate during the warm up should be between 50 to 60 percent of your HRmax. This means that if your HRmax is 190, then your lower limit should be 95 (190x0.5) and your upper limit should be 114 (190x0.6). The ideal Fat-burning zone, also called the fitness zone, represents 65 to 75 percent of your HRmax. Again, if your HRmax is 190, than your lower limit would be 123(190x0.65) and your upper limit would be 142 (190x0.75). Here are the five primary training zones along with their lower and upper limits.

Warm up Zone - (50 - 60% of HRmax): This is the easiest zone and probably the best for people just starting a fitness program or for those who power walk. It is also used as a warm up for more strenuous workouts. This zone has been shown to help decrease body fat, blood pressure and cholesterol. It also decreases the risk of degenerative diseases and has a low risk of injury. 80% of calories burned in this zone are fats!

Fitness Zone (65 - 75% of HRmax): This zone provides the same benefits as the warm up zone, but is more intense and burns more total calories. This is should be your zone of choice since it maximizes the amount of fat calories your body burns (85%.)

Endurance Zone (75 - 85% of HRmax): The endurance zone will improve your cardiovascular and respiratory system and increase the size and strength of your heart. Once you feel comfortable in the fitness zone, you can gradually slide to the endurance zone. However, only about 50% of the calories your body burns will come from fat.

Anaerobic Zone (85 - 95% of HRmax): We have moved into the sugar burning zone. Here you will improve your VO2 maximum (the highest amount of oxygen you can consume during exercise) and you'll develop higher lactate tolerance ability but only 15 % of the calories you'll burn will come from fat.

Red Line Zone (95 - 100% of HRmax): Most people can only stay in this zone for very short periods. You should only train in this zone if you are training professionally in order to achieve maximum performance in a competitive setting. Training in this zone makes you susceptible to injuries and system shock and must not be done without to supervision of a coach or a physician.

Structure & Simplicity

Fat-burning workouts have very simple and easy to follow structures yet they require discipline. The workouts consist of three interconnected segments that are designed to keep you in the Fat-burning zone (or any other zone for this matter,) for at least 40 minutes. Why so long? Because it takes your body approximately 20 minutes of exercise in order to begin to burn fat efficiently. That means that in a 40 minute workout, what you are really getting is 20 minutes of Fat-burning time.

Stage I:
The first 5-minutes

The first five minutes represent what should be done in the warm up zone. Here, you will perform the activity of your choice at a low pace while breathing unusually deeply. In this zone, you are exercising the lungs and increasing the blood circulation throughout your body. Your heartbeat will begin to pick up as well. The purpose of the warm up is to signal your body to prepare itself for a more demanding activity.

Stage II:
The 40-minute Cruise

In the cruise stage you will reach your fitness zone. This is where you'll reap most of your rewards, both physically and emotionally. When working out in the fitness zone your body exchanges oxygen and carbon dioxide with tremendous efficiency. The cells are getting freshly pumped, oxygenated blood that rejuvenates and invigorates their functioning. Your metabolism increases as well as the functioning of your liver and kidneys. Your brain is receiving oxygen- rich blood, which allows you to feel maximum clarity and awareness.

Stage III:
The last 5-minutes

The last five minutes of the work out represent the cool-down stage. This is the time to slide back to your warm up zone. The cool-down stage is designed to let your internal organs get back to normal functioning with ease and comfort after the rigors of the cruise stage. In this stage you will gradually move from the upper limits of the warm up zone to the lower limit. This will allow your heart-rate and breathing to stabilize until your body comes to a complete halt.

The Nose Knows Best

When we work out, most of us are unaware of our breathing. Nevertheless, breathing correctly is a key function during fat-burning workouts. Our body has two ways of inhaling oxygen: The first is through the mouth and the second is through the nose. John Douillard, the author of *Body, Mind, and Sport : The Mind-Body Guide to Lifelong Health, Fitness, and Your Personal Best* explains that "an analysis of the anatomy of the nose leaves no question that it is the primary breathing apparatus for humans. Inside it is made up of turbinates, or ridges, which act as turbines to swirl the air into a refined stream most suitable for oxygen exchange. The entire passageway is lined with protective mucus-producing membrane, to keep it moist and ward off infection. The mucous membrane works together with small hair-like cilia to clean, filter and prepare the air for maximum oxygenation. The air is warmed, cooled, or moistened, depending on the conditions, by the highly sophisticated design of the nasal passage."

The mouth on the other hand, serves only as an emergency inhalation system. It is primarily designed for eating, not breathing. In fact, we do not even have the voluntary ability to breath through our mouths. It's a learned response triggered by emergencies such as nasal congestion or extreme distress.

When we work out, our heart rate increases and our muscles demand more oxygen. So instinctively, we begin to breathe through mouth in order to let more oxygen in. But is that really what happens?

When we breathe through the mouth, we breathe mainly in the chest. And according to Douillard, "Chest breathing fills the middle and upper portions of the lungs but doesn't efficiently engage the blood-rich lower lobes. Although it is easier to get large quantities of air in and out of the upper and middle lobes, the ample blood supply needed for a quality exchange, especially during oxygen-demanding exercise is in the lower lobes." So it's clearly a case of quantity versus quality. We might get more air in by breathing through the mouth but both breathing and heart rate must be faster.

Douillard points out that kangaroos can run at 35 miles per hour while comfortably breathing through the nose. And so can elks, zebras and horses. Even carnivorous animals such as dogs, lions, cats, and wolves, who must cool the blood supply to their brains by panting, are essentially nose breathers who breathe through the mouth only when they become overheated.

The most important benefit of nasal breathing during workouts is that it promotes diaphragmatic breathing. During diaphragmatic breathing, the diaphragm tightens and flattens out while the lower rib cage expends. This action is extremely important because it pulls air into the lower lobes of the lungs. And since blood supply is gravity dependent, there is far more blood available for oxygen exchange in the lower parts of the lungs.

At first, paying attention to your breathing while you work out seems annoying. At least it did for me in the beginning. But after about two months of doing so, I began to see a measurable difference in my performance. While I still stayed well within the comfort of my training zone, my pace was significantly faster. That meant my body was getting more out of each breath than it used to. And that's our ultimate goal. To absolutely maximize each and every breath you take in, especially during workouts.

But you don't have to pay attention to your breathing. Not long ago, I discovered that as long as I could handle a conversation while I was working out, my nose would naturally take care of my breathing (in order to speak you must exhale, which means no air is coming in through the mouth.) This should be your incentive: to invite a friend to tag along for an afternoon jog.

Mix it Up

When people commit to a long term workout program, they tend to use the same type of physical activity for the entire duration of program. The either run, swim, bike or walk, but they rarely mix things up. Limiting yourself to a single type of physical activity can be redundant and boring. I know it is for me. Running dominates my workout program but I always mix it up with swimming, biking (both on and off road,) rollerblading, and jumping-rope in order to keep my body and mind agile.

There are several important benefits to cross-training that go beyond the need to overcome boredom. The first is injury prevention. Most of the injuries we experience are caused by muscle and joint overuse. By cross training, you significantly reduce the amount of impact your body absorbs.

Second, cross-training lets you rehabilitate quicker. Of course, your immediate goal with any injury is to resume normal training as soon as possible. But if you can't resume normal training immediately, your best option is to adopt a modified training program that allows you to maintain your goals without exacerbating your injury or prolonging the recovery process.

Third, it gives you the chance to enjoy other sports. Endurance is a highly transferable capacity. The strong heart and good lungs that serve you well as a runner or a swimmer could serve you equally well in bicycling, skating, cross-country skiing, and other endurance sports. This gives you a chance to be a little creative and really add variety to your workouts. Use this list as a starting point:

Cross training options
Running
Walking/hiking
Swimming
Biking/ road biking
Trampoline jumping
Mountain climbing
Soccer
Ice/field hocky
Rollerblading
Jump rope
Surfing
Skateboarding
Kayaking\rowing
Dancing
Sailing
Stair stepping
Tennis
Squash
Aerobics

The key thing here is to enjoy your self. Working out shouldn't be something rigorous and painstaking. On the contrary, it should be something that enhances your mind-body relationship and liberates you from the stresses of everyday life. It should also be something that allows you to relate to other people and the choices they make about different types of workout strategies. All in all, it's important to remember that regardless of your choice of workout type, your purpose should always be to be healthy and feel energetic and alive. Which workout can do that for you? That's something you'll have to figure out on your own. I'm suggesting that you let your curiosity guide you because you can never really know what it's like to surf or rollerblade if you've never done it before.

Let's quickly recap the last two chapters. In the previous chapter, we talked extensively about stress and how it affects your body. Then we learned how to let your body rest and recover properly; we talked about the importance of eating raw and water rich foods, we saw how decreasing the amount of calories you consume and fasting can critically improve your metabolism and help you lose fat; we learned about the effects refined sugar has on our system, and we discovered the magical healing power of laughter.

Then, in chapter 10, we explored specific workout strategies that are designed to let you enjoy the multiple benefits of using your aerobic fat-burning system. Here, we learned how our body creates energy, we learned about different workout zones, we understood the importance of letting our hearts lead and guide through our workouts, and we discovered the benefits of nasal breathing and cross training.

If you already work out regularly, then I applaud you and hope the distinctions and strategies we covered will bring you greater results. In case you haven't been working out lately, now would be the perfect time for a new commitment. Remember that I can push you and cajole you all day long but in the end, it's up to you to take charge and do the work. And I truly trust that you will.

Every year, the market is flooded with new literature about better training regimens, better equipment, and even new methods for achieving greater results. I strongly urge you to glance over at the health and fitness section next time your in a bookstore. Also, I hope you'll read *Body, Mind and Sport* by John Douillard, and *Slow Burn* by Stu Mittleman in order to further develop your understanding and achieve even greater results than those we have discussed.

Always remember that your body has unlimited potential for health and energy. And as long as you listen to its needs and treat it with respect and care, you are destined to enjoy power, vitality, energy and passion, literally everyday. I'll sign off this section by wishing you unbounded health and energy and hoping you'll truly discover what the French mean when they say "joie de vivre."

Alright, we are about to begin the last section of *Being Great*. And I'd like to think I saved the best for last. So let's talk about something that at the end of the day, matters more than anything else. Obviously, I'm talking about...

Section V.
Communication & Relationships

Chapter XIII

Relationships:
Traps of Pain or Ties of Pleasure?

"The most effective way to achieve right relations with any living thing is to look for the best in it, and then help that best into the fullest expression"

~ Allen J. Boone ~

The Cookie Thief
by Valerie Cox

A woman was waiting at an airport one night,
With several long hours before her flight.
She hunted for a book in the airport shops.
Bought a bag of cookies and found a place to drop.
She was engrossed in her book but happened to see,
That the man sitting beside her, as bold as could be.
Grabbed a cookie or two from the bag in between,
Which she tried to ignore to avoid a scene.
So she munched the cookies and watched the clock,
As the gutsy cookie thief diminished her stock.
She was getting more irritated as the minutes ticked by,
Thinking, "If I wasn't so nice, I would blacken his eye."
With each cookie she took, he took one too,
When only one was left, she wondered what he would do.
With a smile on his face, and a nervous laugh,

He took the last cookie and broke it in half.
He offered her half, as he ate the other,
She snatched it from him and thought... oooh, brother.
This guy has some nerve and he's also rude,
Why he didn't even show any gratitude!
She had never known when she had been so galled,
And sighed with relief when her flight was called.
She gathered her belongings and headed to the gate,
Refusing to look back at the thieving ingrate.
She boarded the plane, and sank in her seat,
Then she sought her book, which was almost complete.
As she reached in her baggage, she gasped with surprise,
There was her bag of cookies, in front of her eyes.
If mine are here, she moaned in despair,
The others were his, and he tried to share.
Too late to apologize, she realized with grief,
That she was the rude one, the ingrate, the thief.

Did you ever make an assumption about somebody only to discover a little while later that you were completely wrong? Remember how you felt? Pretty embarrassed, right? Trust me, I know first-hand. I can't even count the number of times I've been the cookie thief.

This parable by Valerie Cox represents what in my opinion is the most stimulating, exciting and fun, but also the most challenging, difficult and painful aspect of being a human being. Obviously, I'm talking about relationships. Since we are approaching the end of our journey, I decided that we should focus and explore the subject of human relations because when this area of your life is handled properly, it can be a tremendous source of joy, fun, pleasure, love, and ecstasy. Relationships give life meaning and value. In fact, if you think back to the some of the peak moments of your life, I'm sure you'll find that the presence of other people played a significant role in how you felt. On the other hand, when relationships are handled poorly, they become a source of massive pain and misery. Author Margaret Atwood compared relationship pain to an amputation when she said "you survive it, but there's less of you."

Life seems to go by so quickly with its thousand and one demands that can leave you exhausted as you try to balance work, family, health, leisure, social life and contribution to the community. Among all this activity it can be easy to ignore the significance of the changes and transformations that may be occurring in your relationships. It therefore becomes vital to make time to pay attention to this aspect of your life. In doing so you enrich and deepen your experience of the relationship, you honor the stage you are going through, you affirm the transformations taking place and you celebrate and share this aspect of your lives with others.

It's important to understand that as human beings, we are wired for relationships. It was Dr. Elliot Aronson who recognized the importance of relationships in our lives when he astutely labeled us, "Social animals." He noticed that we live in groups, fight in groups, pray in groups and eat in groups. We even bury our dead in groups. Many sociologists believe that it's our ability to relate to one another, to cooperate and to share, that has allowed us to conquer diseases, build skyscrapers, fly to the moon and come as far as we have as a species.

Several studies have revealed that relationships directly affect our mental and physiological health. In a Yale University study of 194 heart-attack patients, those who reported having emotional support were three times more likely to live six months after their attack than subjects who had no such support. In a different study at Carnegie Mellon University in Pittsburg, researchers rounded up 276 volunteers, dripped cold viruses into their noses, and then quarantined them for five days. Subjects who had a wide range of friends and acquaintances had one-fourth the chance of catching a cold as those whose social networks were minimal. Many studies strongly suggest that the way in which the brain develops is linked to early infant relationships, most often those with the primary care taker. Babies that do not receive proper attention and enough tactile stimulation fail to develop normally and may even die, a condition known as Failure to Thrive syndrome.

"We need others. We need others to love and we need to be loved by them. There is no doubt that without it, we too, like the infant left alone, would cease to grow, cease to develop, choose madness and even death"

~ Leo Buscaglia ~

We as human beings have specific emotional needs that we are trying to fulfill from the moment we are born. We have a need to feel secure and protected. We have a need to know that other people understand and appreciate us. We have a need to be loved and supported and we have a need to grow and contribute. And the only way for us to fulfill these primary emotional needs is by interacting with other people at various levels.

The relationships we develop can be divided into four categories, in accordance to how they fulfill our emotional needs. Family relationships fulfill our need for protection and security, professional relationships fulfill our need to grow and contribute, friendships fulfill our need to belong and be understood and romantic relationships fulfill our need for love and sharing.

Since human relationships are dynamic in nature, some relationships can fulfill more than one group of needs. For example, a husband and a wife may operate a business together and so, they have a business relationship as well as a romantic relationship. Family members can also be friends and even work together and thus, the relationship can fulfill several needs at once.

The important thing to understand about all types of relationships is that they are need-based interactions. What does that mean? It means that relationships are a form of emotional exchange; an unwritten accord between two people (or more) who agree to fulfill each others needs.A healthy relationship is one that fulfills the needs of all parties invovled. When a relationship does not fulfill our needs, it gradually begins to drain our energy and eventually make us miserable.

Healthy relationships are based on the assertion and appreciation of each person's individuality and need for growth. In healthy relationships, partners actively encourage each others' pursuit of personal interests even when that requires taking chances and risking failure. In healthy relationships, partners appreciate differences, thereby giving room for creative self expression. Although partners may look very different on the outside, on the inside their strategies for handling conflicts and problems are similar. In healthy relationships partners don't try to change one another but respect each other's uniqueness. In healthy relationships there's an atmosphere of trust, honesty, mutual respect and fairness that encourages sincere sharing and personal growth. Partners don't lie, deceive or compete with each other. They behave like team-mates or shipmates. Both sides tend to feel emotionally secure and are comfortable enough to show their real self without facades or pretences. And although conflicts may occur, both parties use them as opportunities to learn about the other side instead of an opportunity to win one over.

Through their research, Alicia Fortinberry and her husband, psychologist Bob Murray, identified three distinct characteristics that exist in all healthy relationships, both professional and romantic. They claim that in the past, every tribe, or band, had its taboos, roles and rituals, which enabled members to stay together and survive. And since our brains are still those of hunter-gatherers, the essence of relationship-making is much the same for us modern humans.

The first characteristic they found to exist in all relationships is the clear presence and awareness of rules and boundaries. We all have our own individual rules that determine what needs to happen for us to feel either pain or pleasure. We have rules for the things that need to happen in order for us to feel successful or loved or understood or appreciated. Would you like your colleagues to acknowledge your contribution on a joint project to your supervisor? Do you need your partner to let you know if he's running late? Do you want your date to pay for dinner or share the bill? Relationships are need-based interactions. And it's your responsibility to find out what your partner's rules are if you want to avoid unnecessary friction. It is when the rules are unstated, when we keep others guessing, that relationships become inconvenient and even stressful.

Every relationship also needs clear boundaries for safety and emotional security. Boundaries clarify where one party ends and the other begins, and which problems belong to whom. Relationships expert Dr. Henry Cloud explains that "Just as homeowners set physical property lines around their land, we need to set mental, physical, emotional, and spiritual boundaries for our lives to help us distinguish what is our responsibility and what is not." Each of us has boundaries, some of which go unspoken, in many areas of our lives. We set boundaries in regard to physical proximity and touch, the words that are acceptable when we are spoken to, honesty, emotional intimacy (such as how much we self-disclose to others). When one or both people in a relationship have difficulty with boundaries, the relationship suffers. That's why it's important to be assertive and make your personal boundaries well known and clear. Stand up for them. Make sure your partner knows when he ends and where you begin. Many people have the tendency to allow romantic relationships to dominate and control their lives, thus robbing them of their sense of individuality. Declaring your boundaries will prevent that from happening.

The second characteristic of healthy relationships is clear and identified roles and expectations. In healthy relationships, whether professional or romantic, each person has a clear vision of his roles and responsibilities. The operating dynamics in healthy relationships resemble a basketball or a football team where each person knows his position and is aware of what he is supposed to do. In romantic relationships it means having mutual awareness and respect for emotional needs as well as clear division of responsibility when it comes to cooking, shopping, cleaning, or doing laundry. In professional relationships it means clear division of responsibility for different aspects of a project i.e. John is in charge of information gathering and analysis, Mark is responsible for managing the budget, Michelle is in charge of customer support and Donna takes care of administrative transactions. Roles in relationships define our identity. They tell us who we are to the other person. Expectations determine how we should perform our roles. What does it mean to be a dad? What does it mean to be a manager? What does it mean to be a good friend? Expectations set the standard of behavior. They ultimately determine the quality of the relationship and the direction it is going to go.

When parties do not match expectations, disappointment and friction are inevitable. When parties match expectations and are aware of what it takes to satisfy one another, then the relationship has a good chance of flourishing.

The third characteristic of healthy relationships is rituals. Rituals are the glue that bonds relationships together. They form the sub-culture, the little things we do by mutual agreement in order to signify and enhance our relationships. For example, going out with your friends to a local bar or club every Friday night is a ritual. Going out to a special dinner twice a week with your spouse is a ritual. When I was an undergrad, we had a ritual of going to Busch Gardens right after mid-term and finals. It was something everybody enjoyed and talked about the entire semester. You probably already have rituals in your romantic relationship (the good-bye kiss, the daily phone call from work) but may not realize how important these simple actions are in binding you together. Rituals tend to get lost in hard times, and that's when we need to consciously keep them up, even maybe making up new ones and sticking to them.

"A loving relationship is one in which the loved one is free to be himself — to laugh with me, but never at me; to cry with me, but never because of me; to love life, to love himself, to love being loved. Such a relationship is based upon freedom and can never grow in a jealous heart"

~ Leo Buscaglia ~

There is no doubt that the deepest fulfilment in life comes from romantic relationships. Yet, many of us discover these relationships to be extremely difficult to manage. The media frequently reports that 50% of American marriages will end in divorce. This number appears to have been derived from very skimpy data related to a single county or state. However, it appears to be reasonably close probable. The Americans for Divorce Reform estimates that "Probably, 40 or possibly even 50 percent of marriages will end in divorce."

A recent study by the Creighton University Center for Marriage and Family suggests that time, sex and money pose the three biggest obstacles to satisfaction in the lives of newly married couples. The study found that debt brought into marriage, the couples' financial situation, balancing of jobs and family, and frequency of sexual relations was of greatest concern to those ages 29 and under. Those age 30 and over shared with the younger study group the concerns of balancing job and family and frequency of sexual relations, but also added as problem areas constant bickering and expectations about household tasks.

So what then makes relationships difficult? Relationships are difficult because people are different. We communicate differently. We have different ways of handling stress and different ways of resolving conflicts. Plus, we have different values, different beliefs, different friends and different roles to fulfill in society. Without the ability to communicate and bridge those differences clearly, relationships tend to become toxic.

Scientists have long acknowledged the biological differences between men and women. It turns out that men's and women's brains, for example, are not only different, but the way we use them differs too. Women have larger connections and more frequent interaction between their brain's left and right hemispheres. This accounts for women's ability to have better verbal skills and intuition. Men, on the other hand, have greater brain hemisphere separation, which explains their skills for abstract reasoning and visual-spatial intelligence. Poet Robert Bly describes women's brains as a "superhighway" of connection while men's brains connections are compared to a "little crookedly country road.'"

Different habits of men and women are explained by different roles in the process of evolution. Although life conditions have changed, both men and women tend to follow their biological programs. Men tend to retain a firm sense of direction – they need to trace the game, catch the ball, and find the way home, while women have a better peripheral vision that helps them to see what's happening around the house, to spot an approaching danger, to notice changes in the children's behavior and appearance. Men's brains are programmed to hunting, which explains their narrow range of vision, while women's brains are able to decipher a wider range of information. When entering a room, men tend to look for exits, estimating a possible threat, and ways of escape, while women pay attention to the guests' faces to find out who they are and how they feel. Men are able to sort out information and archive it in their head. Women tend to 'rewind' the information over and over again.

The task that men and women face is to learn to accept their differences, avoid taking their differences as personal attempts to frustrate each other, and to compromise whenever possible. Many people believe that love and physical attraction are enough to sustain a healthy relationship and overcome all those natural differences between men and women, but according to Dr. John Gray, that's far from the truth. In *Men Are From Mars, Women Are From Venus*, he writes: "Falling in love is always magical. It feels eternal, as if love will last forever. We naively believe that somehow we are exempt from the problems our parents had, free from the odds that love will die, assured that it is meant to be and that we are destined to live happily ever after. But as the magic recedes and daily life takes over, it emerges that men continue to expect women to think and react like men, and women expect men to feel and behave like women. Without a clear awareness of our differences, we do not take the time to understand and respect each other. We become demanding, resentful, judgmental, and intolerant. With the best and most loving intentions love continues to die. Somehow the problems creep in. The resentments build. Communication breaks down. Mistrust increases. Rejection and repression result. The magic of love is lost."

"When men and women are able to respect and accept their differences then love has a chance to blossom"

~ John Gray ~

When two or more people are in a relationship, there is bound to be conflict of interests at some point. No two people can see eye to eye on every subject. Therefore, conflict between people is a fact of life – and it's not necessarily a bad thing. In fact, a relationship with frequent conflict may be healthier than one with no observable conflict. Conflicts occur at all levels of interaction – at work, among friends, within families and between relationship partners. When conflict occurs, the relationship may be weakened or strengthened. Thus, conflict is a critical event in the course of a relationship. Conflict can cause resentment, hostility or even rupture the relationship. If it is handled well, however, conflict can be productive – leading to deeper understanding, mutual respect and closeness. Whether or not a relationship is healthy or unhealthy depends not on the number of conflicts between participants, but on how the conflicts are resolved.

Clifford Notarius and Howard Markman have researched couples at various stages of their marriages for over twenty years and they validate this point. In their book, *We Can Work it Out*, they report that contrary to conventional wisdom, personal preferences and character compatibility are not reliable variables in determining relationship success. What ultimately determines whether a relationship will last or crumble, according Notarious and Markman, is how both parties handle differences when they arise. In other words, they found that relationship success depends on the ability of two people to manage the conflicts that inevitably occur in all relationships.

Most people have no interest in creating conflict with others. Most of us know enough about human behavior to distinguish between healthy communication and the words or actions that contribute to rocky relationships. It is in our interest to maintain relations which are smooth, flexible, and mutually enhancing. The problem occurs when we fail to use a cooperative approach in our dealing with others. We seldom create conflict intentionally. We do it because we may not be aware of how our own behavior contributes to interpersonal problems. Sometimes we forget, or we are frustrated and annoyed, and sometimes we just have a bad day. At times we feel so exasperated that we focus on our own needs at the expense of others'. That's when we find ourselves in conflict.

Many people shy away from conflict. They may, for example, feel that they might lose control of their underlying anger if they open the door to conflict. Thus, they may see conflict as an all-or-nothing situation. Either they avoid it altogether or they end up in an all-out combative mode, regardless of the real severity of the conflict. Or they may find it difficult to face conflict because they feel inadequate in general or in the particular relationship. They may have difficulty in positively asserting their views and feelings. Children who grow up surrounded by destructive conflict may choose, as adults, to avoid any kind of discord. In this situation, the person may never have learned that there are effective, adaptive ways to communicate without conflict.

People adopt a number of different styles in facing conflict. First, it is very common to see a person avoid or deny the existence of conflict. This is also known as "withdrawal" or "shut down." Unfortunately, in this case, the conflict often lingers in the background during interaction between the participants and creates the potential for further tension and even more conflict. A second response style is the attack. This occurs when a person mistakenly equates conflict with anger. This stance does nothing to resolve the conflict and in fact only serves to increase the degree of friction between the two participants by amplifying defensiveness and encouraging retaliation. A third way by which some people resolve conflict is to use force and threats to drive the other side into submission. They welcome conflict because it allows their competitive impulses to emerge, but they fail to understand that the conflict is not really resolved since the "loser" will continue to harbor resentment. Similarly, some people appear to compromise in resolving the conflict, but they subtly manipulate the other person in the process, and this again perpetuates the conflict between the two parties and compromises the trust between them.

Whenever we find ourselves in conflict, we must be very careful. If we disregard or minimize the position of the other person, if fear and power are used to win, or if we always have to get our own way, the other person will feel hurt and the relationship may be wounded. Similarly, if we always surrender just to avoid conflict, then we are not protecting our boundaries and we give the message to the other person that it is acceptable for them to be self-serving at our expense and to be insensitive to our needs. Our feeling of self-worth suffers, resentment festers, and we feel poisoned in the relationship.

"Conflict is inevitable, but combat is optional"

~ Max Lucade ~

Conflicts vary in scope and size from minor, unimportant differences to disputes which can threaten the existence of a relationship. Conflicts with a loved one or a long-term friend are, of course, different from negotiating with someone who does not care about your needs, like a stranger or a salesperson. However, there is an underlying principle that underscores all successful conflict resolution. That is, both parties must view their conflict as a problem to be solved mutually rather than a battle so that both can enjoy the feeling victorious. Each person must participate actively in the conflict resolution process and make an effort to find solutions which are as fair as possible to all parties invovled. This is an easy principle to understand, but it is often difficult to put into practice.

By far, the best way to resolve conflicts is by a process of negotiation. Negotiation is an agreed compromise. It is something we do all the time in our social, personal and business life. For example, we use it for deciding on a time to meet, or where to go on a rainy day, or what movie to watch on the weekend. Charles Craver, author of *The Intelligent Negotiator* affirms that "We negotiate our way through life. Everyday we negotiate with family, friends, members of our community, business associates, salespeople, and complete strangers. Still, many of us are uncomfortable with the idea of bargaining. We dread the psychological battle of wills, the exploitive rituals, and the deception it normally entails. We tell ourselves that bargaining is not a normal part of life, even believing that most things in life are not negotiable." Craver hits the nail on the head. In the real world, most negotiations and conflict revolve around the give and take of monetary possessions. But relationships have their own unique currency: emotions. In relationships, especially romantic relationships, parties are emotionally invested. And if there's a breach of trust, or the relationship ruptures, both will suffer.

Negotiating in relationships is considerably different than negotiating in business. While in business we tend to view the other side as the opposition and try to get as much as we can by giving as little as possible, in relationships we must be considerate of the other side's emotions and point of view. It's important to remember that in most conflicts, neither party is right or wrong; instead, different perceptions collide to create disagreement. When interpersonal conflict arises, it usually indicates a missing link in communication—that two people have different pictures of the same situation. And since these pictures do not match, an ensuing argument revolves around whose picture is right. Another instance where conflicts break out is when ones rules or expectations have been violated. On the next page, you'll find five steps that will help you negotiate conflicts calmly and effectively through understanding and mutual agreement.

Step 1:
Defuse the attack and acknowledge the problem

Sometimes people argue about one thing and before they know it, they argue about something totally different that happened six months ago. That's the nature of relationship conflicts. Whenever conflict arises there's usually some anger and resentment involved. The other person might be upset and may come to the situation armed with a number of arguments describing how you are to blame for his or her unhappiness. Your goal is to address the other person's anger by agreeing with them, even if they are dead wrong. Why agree? Because when you acknowledge somebody else's point of view, it is difficult for them to stay angry. For example, "I know that I said I would call you last night. You are absolutely right. I wish I could be more responsible sometimes." The accusation might be completely unreasonable from your viewpoint, but by agreeing, you are communicating that there is some sense of truth to what the other person says. This does not mean that you have to compromise your own basic principles. You simply validate the other person's perceptions so you can move on to a healthier and more conducive position in the resolution process. This may be hard to do in a volatile situation, but a sign of individual strength and integrity is the ability to postpone our immediate reactions in order to achieve positive goals.

Step 2:
Allow feelings to be expressed

Before any kind of problem-solving can take place, emotions such as anger, disappointment, frustration or loss must be expressed and acknowledged. This step is vital in creating an emotionally open atmosphere. It is an important step in the negotiation process and must not be overlooked. By calmly asking the other side to express how they feel, you show that you care for their emotional well being and that you are sincerely interested in avoiding combat and making positive progress.

Step 3:
Determine underlying needs

It's important to remember that the goal of conflict resolution is not to decide which person is right or wrong; the goal is to reach a solution that everyone can live with. Looking for needs first rather than solutions is a powerful step because conflicts arise when someone's needs have been violated. Once the violated needs have been revealed, we can address them directly, apologize if necessary and move on to finding solutions.

Step 4:

Build solutions on common areas of agreement, no matter how small

The key to solving conflicts effectively is finding common areas of agreement and gradually building on them. First, agree on the problem. Second, agree on the procedure to follow. Third, agree on worst case scenario. Fourth, agree on some small change that will gradually lead to success. And fifth, agree on mutual concessions.

Step 5:

Find solutions that satisfy needs on both sides

At the heart of interpersonal conflicts is the assumption that one person must be right, and the other wrong. The problem with this "winner take all" belief is obvious. Here, conflict becomes a matter of two people defending their respective positions without gaining any insight into the opposing party's point of view. Using conflict constructively requires a shift from the perspective that "only one person can be right" toward one of seeking mutual understanding. This perspective acknowledges that both people can be right. By using this as a starting point, conflicts that were previously insurmountable can now actually resolve themselves and relationships can be strengthened. The key to successful relationship negotiation is for both sides to be satisfied with the resolution. Remember that you and your partner are in the same boat, even if you may seem to oppose each other. Therefore, any solution that leaves one side resentful or dissatisfied will end up hurting the relationship long term. You must reach a win-win solution or the ship will sink.

Letting Go

Many times when we are unhappy in a relationship we try to change how we feel by changing our partner. But expecting to become happy because we've placed the responsibility for change on someone else is akin to pushing a string: at best, lots of energy for little or no progress. At worst, an ongoing campaign to "make" someone change can cause friction or even destroy a relationship. The most important change we can make when faced with an unfulfilling relationship is to heal our own need to change the other person in order to make us happy. But what if we do change ourselves and we are still not happy?

Earlier, I implied that every relationship has a life of its own. Some relationships may last a life time and others only a few weeks. When relationships no longer fulfill our needs, we need to be honest about it, acknowledge it, and let go. This is true for romantic relationships, professional relationships and friendships. I'm not saying this is an easy decision. Letting go, saying good bye or terminating a relationship is never easy. But we must remember that a relationship that doesn't nurture who we are and doesn't fulfill our needs will eventually drain our energy and make us miserable. Relationships either grow or decay. When a relationship no longer fulfills the needs it once used to, it is time to let it go. And as hard as it may be, it is a sign of growth and maturity to let go of a decaying relationship in order to make room for a new one that will allow us to grow and develop.

The Secret Ingredient: Unlimited Sharing

There are a few things we must always keep in mind if we want our relationships to thrive. First, we must remember that relationships are a place we go to give, not to get. They are a place we go to share our emotions, experience, dreams and hopes. That's what makes relationships unique and meaningful. It is when we enter relationships in order to *get* something, be it adoration, respect or even love, that we ruin the true meaning and purpose of relationships. You can't take love or get love. You can only give and receive it. Second, we must remember that we can only give what we have inside. If we bring resentment and negativity into a relationship, we can't expect to receive love, care and support. Whatever it is we want in a relationship, we must make certain that we have it, and then give it, first. If you want love, be loving. If you want excitement, be exciting. If you want passion, be passionate. Don't hold back or wait for the other side to make the first step. Be courageous. Take the initiative. Always remember that the purpose of relationships is to share your life.

I truly believe that relationships, the ability to connect with people on a deep human emotional level, are the essence of life. I believe that in my life time, what really matters is not how much money I make or how many things I own but how many people I am able to connect with on a deep emotional level. To me, that's what life is all about. The rest is just details. And I'm not saying this should be your life's purpose, but from my personal experience, if you can't share your life openly with other people and create deep, loving emotional bonds, you are missing the point of living. You really are. Everything in our lives can be replaced expect the existence of other people. Human beings are finite and fragile. We never know when somebody will pass on from our lives or when we will have to say goodbye. Therefore, cherishing every moment and every person we come in contact with, regardless of how different they may be, is of supreme importance.

Remember that in order to enjoy ourselves and feel passion and excitement, we need other people. What's a football game without a crowed? What's a rock concert without an audience? What's a writer without his readers? What's a politician without his voters? What's a CEO without his employees? And what's a government without its citizens?

There's something magical about people relating to one another and connecting on the same level, whether as a family or in the workplace, that generates an indescribable energy. It's something you can't buy. It's like the feeling of being in love. You can't see it with your eyes or touch it with your fingers, but you can feel it vibrating in every cell in your body. That's the power of relationships. Invest in it. Use it. Own it.

The next chapter builds upon the distinctions and strategies we covered in this chapter. In chapter 14, we are going to take a look at some of the best communicators and learn how they use...

Chapter XIV

Influence:
Moving People to Action

"Not only to say the right thing in the right place, but far more difficult, to leave unsaid the wrong thing at the tempting moment"

~ George Sala ~

A long time before man knew how to speak, a band of frogs were traveling through the woods when two of them fell into a deep pit. Mystified, the remaining frogs quickly gathered around the pit. They peered anxiously down, hoping the pit wasn't too deep for their friends to jump back out. But when they saw how deep the pit was, they figured the two frogs were as good as dead. "There's no chance they are coming out of that pit," said the frog with the black dots on his back, and the surrounding frogs nodded in agreement. "Hey", he shouted, "You two better give up right now. There is no way you'll be able to jump out of this pit."

The two frogs ignored the spiteful comments. They tried to jump out of the pit with all of their might, but to no avail. The pit was just too deep. Seeing their persistence, the frogs at the top of the pit became angered and started shouting malicious obscenities.

"We are going to die in this pit," mumbled one of the frogs in frustration and after a short while, he slumped to the ground and died of desperation. He just couldn't take it. But the other frog refused to give up and continued to jump. Strangely enough, it appeared as though the louder the frogs outside the pit shouted, the higher he jumped. Seeing this, the frogs shouted even louder and began to wave their hands, motioning the frog to give up the effort and accept his fate.

Suddenly, as if it was a miracle, the frog jumped so hard that he cleared the pit and landed safely on the ground. "Hey, didn't you hear us?" asked the frog with the black dots on his back in amazement. "I'm sorry but I can't hear you," answered the frog. "I'm deaf. But thanks for the encouragement; I couldn't have made it without you guys."

"It's not about you say, it's about what they hear." This was the first lesson I learned as a public speaker. This maxim is the essence of what it takes to be an effective communicator. But unfortunately, even though it sounds simple, implementing it effectively is a bit more difficult. Let's say you are telling a motivating story. One person gets inspired and energized while another person gets bored out of his mind. You tell a joke and one person laughs till he cries while another remains stony faced. How is this possible? How can the same message affect people so differently?

Let me ask you, were you ever in a situation where you really wanted your communication to be meaningful and to make a difference, but somehow, what you said (or didn't say) went by unnoticed, or even worse, it ended up exploding in your face? Maybe you were trying to cheer up a friend who was depressed but ended up depressing him even more, or maybe it was a new idea you thought would be really good for your department but your boss just didn't seem to care, or maybe you were trying to explain to your spouse why you don't want to go out on Friday but somehow you found yourself arguing about things that happened months and months ago. The reality is that we all have been ignored or misunderstood on occasion. But whether we are trying to influence somebody to buy a car or go out with us on Saturday night, the bottom line is that we all want our communication to have an impact on our listener.

Human communication is very powerful (and so is frog communication, apparently,) because, when used effectively, it has the ability to influence our emotions in many different ways. It can encourage, inspire, empower, entertain, heal, comfort, bore, humiliate, injure, and even terrify. But most of us tend to take this incredible power for granted. All we have to do is open our mouths and the words just seem to fly out. But influential communication is much more than just letting words fly. Bruce Barton once observed that "Every time you open your mouth you let other people look into your mind." That's a clever insight. Burton understood that language, be it written or spoken, is only a medium. It's a coding system we use to translate our thoughts and feelings into sounds, utterances, and characters, so that other people will be able to understand our intentions. The real power is not in the words themselves, but in the experience, stories, lessons, logic and emotion they represent.

Why do we communicate with each other? I know the answer may seem obvious but seriously, take a minute to think about it. Is it to share ideas? To be understood? To empower? To teach? To control? Perhaps. But the ultimate purpose of human communication is to influence other people, to make them do things. The politician wants to make people vote, the actor wants to make people go to the cinema, the teacher wants to make the child learn, the comedian wants to make you laugh, and the salesman wants to make you buy. Many people say they communicate because they want to be understood. But the truth is that you can be understood and still be ignored, right? Think about the last election as an example. Think about the candidate you didn't vote for. Why didn't you? It wasn't because you didn't understand him, was it? Or let's say you have a friend who's using drugs. How would you feel if just after you had a conversation with him about quitting, he went off to score? Would you feel you'd made an impact? Probably not. In fact, my guess is that you'd probably feel disappointed and ignored. Why? Because even though your friend understood you, he didn't take any action. You may have succeeded in making him think about the issue but the reality is that he just kept doing what he always does. In other words, what you said didn't move him.

When we look at the greatest communicators in our culture, be they leaders like Bill Clinton or Nelson Mandela, artists like Michael Jackson or Madonna, actors like Al Pacino and Tom Hanks, talk show hosts like Oprah Winfrey or Dr. Phil, or athletes like Andre Agassi or Tiger Woods, the first thing we notice is that when they speak, people listen. The second thing we notice is that they have a remarkable ability to bond with people from every walk of life. They are able to transcend gender and racial differences and connect with people on a deep emotional level. And lastly, they have an uncanny ability to influence people to make decisions and take action. That's a powerful skill. It doesn't matter what you are trying to achieve, whether it's getting into graduate school or starting your own business, chances are there's somebody out there who can help you. And unless you create a bond and find a way to fill their needs, they're not going to fill yours. That's why we want to learn how to communicate in ways that are attention grabbing, inspiring, influential, moving, and memorable.

In order to be an effective communicator, you must be able to do two things. First, you must be able to develop a rapport with different types of people. A rapport is a way of bonding with your listener on an emotional and intellectual level that's intimate and trusting. You may recognize it as that "in-synch" experience you feel when you are reminiscing about the past with a childhood friend and the conversation seems to flow effortlessly. The second thing you need to know is how to use different motivational elements that encourage your listener to take action.

In essence, these two steps are an empowerment process. And when done properly, your listener will feel stronger, energized, hopeful, and motivated to take action. There are just no words to describe how rewarding it is to see the results of this type of communication because it seems to elevate the human spirit and inspire people to greatness and growth. One of the best examples of the type of communication I'm talking about is John f. Kennedy's famous "Why go to the moon?" address at Rice University back in 1962. In his speech, Kennedy did far more than just answer a question. He made us believe. He made us believe in the space program, he made us believe the efforts were worth it, and he made us commit to the effort. That's what influential communication is all about. Here's a small piece of that address:

> " No man can fully grasp how far and how fast we
> have come, but condense, if you will, the 50,000 years
> of man's recorded history in a time span of but a half a
> century. Stated in these terms, we know very little about
> the first 40 years, except at the end of them advanced
> man had learned to use the skins of animals to cover
> them. Then about 10 years ago, under this standard,
> man emerged from his caves to construct other kinds of
> shelter. Only five years ago man learned to write and
> use a cart with wheels. Christianity began less than
> two years ago. The printing press came this year, and
> then less than two months ago, during this whole 50-
> year span of human history, the steam engine provided
> a new source of power. Newton explored the meaning
> of gravity. Last month electric lights and telephones
> and automobiles and airplanes became available. Only
> last week did we develop penicillin and television and
> nuclear power, and now if America's new spacecraft

succeeds in reaching Venus, we will have literally reached the stars before midnight tonight."

"This is a breathtaking pace, and such a pace cannot help but create new ills as it dispels old, new ignorance, new problems, new dangers. Surely the opening vistas of space promise high costs and hardships, as well as high reward."

"So it is not surprising that some would have us stay where we are a little longer to rest, to wait. But this city of Houston, this State of Texas, this country of the United States was not built by those who waited and rested and wished to look behind them. This country was conquered by those who moved forward—and so will space..."

It's hard to stay indifferent to this formof communication. And sure enough, we didn't. By 1969, we embraced Kennedy's vision and became the first nation to put a human being on the moon.

If you'll notice, the way Kennedy condensed the last 50,000 years into a half a century gave his audience the impression that reaching space was just around the corner, only a few hours away. On top of that, by comparing the space quest to the inventions of the steam engine, penicillin and nuclear power, he made it appear as though reaching the moon was a natural step in the progression of humanity. But Kennedy knew that sophisticated metaphors and analogies were not enough. In order to move his audience to action, Kennedy used the "pain-pleasure" principle in the form of a subtle decision: either commit to the challenge and lead the field (pleasure) or lag behind and let the other nations of the world get to the moon first (pain). This was brilliant from Kennedy since he was well aware of the collective American ego at that time (the cold war years) and Rice University's in particular, which greatly valued winning and leadership. By framing the space quest as a "race" and using competitive terms such as "leading," and "being first," Kennedy stirred the hearts and minds of his listeners. He spoke a language they understood. That's influential communication at its best. Would he have achieved the same effect by comparing the space quest to a hunting expedition? I'm sure he wouldn't have. Because it's not what you say, it's what people hear.

Effective communication is listener oriented. That is, it takes into consideration the listener's beliefs, values and concepts of the world as well as his level of attention and receptivity. Too many times I see people rush into important conversations without setting the stage and checking their listener's level of attention. This is something very basic but sometimes we get so self-centered that we forget to see if the person we want to talk to is prepared to listen. For example, if your boss has just finished yelling at the marketing director, now would probably not be the best time to complain about the parking situation or ask for a raise. If your cousin is crying hysterically and gasping for air because her boyfriend just broke up with her, she won't be able to hear your soothing words and wise advice. Let her calm down first. Get her some water. Wait until she regains her composure and then talk to her. If you are in a crowded or noisy environment with cell-phones going off and people constantly moving around, that may not be the best time for a heart to heart conversation with someone about their drinking habits.

Many times, you may get negative feedback because the person you are communicating with is not responding to you but to an event that happened earlier in the day. He may be anxious, tired, scared or frustrated by things that have absolutely nothing to do with you. That's when paying attention to physical cues may prove invaluable. If you notice your listener is shifting his eyes, dropping his head, tapping his foot or fingers, perspiring, yawning, getting dry mouthed or stressed, then he may be feeling sick or nervous and probably won't be very receptive to your message. That's why you must pay attention.

Timing is everything. Always be considerate and ask "I wanted to talk to you about a few things that are really important to me and I was wondering if now would be a good time to discuss them with you?"

Once, I wanted to consult with one of my professors about an important decision I had to make in my personal life. The problem was that he had an annoying habit of using his office hours in order to prepare himself for his lectures. Whenever I came to his office, he was always rushing the conversation in order to get rid of me. I didn't like that at all. But still, I wanted quality communication because I knew that if he would take the time to listen to my little dilemma, he could give me good advice. So what did I do? I asked. I told him that I have a very important decision to make and that I greatly valued his opinion. Then I said that I would be forever grateful if he could give me thirty minutes of his time to hear my dilemma, outside his office hours. To my surprise, he immediately agreed. We eventually met for lunch the day after and I got to pick his brain for about an hour which was great. But it only happened because I took the time to set the stage.

As I said earlier, there are two things we must do in order to influence people to act. The first is to establish a rapport, and the second is to encourage them to make independent empowering decisions. Let's first focus on how to develop a rapport since most people find this to be particularly challenging.

Rapport is a two way flow of communicated emotions that establishe trust and connectedness. Being able to bond and connect with people quickly is the first ingredient to influential communication. That's because unless people feel you are respectful, sincere and trustworthy, they are going to have their defenses up and are not going to be receptive to your message. In fact, if you don't take the time to bond and build a rapport, they'll probably resent you for being intrusive.

The key to establishing a rapport is realizing that most of us are attracted to the similar and familiar while we stay away

from what's different or unusual. That's just part of our genetic self preservation mechanism. We tend to move toward
things that are like us because unconsciously we presume they
are safe, while we move away from things that appear different from us since we presume they may be harmful. Let me
give you a few examples. Take a look at your friends. If you are
like most people, your friends are usually of your age group.
You probably dress alike, enjoy going out to the same places
and share interests. Think about a person you really like and
notice what makes him appealing. Is it the way he is like you or
unlike you?

On the other hand, how do you feel around people that are
very different than you? How do you feel around people who
do not speak English or eat with their hands? Whom do you
feel closer to, the British or the Koreans? Many people believe
that "opposites attract." Unfortunately, we don't know that's
only one half of the complete phrase. The complete phrase states
that opposites attract, but in the long run they never stay together. How would you feel if every time you wanted to go out,
your spouse wanted to stay home? Do you really want to be
with someone who always disagrees with you and has different interests? Of course not. If you examine any successful relationship between two people you'll discover that initially, they
bonded because they had something in common. Sure, they
may have opposing interests and different ways of doing things
but nevertheless, what brought them together were their com-
monalities.

Do people form on-line communities and social clubs for
people who are different than themselvs? That would be ridiculous. People form communities to share interests or common problems. For example, www.renderocity.com, is a web
community where digital artists can present their work and
exchange tips. Alcoholics Anonymous is a world wide organization that brings together Alcholics who wish to kick the habit.

Do you know what made movies like *Rush-hour, American*

Pie, Shanghai Knights, About a boy, Austin Powers and *Happy Gilmore* into successful comedies? It's the age old comedic formula. Bring together a group of people with opposing personalities and let them solve a problem or overcome a challenge. Do they manage to get along? Hardly. But that's what makes it so funny. It's a paradox. On one hand, they can't stand each other, but on the other, they can't leave each other.

One way to establish a rapport with another person is by discovering things you have in common. This can be almost anything. It can be a similar experience such as bungee jumping or a vacation in Cancun or graduating from college. It can be familiar friends, family members or acquaintances. It can be mundane things such as similar taste in food, music, movies, and clothing brands. And it can be more personal things like beliefs, values, religious persuasion, ethnic background, family heritage, and style of upbringing. The idea here is to become fascinated by what other people can share with you. There's no other way to bring down the barriers and lower the emotional defenses. Remember that most people enjoy talking about themselves but they probably don't do it as often as they would like to. If you can stimulate your listener with questions about their lives and become interested rather than trying to be interesting, you'll be able to build a rapport in no time. If what interests them doesn't interest you, then you need to find out how they became interested in what they do to begin with. In other words, if you don't like long distance running and the person you are communicating with is a veteran marathon runner, find out what got him so enthusiastic about running to begin with.

A few years ago, I sat next to a big-shot mathematician while flying across the country. I recognized his face immediately since there had been a big article about him in the paper just the day before. The article was very interesting and I really wanted to converse with him and ask him a few question. But, I had a tiny problem: I hate math. I find it cold and indifferent. It's not that I'm not good at it; I just don't find it very applicable to my daily life. I like to work with people, not numbers. Nevertheless, I wasn't going to let my personal preferences prevent me from creating rapport and having an interesting conversation.

Looking over, I noticed he was busy jotting numbers down and playing with different equations. I figured he probably didn't want to be disturbed but as the time passed my fascination grew stronger and stronger. I just had to find out how somebody could get so excited about something that appeared to me boring and dull. Finally, I couldn't resist any longer. I turned to him and asked," Excuse me, I saw the article about you in the paper yesterday and since I don't really understand numbers, I was wondering what do you find so fascinating about mathematics?" He smiled, and then began sharing his life story of how when he was just a little kid he became fascinated with solving problems and how he always tried to give things numerical values so he could measure and compare them to one another and decide which one was better and so on. We had a great time. I kept asking questions teasing him about being a nerd and he told me about black holes and time travel. The conversation was definitely an eye opener. And while I didn't understand his profession, I certainly changed my opinion about mathematics. I'm sure you get the point. Fascination will make you a diverse communicator, one who is able to communicate with people on all levels.

Another way to develop a rapport is by disclosing a personal mistake or weakness. Oprah has built a special relationship with the public by sharing her struggles and victories over obesity. She wasn't afraid to expose her weaknesses even though she was a world famous celebrity. By sharing, she appeared real and humane rather than aloof and mysterious like most other celebrities. And because Oprah was willing to share her problems, we gladly share ours with her.

Sharing a personal weakness is an especially powerful way to create a rapport in tense situations. When I was in my senior year in college, I was involved in an experiment in which fresh-men and sophomores had to share a personal experience. They were given a piece of paper on which was a written paragraph describing an argument between a child and his parents. Amaz-ingly, 90 percent of the 370 participants shared a troubling ex-perience they had with their parents. How come? Reciproca-tion. Remember, we are constantly comparing and evaluating ourselves because of our need for self-validation. When we share a personal weakness with another human being, we are prac-tically saying "Here, I'm not perfect. But my heart is open and I trust you not to take advantage of me." And in most cases, because of the need to reciprocate, the listener will disclose a personal weakness in return. That creates a strong sense of trust.

Please remember, that tempting as it may be to try and im-press people by sharing a triumph or an outstanding achieve-ment, you must resist it. While people may be impressed by your success, they'll find it difficult to identify with it. That's because struggle and difficulty are much more common than triumph and victory. Everybody knows what it's like to lose or fail, but not everybody knows what it feels like to win. Besides, flashing your success can make you seem arrogant and un-friendly which only ruins the rapport and minimizes influence.

About two years ago, I was speaking with a group of kids who got involved with drugs and dropped out of high school. Now, those kids were almost down and out. They had fallen behind considerably and lived in environments that were unsupportive of their needs. What do you think would have happened if I would have started my talk by sharing tales about my athletic scholarships, world travels and media appearances? Would that have done anything to build a rapport? Of course not. So how did I begin my talk? Well, while I wasn't a high-school drop out, I did get suspended several times for disrup-tive behavior and had my fair share of problems and clashes with authority figures. So I started with that. Then, I shared a few stories about the mistakes I made, the people I hurt, and the opportunities I missed. That created an immediate bond between us. They started asking questions and getting involved and soon, a conversation that was meant to take no longer than thirty minutes turned into a two-hour, life-changing encounter.

When trying to create a bond, remember to meet people where they are before you take them where you want them to go. If somebody is hurting, start with hurt. If somebody is disappointed, start with disappointment. Communicating mistakes and struggles go a long way in creating instant bonds because they are an integral part of the human experience. Everybody makes mistakes. So when you are trying to create a bond, be real, be honest and don't be afraid to open your heart.

"They may forget what you said, but they will never forget how you made them feel"

~ Carl W. Buechner ~

One of the most important things you need to be aware of while you're engaged in conversation is the frequency with which your partner uses verbs and emotional words. Verbs and emotional words form what is known as **word themes**. Word themes are contextually related verbs and predicates that we use to describe our experiences. For example, many salesmen and lawyers tend to use combative or aggressive terms such as "destroyed," "battle," "maneuvered," "nailed," "confront," "relentless," "take him out," "trapped," "on fire," and so on. Other people may describe their experiences by using sports terms like "score," "he dropped the ball," "he's out," "keep the numbers up," "goal line," touchdown," "all the way to the finish," and "he had his back against the ropes."

Remember what Bruce Barton said? He said "Every time you open your mouth you let other people look into your mind." Word themes do just that. They give us a unique insight into a person's inner world by revealing the patterns and language he understands and is comfortable using. When people use word themes, they are telling you how they would like to be communicated with. If someone is a non-confrontational laid back type of guy who uses passive word themes like "relax," "take it easy," and "there's no rush," and you try to establish a rapport by using bombastic battlefield jargon, you're not going to be very successful. Why? Because you're not using a language style he appreciates. It is one thing to say, "Danny defeated the other player," and another to say, "Danny murdered the other player." Same meaning, but the emotional intensity is different. You can easily drive your listener into a tight corner by using a language style that's too intense or bore him to death by using a style that is too passive. The key here is to use the same word themes that he is using. That's how you guarantee a rapport. By mirroring word themes, you connect with your partner's inner world and make him feel emotionally secure and comfortable.

If you recall, I started this chapter by stating that communication is not about you say, it's about what the other side hears. What this phrase really means is that *you* are responsible for communicating in a way that reaches the other side. If you are trying to influence a child to do one thing and she does something else, then you're responsible because you didn't find a way to get your message through. Mirroring word themes help you do just that: get on the same wavelength as your partner.

"Rapport? You mean like, 'You run as fast as you can, and I'll throw it as far as I can'?"

~ Jeff Kemp ~
(When asked about his rapport with wide receiver Jerry Rice)

The rapport building skills I shared with you so far have

one thing in common: they're communicated through words. And that's the most common way of building a rapport. However, in 1967, a UCLA professor Albert Mehrabian, completed research showing the significance of non-verbal cues in communications. He concluded, in part that, "The combined effect of simultaneous verbal, vocal and facial attitude communications is a weighted sum of their independent effects — with the coefficients of .07, .38, and .55, respectively." What this actually means is that in face-to-face conversation, 38 percent of communication is inflection and tone of voice, 55 percent is facial expression, movement and body language, and only 7 percent is based on what you actually say.

Meharabian's findings help us understand how stand up comedians like Jamie Foxx and Chris Rock can shoot four letter words left and right and make us laugh. Or how talk show hosts like Conan O'Brien can communicate in a seemingly boring manner and still appear viciously funny. Because it's not about what they say, it's about how they say it. It's the physiology, the gestures, the tone of voice and facial expressions that make us laugh.

According to Mehrabian's research, most of us try to create a rapport by talking. That means we are missing out on 93 percent of our ability to communicate commonality to the brain of the other person. The truth is that some of the most effective ways to develop a rapport are actually non-verbal. Take physical appearance for example. Scientists have long known (and proved) that clothing can make a person feel either comfortable or out of place. The way we dress in different situations largely determines how much people will trust and like us.

When I was 22, I was hired as a counselor in a juvenile treatment center. On my first day at work, I wore new dress pants, shining black shoes and a stylish leather coat. Obviously, I wanted to make a good first impression. As I came through the main door, the head counselor spotted me and motioned me to step into his office. "Nice clothes," he said. "Thanks," I replied. Then he added "You know the kids are not going to talk to you looking like this, right? They're going to think you're acting flashy." "What? Why? What's wrong with my clothes?" I answered defensively. "Well," he said, "just think about it. You're dressed like a businessman. Most of the kids here have no more than five T-shirts, a pair of jeans and some old beat-up sneakers. Chances are they've never even seen a jacket like the one you're wearing except on television commercials. How do you expect to develop rapport this way? You're a counselor, remember?" "My God, he is right," I thought to myself. I was about to make a lousy first impression on the kids, one that would be very hard to erase. I jumped in my car, drove home and changed into a pair of khakis and an old T-shirt.

Our appearance also influences how people treat us in the business world. As a sophomore in college, Kevin Hogan, author of *Talk Your Way to the Top*, did an interesting little experiment. He and a friend went to several jewelers dressed in jean jackets, tee-shirts and blue jeans and measured the time it took them to get served. They also asked the value of the most expensive diamond the clerk could take out of the vault without calling the security person. A little while later, Kevin and his friend exchanged the tee-shirt and jeans with coats, ties and dress shoes and visited a few more stores. Guess what happened? When dressed in coats and ties, they got served three times as fast as when they were wearing jeans and tee's. Not only that, the diamonds they were shown were almost five times as expensive.

I'm not telling you how to dress here. There's a time to wear a tie and there's a time to wear an NBA jersey and I'm sure that you're intelligent enough to know when to wear what. The key here is to dress in a way that makes the people you're communicating with feel comfortable. If you insist on making fashion statements, that's fine. But you'll find it hard to develop a rapport with certain people that way. Keep in mind that effective communication begins by considering the comfort of the person you're communicating with. It's a sign of respect and consideration which most people value greatly.

The most powerful way to achieve a rapport with other people is by mirroring their physiology. Words build rapport on a conscious level. Physiology on the other hand, creates rapport on an unconscious level. That's when the brain goes, "I like this person. I don't know what is it exactly about him but I feel he is just like me." When this happens, there's a click, a powerful attraction that neither side can explain but which both can feel.

When mirroring physiology, we match our partner's physiological cues such as voice tonality or body posture. This is not the same as mimicking. Mimicking or impersonating someone by repeating his words back or by exaggerating his tonality would of course, be disrespectful. Mirroring is much more delicate and subtle because we aim to create a sense of synchronization and flow, much like dancing.

What physiological traits could you mirror? Let's start with the voice. You can easily mirror your partner's tempo, tonality, volume and pitch. You don't have to match it perfectly, but if your partner is a fast talker, who tends to swallow vowels and make verbal shortcuts, then by all means, pick up the pace. If your partner has a deep, low voice like Morgan Freeman and he tends to speak rather slowly, then get on his level. Tone down your voice and slow it a little.

Remember that effective mirroring is a lot like tuning in a radio with an analog dial. You need to find the right spot on the dial where the reception is clear and flawless. That's why when somebody doesn't understand us we say he's not on our "wavelength." What else could you mirror? How about facial expressions and eye movements? Certainly. Children rely on non-verbal communication more than adults. They can conduct an entire conversation by nodding their heads and making faces. They don't even need to use words. In your next conversation, pay attention to smiles, frowns, blinking, twitching of the forehead and use of the eyebrows. Remember that people tend to show how they feel through their facial expressions and what they think through words. Can you mirror body posture, hand gestures and movement? Sure. In fact, by sitting, standing or moving like the other person, you create a strong sense of symmetry and unity that considerably strengthens rapport. Breathing pattern is another powerful trait you can easily mirror. When people breathe at the same rate they are usually in synch with each other. If you pay attention, you'll notice that people naturally breathe at the same rate when they are making love or dancing or watching a scary movie.

Know that you don't have to mirror everything about a person in order to create a rapport. Sometimes it's enough just to match voice cues or breathing patterns. The key thing here is to set the stage for meaningful communication by achieving a certain level of comfort, one that's tension free. That's all. And all you really have to do to achieve that is observe, listen carefully and stay flexible.

"Speech is power: speech is to persuade, to convert, to compel. It is to bring another out of his bad sense into your good sense"

~ Ralph Waldo Emerson ~

So now, the stage is set. We have achieved a comfortable level of rapport and are ready to communicate an empowering message that will encourage our listener to move in a particular direction. But how do we do that? Do we threaten? Tell a story? Ask a question?

In order to influence people to take action you must know what motivates them. What drives all human behavior? That's right, emotions. All human behavior, from the criminal to the altruistic, is primarily driven by two basic emotions, either the need the avoid pain or the need to gain pleasure. But in reality, no person is equally driven by both needs. Some of us are driven more by our need to avoid pain and some are driven more by the need gain pleasure. Think about dieting. Some people diet because they want to look great and get noticed while others diet because they don't want to be called names or shop for oversized clothes. Both groups of people want to lose weight but their motivations for doing so are different. Have you ever procrastinated? Who hasn't? I know I sure have. Procrastination is an ineffective way of dealing with things you don't want or don't like to do. Remember finals in college? Did you procrastinate then? Well, why did you? Because at some emotional level, you associated pain with studying for finals. It just wasn't something you wanted to do. So you moved away from it until the pain you associated with failure overcame the pain of studying and you got busy.

Motivation Strategies are internal emotional patterns that we use in order to take action. In essence, motivation strategies are a systematic way in which we use pain and pleasure in order to function in everyday life. There are two primary motivation strategies that we use in order to act. The first is a *moving a way from* strategy and the second is a *moving towards* strategy. People who rely on the moving away from strategy are more driven by the need to avoid pain than they are by the need the gain pleasure. On the other hand, people who use the moving towards strategy are driven primarily by the need to gain pleasure. Getting into relationships because you don't want to be alone is a moving away from strategy. Getting into relationships because you want to feel the thrill and excitement of being in love is a moving towards strategy. How about sports? You would think that college athletes would be motivated by victories and trophies but that's not always the case. Many athletes play college sports because it covers their tuition. That's a moving away from strategy.

Human beings are complex. Everyone moves towards some things and away from others. But throughout our lives, all of us develop a tendency to use one strategy more than the other. Some people are naturally curious and are comfortable taking risks and so move towards things that excite them. Other people may be more cautious and protective. They tend to move away from harmful situations and prepare for a rainy day.

It is nearly impossible to influence people to take action without knowing their motivation strategy. Let's say you're trying to influence a friend to purchase a new computer. How would you do that? Well, you could point out all the great features it has and all the things it can do or you could focus on all the things it doesn't do. You could say that a specific system is great because it can burn CD's, play DVD's, and run the latest games or you could emphasize that it doesn't break down, doesn't make noise, and requires no immediate upgrades. How would you know which strategy to use? That totally depends on your friend's motivation strategy.

Understanding motivation strategies is something that marketing and salespeople figured out a long time ago. They know that "moving towards" people are interested in benefits and "moving away from" people are interested in minimizing potential loss. Therefore, they know that they can promote a product in two ways. They can either advertise what it can do or what it can't. Let's take tooth paste as an example. You could either advertise how your particular brand is great at whitening teeth and fighting cavities or you could emphasize how it prevents bad breath and tooth decay.

Remember, a dime has two different sides, but both have the same value. It's just a matter of which side you prefer, heads or tails. Let's say you'd like to go out with a particular girl on Saturday night. How would you approach her? If she is a moving towards person, you would probably say, "I think that if we go out on Saturday night, we are going to have a blast. We'll have a nice dinner and then we'll catch a movie and it will be great." But what if she is a moving away from person? Then you'd have to say something like "If we don't go out together on Saturday, we are going to miss out on a lot of great things…" I'm sure you get the point.

So how do we find out someone's motivation strategy? You find out what their values are and how they are trying to meet them. You do that by asking: "What's most important to you in life right now?" The answer may be "my family," or "my job" or "my health," or to have "peace of mind." The next question you need to ask is "How are you trying to meet this value?" The answer is either what they are doing to meet their value or what they avoid doing. That's a clear indication of the motivation strategy they are using. Let's say I wanted to influence you to get a new job. I would probably ask, "What do you value most in a job?" If your answer were something like, "I want it to be a good place to grow and develop," or "I want to be compensated really well," then I would know that you are using a moving towards strategy. But if you said something like, "I don't want a place where there's a lot of competition and a lot of pressure to perform," then I would clearly know that you are using a moving away from strategy. Knowing your motivation strategy tells me exactly what you are looking for. And when I know what you're looking for, I can weave it into my message and help you take action towards your value.

Taking the time to find out people's values has two significant benefits. Obviously, we get to learn their motivation strategy. But also, we get to bond and connect with them even more deeply. People tend not to disclose their values to people they neither love nor trust. By asking about values, you show that you care about what's important to the other person. This amplifies what Theodore Roosevelt said a long time ago: "Nobody cares how much you know until they know how much you care." That is absolutely right. Just think about it, when something is troubling you, do you go to see a therapist or do you talk to a friend? Most of us tend to listen to people who know what's important to us. So don't miss this step.

I have four young nephews. Three of them usually move

away from things and one tends to move towards. This can make simultaneous communication with all four a bit challenging at times. Especially when dinner time rolls by and my sister, their mom, wants them to turn the tube off and come to the table. How would you influence all four children to leave the T.V and go to the table? Let's say you decide to influence them by using a moving away from strategy. So you say something like, "If you guys don't come to dinner right at this moment, then you'll lose T.V privileges tomorrow." That's a good moving away from message but it's probably going to influence only three of them. The middle kid, the one who's a moving towards person, just doesn't respond to this type of communication. "I don't care," he'd say, "There's nothing interesting tomorrow on T.V. anyway." This is where my sister usually loses it. She begins to threaten and bully him around. But that doesn't faze him. In fact, he even seems to enjoy the battle. At this point, I usually decide to interfere before the whole situation gets out of hand. So I say to him, "Listen, I really think you should go to eat right now because if you do, you'll get to watch T.V. tomorrow. And that's something you really want, isn't it?" What did I do here? First, I respected something he values. Second, I invited him to do something by rewarding him with more of what he likes. Needless to say he could have gotten smart about it, saying he could watch T.V. anytime he wanted to but he didn't because I didn't threaten him, I invited him. That's extremely important, even to little children. Remember, people of any age will listen when they know you understand what's important to them. When you respect their values and let them make their own decisions, they feel empowered and strong.

Alright, let's stop here. The subject of influential communication is as vast and deep as the Pacific Ocean. I wish I had the book space to talk to you about more strategies and techniques but that's not the essence of our journey. I've given you the essentials. The rest is up to you to discover. If you want more, I recommend you check out books like *Reading People* by Jo-Ellen

Dimitrius, *Influence* by Robert Cialdini and *The Psychology of Persuasion* by Kevin Hogan. These books focus on different communication and persuasion strategies, both verbal and non-verbal which I'm positive you'll find extremely helpful.

We are approaching the end of our journey. We have one more chapter to go and that's it. You've been doing great so far. Let's keep the momentum going. I'll meet you on the next page.

Chapter XV

Living Greatness:
The Ultimate Challenge

"No man is truly great who is great only in his own lifetime. The test of greatness is the pages of history"

~ William Hazlitt ~

Several years ago, I went to see Itzhak Perlman, the violinist, in a concert at New York City. If you have ever been to a Perlman concert, you know that getting on stage is no small achievement for him. Itzhak contracted polio as a child, and so he has braces on both legs and walks with the aid of crutches.

I remember vividly the way he walked slowly across the stage until he reached his chair. Then he sat down, rested his crutches on the floor, undid the clasps on his legs, tucked one foot back and extended the other foot forward. Then he bent down and picked up the violin, placed it under his chin, and nodded to the conductor. All this time, the audience remained reverently silent, patiently waiting to hear the first bars.

But this time, something went wrong. Just as he finished the first few bars, one of the strings on his violin broke. The snap was so loud and sudden that even those sitting in the back rows (where I sat) were taken by surprise. There was no mistaking what that sound meant. The question was what was

Itzhak going to do? I figured he would have to get up, put on the clasps again, pick up his crutches and slowly walk off stage, either to find another violin or find another string for this one. But Itzhak thought otherwise. Instead of getting up, he waited a moment, closed his eyes and then signaled the conductor to start again.

Now, most people in the audience knew that it was nearly impossible to play a complete symphonic piece with just three strings. It just couldn't be done. But that night, Itzhak Perlman cared not for the possible. As the orchestra began to play, Perlman picked up from where he had left off. He played with such passion and power that the music seemed to physically penetrate every person in the audience.He played like a man possessed, as if he was fighting a ravenous grizzly bear. You could see him modulating, changing and re-composing the piece in his head. At one point, it sounded like he was de-tuning the strings to get new sounds from them that they had never made before.

When he finished, there was an eerie silence in the room. You couldn't even hear people breathe. But then, people slowly rose to their feet and an extraordinary outburst of applause broke out from every corner of the auditorium. We were all on our feet, screaming and cheering, doing everything we could to show how much we appreciated what he had done.

He smiled, wiped the sweat from his brow, raised his bow to quiet us, and then he said, not boastfully, but in a quiet, pensive, reverent tone, "You know, sometimes it is the artist's task to find out how much music you can still make with what you have left."

What a powerful statement that is. It has stayed in my mind ever since I heard it. And who knows? Perhaps that is the definition of living, not just for artists but for all of us. Here was a man who has prepared all his life to make music on a violin of four strings, who, all of a sudden, in the middle of a concert, finds himself with only three strings; so he makes music with three strings, and the music he made that night with just three strings was more beautiful, more sacred, more memorable, than any that he had ever made before. So, perhaps our task in this shaky, fast-changing, bewildering world in which we live is to make music, at first with all that we have, and then, when that is no longer possible, to make music with what we have left.

You and I have come a long way together. How much further you'll go from here is your decision. I sincerely hope that the stories, insights, distinctions and tools I shared with you will help you to be who you really want to be and to have what you really want to have. I believe you have plenty of music in you. And I believe the time has come for you to play it live and loud. Not tomorrow, not someday, but right now. Everyday you live can be concert day, if you choose to make it so. Everyday can become an opportunity to grow, inspire, create, innovate and contribute, if you decide to. The message of being great has been simple all along: Do what you can with what you have, all the time. Take action. Live your life fully, every day, every minute. Strive. Play your music hard. Make the world hear it. And don't settle for less than you can be even if on some days, you only have three strings to play with.

"The greatest thing a man can do in this world is to make the most possible out of the stuff that has been given him. This is success, and there is no other"

~ Orison Sweet Marden ~

Before we part ways, let's take a quick look back at all the things we've learned and the people we've met throughout our journey. We started off by talking about the importance of taking action. We then met the four young guys who founded Mirabilis and created I.C.Q. Then we met the greatest baseball player that ever lived, Pete Gray, and we discovered three myths about greatness. Then we had a reality check and learned about the pace of change. We learned about our need for significance and the different ways people go about achieving it. We explored the concept of identity and understood that our identity is only a concept of who think we are. We then crossed the Pacific Ocean with Gerard Daboville and learned about what drives human behavior. We met Jaime Goldman, Candy Lightner, Scott O'Grady, Brenton Butler and Ray Gatchalian and learned that every winner has scars. We discovered that events by themselves have no meaning except the meaning we choose to give them.

We then traveled to Canada and watched Charles Blondin cross the Niagara Falls on a tightrope. We learned about the potency of beliefs and we explored seven empowering beliefs that characterize great people.

In section two, we learned about wealth wounds and the various barriers that prevent people from attracting wealth into their lives. We watched Jonathan Lebed make hundreds of thousands of dollars at the age of 14 and we learned about entrepreneurship and the bucket system.

In section three, we dove into the depths of the human mind as we explored creativity and concepts. We learned that the human mind is a unique pattern making system that organizes and structures information for easy retrieval. We then went on to rescue the princess that locked in the northern tower and we learned about the bulldozer, the tactician and the magician strategies for solving problems.

Section four focused on the battle against stress and the preservation of energy. We joined Elvis in his last moments before he died and we learned about the importance of deep sleep and the impact of processed sugar and cooked foods on our body. We joined Rick and Dick Hoyt in the Ironman and we learned how our body produces energy. We explored different workout styles, training zones, and breathing techniques.

Finally, in section five, we explored relationships and communication. We met a highly optimistic deaf frog and the all too common cookie thief that resides in us all. We learned about the power of relationships and how to resolve conflicts through negotiation. We covered subjects such as motivation strategies, rapport and communication tools that will allow you to influence other people to make decisions and take action.

By now you know that greatness is not something you can buy or achieve or get, it's something you choose by the way you live your life. An extraordinary life doesn't just happen out of the blue. It's something you have to create by taking the initiative and being a doer, by taking action.

In this book, I did my best to show you how other people have chosen to deal with adversity and what they have done in order to turn their lives into a unique creation. Now it's up to you to step up and do the same. I don't expect your life to transform over night. But I hope your mind has. I hope you'll begin to make changes in how you live, how you manage your emotions, how you deal with your finances, how you solve your problems and how you connect with other people. I hope you'll make the commitment to march to your own rhythm and dance to your own music and not become complacent by what you have already achieved.

Greatness is about listening to your internal voice, following your own rules and living up to your own standards and capabilities, instead of those of the people around. Many times, out of our need to belong and connect, we tend to compromise our abilities and settle for mediocrity. We convince ourselves that the results we are getting are good enough just because they're better than the next man's. That's when we have to take an honest look at ourselves and ask "Can I be more? Can I do more? Can I know more? Can I give more? Can I create more?" Great people do not compare or measure themselves against other people. They know that comparison is nothing but mediocrity in disguise. They know that the only true measurement of a human being is whether he is committed to his internal code, his own sense of growth and purpose.

"Greatness lies, not in being strong, but in the right using of strength; and strength is not used rightly when it serves only to carry a man above his fellows for his own solitary glory. He is the greatest whose strength carries up the most hearts by"

~ *Henry Ward Beecher* ~

The final point I want to make is about a subject most people would rather to avoid at all costs: death. It is said that we learn the most about life when we face death. I'm not sure that's true for every person but in my case, a quick brush with death taught me something extremely important about living.

Let me take you back to the summer of 2002. By that time, I had managed to get my life back on track and create a healthy momentum, going forward in my personal and professional life. I was in the middle of preparing for my biggest seminar to date and everything seemed to be flowing smoothly.

I remember that day clearly. It was the day that Lance Armstrong won his fourth Tour de France. I watched him ride to victory and felt really happy for him. In fact, I was so happy and inspired that I decided to fetch my bike and go for a late afternoon ride. The sun was still up so I figured that if I were to ride my regular course (about 30 miles) a little faster than usual; I would be home before sundown and avoid the rush hour. And so, I geared up, loaded my mp3 player and headed out.

That day, the weather was beautiful. The sky was clear and the temperature was in the mid 80's with a slight breeze from the east. The music was pumping loud in my ears and my legs were pounding in perfect rhythm to the music. I felt free and alive. The miles seemed to fly by effortlessly. I remember feeling really lucky for having the time to enjoy myself that way.

About half way through my ride the sun began to set. I didn't pay attention to it at first. But as it got darker and darker and the traffic got heavier, I started to worry. I still had more than half an hour of cycling ahead of me, some of it through a highly populated urban area. So with less then 15-miles to go I decided to pick up the pace.

About 3 weeks earlier, I rode my bike along the exact same route. Back then, I noticed that just before the last overpass, a new road was being completed. It was supposed to run parallel to the main road in order to release the pressure on the main intersection to my town. I figured that by now, the road would have been completed and while it probably didn't have any road marks or lights yet, I could still use it to avoid the heavy traffic. And so, with my head down, legs pounding and lungs burning I made the turn on to the new road.

By now there was hardly any light. The new asphalt road was pitch black and there were no lights or road marks. Just as I thought. I was still going relatively fast because of the momentum I'd built earlier on but I began to feel very uncomfortable with the fact that I couldn't see much of what was going on ahead of me. All of a sudden, the asphalt became rough and bumpy and I felt that something was about to go terribly wrong. I put my fingers on the brakes and before I had the chance to slow down, I saw it. Approximately 20ft down the road, a roll of red barbwire had been stretched out from one side of the road to the other about 4 feet above the ground.

There was no time to think. I slammed the brakes instinctively as hard as I possibly could. Because of the sheer velocity the front wheel got twisted and jammed and the back wheel lifted high in the air as if the bike were trying to do a summersault. I was catapulted forward at about 30mph, in much the same way an unbuckled person flies through the windshield of a car in a head on collision.

The next few moments lasted a life time. Everything seemed to be moving in slow motion, except my thoughts which were racing at the speed of light. "I've ruined the seminar. What will my parents say? I can't make it to dinner with my friends tonight. Why did I even get on the bike?" But deep within the turmoil, I remember a confident voice in my head going, "Don't worry, whatever happens, we are ready." Then an unexplainable calm filled my body. "Just relax and let go," the voice add, "Everything is taken care of." At that point, I was certain I was going to die.

I flew over the barbwire and slammed violently into the asphalt, headfirst. Luckily I was wearing a protective helmet but nevertheless, the blow was overwhelming. I rolled on the ground several times until my body came to halt and then I lost consciousness.

Moments later, I opened my eyes. I was lying flat on my back, eyes starring directly at the moon. I was not dead. But I had an unbelievable headache. I struggled slowly to my knees and noticed it was hard for me to breathe. I was also bleeding from my elbows, my knees and my chin but other than that, everything seemed to be in working order. My bicycle on the other hand was a different story. The front wheel was broken and my rear wheel was violently twisted. I found my MP3 player about 15ft from where I landed. It was broken in three pieces.

Suddenly, for the first time in my life, it dawned on me that I was mortal. My life could have ended right then and there. This was no game, it was real. Death is something I've always acknowledged intellectually but have never internalized emotionally because I always felt invincible. But now, after sensing mortality in every fiber of my being, something in my awareness has changed.

Something very powerful happens when we come to grips with your own mortality. When we truly accept the fact that our life is temporary and that the end could come at any time and any place, we begin to cherish and savor time, our life force, above all else. That's what happens to people who discover that they have a terminal illness. Suddenly, they begin to set goals. They find their passion. They cut the nonsense and make a commitment to live every minute and every second fully because they know the show is not going to last forever. But let's ask ourselves, "Do we really have to be terminally ill to realize that our time here on earth is limited? Do we have to wait for death to be around the corner to remind us how to live?"

The truth is that you don't have to be diagnosed with cancer to find passion and purpose in your life. You don't have to be involved in a car wreck to realize that every day that you live actually brings you one step closer to the end. You can develop awareness for your mortality right here and now, and let it propel you to live the rest of your life fully, without holding back. You can make a decision right here and now that you are going to start searching for purpose and meaning and that you will not stop or slow down until every dream and every aspiration that resides within your soul becomes a living, breathing reality. Nobody stops you from making this decision.

In the unforgettable movie *Braveheart*, Mel Gibson's character, William Wallace, is destined for execution by the British for courageously opposing their occupational rule of Scotland. On the night before the execution, the royal British princess approaches Wallace clandestinely and tries to convince him to confess his sins and swear allegiance to the King so he may spare his life. But William refuses, saying "If I swear to him, then all that I am is dead already." The princess then begins to cry because she realizes that William is ready to die and that by dying, he actually lives his purpose- to be a free man. Wallace looks deep into her eyes, and says "My lady, every man dies, not every man really lives." No truer words were ever spoken.

Death is an enormously powerful teacher. It teaches us, if we are wise, not to wait but to live everyday as if it were our last. It teaches us to get on with what's most important, to find a purpose, and become who we were meant to become. It triggers in us a sense of urgency, to get on with life, to move on and make things happen.

But perhaps death has another powerful lesson to teach us by reminding us that our bodies may perish but our legacy may live on for ages to come. Legacy is the memory we leave behind as we pass away. It is how and what we will be remembered for by generations to come. Think of the legacies of Jesus Christ, Mahatma Gandhi or Socrates. They are ageless. And yours can be too. It is important that we never forget that our legacy in not a measure of how long we lived, but how we lived while we were alive. Were we fearful or courageous? Were we cruel or kind? Were we fair and honest or did we take advantage of the weak and ignorant? Did we realize our growth potential and overcame the hardships or did we give up and settled for mediocrity? Most of us are afraid of death. We'd rather not think about it at all. But when we have the courage to think about the end, when we think about such things as how and what we will be remembered for, we have a unique chance to change and shape our present. I love the story of Alfred Nobel, as related by Randy Alcorn in his book, *The Treasure Principle:*

> *"Alfred Nobel dropped the newspaper and put his head in his hands. It was 1888. Nobel was a Swedish chemist who made his fortune inventing and producing dynamite. His brother Ludvig had died in France. But now Alfred's grief was compounded by dismay. He'd just read an obituary in a French newspaper — not his brother's obituary, but his! An editor had confused the brothers. The headline read, "The Merchant of Death Is Dead." Alfred Nobel's obituary described a man who had gotten rich by helping people kill one another.*
>
> *Shaken by this appraisal of his life, Nobel resolved to use his wealth to change his legacy. When he died eight years later, he left more than $9 million to fund awards for people whose work benefited humanity. The awards became known as the Nobel Prizes.*
>
> *Alfred Nobel had a rare opportunity — to look at the assessment of his life at its end and still have the chance to change it. Before his life was over, Nobel made sure he had invested his wealth in something of lasting value."*

What's your legacy? What do you want to be remembered for? If you were to die today, how would your obituary read? Each of us chooses, either purposefully or passively, how to invest the human currencies of time and talent. The great man invests them in creation and growth, by making couragoues decisions and abolishing fears. The fool waits and hesitates and lets his values slip away, like dripping water from a broken bucket. We don't get a second chance to live. So make this one count. Go and make your mark. Leave no stone unturned and no dream unfulfilled. Live by your own standards and on your own terms. Because when you do, it doesn't matter when death knocks at your door. You'll be ready.

"Somebody should tell us, right at the start of our lives, that we are dying. Then we might live life to the limit, every minute of every day. Do it! I say. Whatever you want to do, do it now! There are only so many tomorrows"

~ Michael Landon ~

Before closing his lectures and seminars, business philosopher and life teacher Jom Rohn encourages his audience to answer four open-ended questions. These questions are very simple but the way you choose to answer them can have profound implications for your life.

The first question is "Why?" Why even try? Why wake up in the morning? Why succeed? Why read? Why learn? Why create? Why climb a mountain? Why reach the moon?

The second question I want to ask you is: "Why not?" Why not see how far you can go, how much you can learn, how many skills you can develop how much money you can earn, how many things you can share, and how many people you can connect with? Why not see all you can see, do all you can do and be all you can be? What are you going to do with the rest of your life? Hang on until the bitter hand?

The third question I want to ask you is "Why not you?" All the remarkable stories I shared with you in this book gave you an insight into how ordinary people achieve extraordinary things. You've learned that you don't have to be Michael Jordan or Bill Gates in order to be great. True success in life comes from making the best out of your own talents and abilities whatever they may be.

So, why not you? Do you lack the drive and motivation? Does your blood run less hot than mine with ambition? I can't buy that. You wouldn't be reading this book if that were true. If you can read, if you can learn, if you can develop the courage to try new things and commit to new disciplines, no challenge can stand in your way. Why not you racing camels between the pyramids in Egypt? Why not you walking through the Acropolis, sitting where Socrates and Plato used to sit? Why not you sailing by the shores of Monaco or diving along the coast of Australia? Why not you having lunch at The Savoy in London or gazing at the Mona Lisa in the Louvre? Why not you rafting in the Amazon or bungee jumping in Costa Rica?

And the last question I want to ask you is: "Why not now?" What's stopping you from taking action right now? You don't have the time? You have too many responsibilities? Not enough money? Be honest with yourself. If you can be more, be more. If you can do more, do more. If you can learn more, learn more. I gave you plenty of leads in this book for other books that I've found valuable. Go and find them. Read them. They will lead to more books, more knowledge and more answers. Let this be the moment that your quest for true greatness begins.

So this is it. We have reached the end of our journey together. The time has come to say goodbye and go our own separate ways. I want to wish you health, wealth, happiness and fulfillment. I hope to hear from you by e-mail or meet you in person and learn about the changes you've made and the lives you've touched. I hope you'll pass on what you've learned in this book and that you'll help other people win their internal battles. Wherever you may go from here, take care, take action, and soar high. Make your life a masterpiece. And until we meet again, I hope you'll remember to let your light shine brightly because when you do, you illuminate the way for all of us. So shine on my friend, and don't forget to stay in touch. Goodbye.

Chapter XVI

Goals:

The Art of Strategic Thinking

"Man is a goal-seeking animal. His life only has meaning if he is reaching out and striving for his goals"

~ Aristotle ~

Hello again!

Congratulations on finishing *Being Great: Winning the battles within!* I hope you will continue your pursuit of greatness by reading chapter 16: *Goals: The Art of Strategic Thinking.* This chapter is only available for download in electronic format through www.being-great.com by registering with the code bellow. You will also have access to additional downloadable resources as well as exclusive previews and screening opportunities of our upcoming products. Enjoy.

Your registration code is:

2006-BGWT-BWSD

About Strength Dynamics

Strength Dynamics was founded in 2003 by Eyal Yurconi and Mark Tulchinski. The vision behind the organization was to become a leading source of knowledge and opportunity for individuals and organizations seeking to improve performance and quality of life. Through its divisions, Strength Dynamics also offers personal development tools and strategies to young people all across the world with the purpose of encouraging learning, leadership and creativity.

Strength Dynamics Foundation

The strength dynamics foundation is dedicated to providing children and adolescence unique opportunities for growth and leadership. The foundation offers yearly scholarships based on outstanding intellectual performance, exceptional athletic abilities, promising creative potential, and extraordinary community involvement. The foundation also offers the "Standards of Greatness" assistance program that gives underprivileged children and adolescents the opportunity to learn life changing skills from today's leading professional coaches and trainers from all walks of life. For more information about the Strength Dynamics Foundation, please visit www.strengthdynamics.com

Strength Dynamics Research

RESEARCH

The strength dynamics research division is responsible for the creation and marketing of cutting edge personal development tools and strategies to a wide range of audiences. The research division offers services in the form of consultation, seminars, and tailored training packages to corporate and small businesses, as well as sports teams, professional athletes, community leaders, teachers, students, and parents. Popular topics include: leadership development, classroom management, adolescent potential development, flow & peak performance, goal setting & strategic thinking, team dynamics & synergy, conflict resolution & negotiation skills, persuasion tools, and problem solving strategies.

Throughout the years, Strength Dynamics Research has developed several corner stone seminars and training programs including: *The Fire Within*: how to live on passion & purpose, *Being Great*: success skills for the 21st century, and *The Teacher's Edge*: how to deliver information, facilitate learning, and manage behavior inside and outside the classroom. For a complete list of available services and further information, please visit www.strengthdynamics.com

Strength Dynamics Studios

STUDIOS

The Strength Dynamics Studios division gives upcoming musicians, composers, directors, graphic artists, and web developers the opportunity to collaborate their talents on unique multimedia projects such as films, soundtracks, website development, and 3D-animation sequences. Through Strength Dynamics Studios, artists receive the knowledge and guidance necessary to maximize their talent and promote their work via the mass media. To view completed projects, samples, applications, and upcoming collaboration opportunities please visit www.strengthdynamics.com

Strength Dynamics Publications

Publications

Strength Dynamics Publications is dedicated to publishing and distributing high quality literary works that add real value to people's lives. The publication house offers writers, poets, literary artists and professional speakers the opportunity to promote their work through many different media venues. Strength Dynamics Publications focuses primarily on fiction and non-fiction literary works in the fields of philosophy, psychology, theology, as well as unique and outstanding life experiences.

Strength Dynamics Publications
Price List

Dear reader,

We hope you've enjoyed reading *Being Great:Winning the battles within* and that you found it valuable and applicable to your life. We invite you to download the 16th chapter: *Goals: The Art of Strategic Thinking* from www.being-great.com and enjoy additional bonus material. Please don't forget to let us know how this book has impacted your life. Your impressions will be published on E-display.

As part of our effort to distribute wisdom and high quality information that makes a real difference in people's lives, we would like to offer you our special discount rates for multiple orders. *Being Great* is a fabulous gift for the graduating senior, the aspiring professional, the newlywed couple and the individual facing a life challange.

Please refer to the price list below when completing the Quick Order Form on the following page. Once you are done, simply detach the Quick Order Form (notice the dotted line) and send it to us along with your payment of choice. Please note that a portion of the proceeds from this product will be used to fund scholarships for disadvantaged junior and high-school students. Thank you for your order!

*Being Great: Winning the Battles Within

No. of copies	Price per unit
1	$ 17.95
2-5	$ 16.95
6-9	$ 15.95
10-59	$ 14.95
50-499	$ 13.95
500-999	$ 11.95
1000+	$ 8.95 (over 50% discount!)

*Each and every copy of *Being Great: Winning the battles within* comes with a unique registration code that unlocks the 16th chapter (available only in electronic format) and allows the reader to download additional bonus material such as Inspirational movie lists, book recommendations and much more.

Strength Dynamics Publications

Quick Order Form

Contact Information:

Name:

Title:

Organization:

Mailing Address:

City: State: Zip:

Billing Address:

City: State: Zip:

Phone:

Email:

Order Information:

Item	Quantity	Unit price	Total Price
Being Great: winning the battles within			

Total cost of all items:

Shipping add 7%($3.95 minimum)

Total Purcahse amount:

☐ Yes, I want to be a part of the Stregnth Dynamics Foundation program. Please use 15% of the proceeds from my order to fund scholarships for disadvantaged junior and high-school students.

Payment Options:

Money/Purchase order #:

Check #:

Mail Your Order to:

Strength Dynamics publications

3030 Ocean Ave. Suite 2-H

New York, 11235

NY

Phone: (718) 501-8658

Fax: (718) 501-8658

Orders@Being-Great.com

www.Being-Great.com